KEITH PENNOCK

Rescuing Brain Injured Children

Compliments of:
The Lazarus Foundation
436 Locust Street
P.O. Box 148
Columbia, Pa 17512
Ph#- 717.684.7511
Fax#- 717.684.7558
Toll Free#- 1.877.684.7511
www.lazarusfoundation.org
email - lazarusfoundation@earthlink.net

ASHGROVE PUBLISHING
LONDON & BATH

This edition published in Great Britain by
ASHGROVE PUBLISHING
An imprint of Hollydata Publishers Ltd
55 Richmond Avenue, London N1 0LX

Ashgrove editorial office: 3 Town Barton
Norton St Philip, Bath BA3 6LN

ISBN 1–85398–111–7

This edition 1999

To my mother, for her love and faith,
To Valerie, for her love and dedication,
To Susie, Judy and Heather,
for their love and willingness
and to Alison,
for all the joy she has given us,
and for helping to shape the lives of so many.

Photoset in 11/12½ Times by
Ann Buchan (Typesetters), Middlesex
Printed in Malta by Interprint

CONTENTS

ILLUSTRATIONS

ACKNOWLEDGEMENTS

I am very grateful to Rita Hodder for her expertise in proof reading and editing the original text of this book. I suspect she will be the only person who will ever read it **aloud** from cover to cover!

I am also grateful to have received the very professional support and advice of Robin Campbell, of Ashgrove Press.

Constant encouragement has come from Pauline and Mike Heawood, Maggie Gibbons, Roy and Wendy Moore, Machteld Linschoten, Dieter van Werkum, and Linda and David Ratcliffe.

Anne Diamond and John Cleese have helped a great deal in getting the message of the book across to the families for whom it was written.

I am indebted to all the families whose stories I have been given permission to relate. This is also true for all those parents who have allowed me to include photographs of their children.

The quotation on Page 64 is taken from *Human Neurological Organisation* by Edward B. LeWinn MD, published by Charles C. Thomas, Springfield, Illinois.

Finally, my grateful thanks to all the children themselves, who have taught me so much, and have given me the greatest challenge so far in my life.

FOREWORD

Westbury-on-Trym,
Bristol.

I first learned in 1984 of Mr Pennock's outstanding work with brain injured children. In 1981, my wife was knocked down and suffered very severe and diffuse injuries to her brain; this was followed by five months in hospital, by which time I had retired fully from medical practice.

Since little progress was expected from further hospital treatment, it was suggested that it might be better for my wife to be at home. By 1984, she had made little progress; she could neither read nor write, and her memory was still markedly impaired. Then an article appeared in one of our daily newspapers, describing the pioneering work being undertaken in Somerset by Keith Pennock, then at the British Institute for Brain Injured Children. This work was based on a new concept to help such children originally developed at an Institute in Philadelphia, USA.

Although I had been a doctor since 1940, I knew very little about the rehabilitation of severely brain injured patients, most of whom either died or failed to recover sufficiently to be able to leave hospital. I was sure, however, that if I met Mr Pennock, I would learn something of value which might speed my wife's progress. I therefore wrote to him, and received a warm invitation to visit him. This visit, and a subsequent one some months later, proved of great help. Both gave me much to think about in determining which of the procedures in use might be adapted to help adult patients. I was encouraged to persevere, and to apply much of what I had observed, what I had learned from Mr Pennock, and what I subsequently read, to help my wife and other adult patients. As a result, she improved very considerably.

We had two sons, and fortunately neither had suffered a brain injury. Had they done so, we would have searched Britain for someone with the experience of having treated many hundreds of children with such injuries, including blindness and deafness, who could now see, hear and function.

Over a thousand children have been helped by Mr Pennock, including his own daughter, Alison. Some could not initially even creep or crawl; now, many of them can walk, run, jump, hurdle, swim, and take part in other outdoor activities. Many can now read and write. An increasing number are accepted for normal schooling, and some older ones are even in regular employment and drive cars.

Over the years, Mr Pennock has built up a remarkable expertise, and a most readable account of his achievements is given in this book. The procedures which have been developed offer the advantage that at no time is the child separated from his family. This, I am sure, is a fundamental need of every developing child. Brain-Net's role is to teach parents what they themselves can do to provide their child with the daily therapy he needs, and it has succeeded in linking together two most powerful tools – its own experience, and the love of the parents for their child.

Dr Geoffrey Tovey CBE MD FRCP
Lately: Founder and Director,
UK Transplant Service

INTRODUCTION

Brain-Net,
8 Cypress Drive
Puriton, Bridgwater
Somerset

No mother or father ever PLANS to have a brain injured child. The thought never enters their heads. They may plan for their child's future – his name, her school, or even his career – but for them to deliberately plan to have a hurt child is out of the question. Yet, if such a disaster should happen, parents are virtually **expected** to learn to live with their problem, and the world often reacts adversely to any mother or father who refuses to do so.

It is for this courageous minority that this book has primarily been written. It is an attempt to tell the truth: that a great deal can be done, by parents themselves, to give their brain injured children a real chance in life, despite their many problems. To some of the older generation of professionals, these mothers and fathers are a thorn in the flesh. They keep on asking what is really wrong with their children. They keep on asking what they themselves can do about it. They won't take 'no' for an answer. These are the very people who are motivated to find the right answer, and for some of them, and those who want to help them, the right answer may lie in the following pages.

This is NOT a 'Do It Yourself' book. The brain, and the many, many control systems in it which can cease to function when brain injury occurs, is far too complicated an organ to be regarded so lightly. And the physical complications which can ensue need careful attention if the problems are not going to be compounded.

Nor is it a 'medical' book. Our work is primarily DEVELOPMENTAL, not medical, and we specialise in the creation, or re-creation of function. Yet our treatment programmes are compatible with much of modern medical thinking.

It is a book about things practical and things positive, and it is a story of what can be done, sometimes against long odds, when ordinary people find themselves facing extraordinary problems.

Keith Pennock
January, 1998

Men stumble over the truth from time to time,
But most pick themselves up
And hurry off as if nothing has happened.
Sir Winston Churchill

PART ONE

Our History

CHAPTER 1
How it all Began

When people hear of our work with brain injured children, they often refer to us as being *new,* and sometimes as being *American*! In fact, the concept of exposing a brain injured child to a high level of sensory stimulation, and giving him a great deal of opportunity to try to use his brain more efficiently, is not new, and whilst being American in origin, its practical application is no longer confined to the nationals of that country.

The story starts with Dr Temple Fay, a gifted neurosurgeon, and professor of both neurology and neurosurgery at Temple University Hospital and Medical School in Philadelphia, USA, between 1929 and 1943. In addition to his neurosurgical skills, Dr Fay was a brilliant observer, and his ability to interpret his observations and to produce from them practical solutions to problems, placed him in a category of being well ahead of his time.

It was one of Dr Fay's responsibilities to operate on brain injured children and, like other conscientious surgeons, he used to monitor the post-operative progress of his young patients. He found that it was possible to divide the children into very distinct groups: those who came from rich families, and those whose parents were relatively poor.

In America, then as now, there was no National Health Service, and if parents wanted their children to receive any post operative treatment, whether hydrotherapy, physiotherapy, occupational therapy, or any other, they had to pay for it. As a result, the children whose parents could afford it received a great deal of rehabilitative support, whilst those for whom such luxuries were well beyond their means, were simply discharged from hospital back to their own homes.

Dr Fay's interest deepened when he discovered that, two years after their operations, those children who had received rehabilitative therapy were achieving only a very limited number of gains: 'Mary can now hold her head up better', or 'Alan has developed more movement in his fingers'. In contrast, the children whose parents had taken them home to recuperate were redeveloping many of their functions, and were making much more progress.

On the face of it, a paradox was occurring, and the maxim – 'you gets what you pays for' was being turned topsy-turvy.

It was clear that something powerful and special was being provided by their parents for the children who were being looked after at home. What was it?

In the end, Dr Fay realised that the special ingredient was so ordinary, so normal, that it had escaped everyone's notice. Once the children had returned to their homes, their parents, determined to keep them safe and secure, had put them **on the floor**!

The floor had provided the children with the same opportunity for movement which it gives to babies. And they had used the opportunity to begin, all over again, to learn about balance, co-ordination, and mobility. They were re-training their own nervous systems.

In the late forties, Dr Fay founded the Neurophysical Rehabilitation Centre, where he was able to devote his time and skills to the treatment of brain injured children and adults. Here, he was joined by Glenn Doman, a skilled physiotherapist, who had become fascinated by Fay's insight, and eagerly seized the opportunity of working with him to construct a new approach to the impossible problems created in children by brain injury. In those days, no-one had ever heard of a brain injured child who had ever become able to function as well as his peer group; in fact no-one was really sure what 'normal' was. Fay and Doman, later joined by Robert Doman MD, Glenn's brother and a specialist in rehabilitative medicine, and Carl Delacato, an educational psychologist, set about establishing what 'normal' was, and discovered that all children develop along identical lines. Since they carry within their brains not only the control mechanisms necessary to ensure their own ability to function, but also those required by all the creatures which preceded man, children complete several specific stages on their journey to functional maturity. Responsibility for each stage lies with a different level of the brain, and if any one of these levels is damaged, then the functions associated with this level are impaired, and any further progress will be inhibited.

Once the team became aware of this new information, they began to develop additional activities which might encourage functional improvements by providing fresh stimuli to whichever brain level might be impaired, and the principles of 'sensory/motor stimulation' became established.

In 1955, The Rehabilitation Centre at Philadelphia was founded, as an in-patient therapy unit which began to practise on a larger scale the ideas which Dr Fay had first proposed, and the subsequent team had developed.

Growing success with both children and adults encouraged the team to improve upon the early and more primitive forms of stimulation which had been used, and in 1963, as more doctors, nurses and clinicians joined them, the Institutes for the Achievement of Human Potential were born.

During the 1960s, following the publication of an article in the *American Medical Association Journal* describing the Institutes' work, and the results they had achieved in the treatment of 76 severely brain injured children, many families sought their help. We were one of those families.

CHAPTER 2
Early Days in England

At this point, the story becomes personal. In 1966, our first child, Alison, was born, and, at the age of four months, received the triple vaccination against whooping cough, diphtheria and tetanus. Unfortunately, she developed an adverse reaction to the injection, and within a matter of weeks was suffering repeated convulsions, and ceased to develop normally. We were told that she might catch up again in time; that she might always remain backward; that she might even deteriorate. No one could answer the one big question: 'Which of these will happen?'

We visited several specialists. Various combinations of drugs were tried to control her fits, but without success. We became more and more frustrated and desperate, whilst Alison grew bigger, and developed very, very slowly.

In 1968, we visited a new specialist. She told us to take our daughter home; to teach her how to feed herself, dress herself, and to become toilet trained. At last! Now we had something positive to do!

Yet within a few days we realised that Alison did not really know where her hands were, and could not understand enough to know how to control her bowel and bladder functions. Our hopes had been raised, only to be dashed again.

By the time she was three years old, Alison still could not see very well; she could hear some sounds, but didn't understand what they meant; in some parts of her body, she was hypersensitive, whilst in others she had no detectable sensation; she had little control of her hands, and didn't play with toys, but she loved to hold Ladybird books, and often grasped a soft piece of cloth with which she would brush her nose (we called it her 'tickler'); her balance and co-ordination were so poor that instead of walking, she simply staggered about. Despite this very inadequate mobility, she was nevertheless hyperactive, and refused to stay still. To complicate matters further, she was having more than two hundred epileptic spasms each day, despite being on **three** anticonvulsant drugs.

Because of her lack of balance, her hyperactivity, and her fits, she fell down many times, and was a frequent visitor to our local casualty department. Her life must have been frightening, painful and frustrating, and, not surprisingly, she cried a lot – the only sounds she could make.

In short, she had a lot of problems, and we could find no solutions.

Our second daughter, Susie, had been born in the meantime, and her quite normal development, whilst a pleasure to us both, helped to highlight Alison's problems. Alison had been gradually overtaken by her younger sister, and while she was theoretically three years old, in fact she was well below that age in almost every respect. We continued to worry.

At the end of 1968 our neighbour, Anne Eastwood, who with her family was to prove a tower of strength during the next six years, showed my wife, Valerie, an article, in what was then the *Manchester Guardian*, entitled 'Hope for Susan'. It was the story of a little girl whose problems sounded very similar to Alison's; her parents had taken her to a clinic in the USA, and she was beginning to make progress.

In 1969, making an international call to the USA was an expensive and rather terrifying operation. Nevertheless, with tape recorder microphone in one hand and the telephone receiver in the other, I called the clinic – the Institutes for the Achievement of Human Potential – and asked for their help. In a one-and-a-half minute conversation, they put me in contact with an English organisation, based in Cheltenham, which was arranging a charter flight to the Philadelphia centre for a group of brain injured children and their parents.

Now we had a decision to make. The cost of a trip to the States was far more than our meagre savings could meet. Susie was two years old, and our new baby, Judy, had only just arrived. Could we cope? My mother-in-law offered to look after Judy (the first of several 'holidays' our younger daughters were to enjoy when Valerie and I had to go to the States with Alison). Our neighbour, Anne, promised to take care of Susie. I sold my pride and joy – a 1937 MG TA sports car – to raise some of the cash needed, and with gifts of money from both our mothers, we had just enough to meet the costs. The Cheltenham organisation was able to offer us places on their flight, and on February 28th, 1970, we flew to America.

We would have expected Alison to sleep at least some of the eighteen-hour journey, or to have been even 'busier' than usual. In fact, much to our surprise, she was much easier to look after, despite the fact that she stayed awake the whole time. She was fascinated by all the lights at Kennedy Airport, and as we travelled in the chartered bus along the Van Wyk expressway into New York, across the Verrazano Narrows Bridge over the Hudson River, and along the New Jersey Turnpike, she seemed to be interested and excited. It was almost as if she knew why she was there, and didn't want to miss a minute of it!

The Institutes consisted of a number of buildings, some very modern and permanent, others more temporary, clustered around a beautiful house in Chestnut Hill, a residential suburb on the northern side of Philadelphia.

On our first day, in company with the other twenty-nine children in our group, Alison was very thoroughly examined – physically, functionally, and medically – by a number of different staff members, and we were asked an exhaustive series of questions about her previous history.

Eventually, at 2 o'clock in the morning of the second day, we saw Glenn Doman himself, and learned that our daughter had moderate, diffuse, and bi-lateral injuries to her cortex and midbrain.

Now, at last we had the answer to our first question. We knew that she was brain injured. Not spastic, backward, retarded, mentally handicapped, hyperactive, or epileptic, but BRAIN INJURED. I am not sure whether we were more relieved or more scared: relieved that at last we had found out what was *really* wrong with her; and scared that we might not be able to put it right.

As the week progressed, we attended two full days of lectures. We learned where her injuries lay, how they might be overcome, and what we ourselves could do to speed the process.

My wife is a physiotherapist. She had already tried everything she could think of to help Alison, and had become more and more despondent when she discovered that 'the book' didn't seem to apply in our child's case. At the end of the second hour of lectures, she turned to me and said 'Of course! Why on earth didn't I think of all this. It's so obvious.'

On the last day of the week we were taught Alison's own, individual programme of activities. Each activity was designed to stimulate her senses, or to give her the opportunity to learn new skills. We had the answer to our second question: 'What could we do to help her?' Through travelling with other families, and talking to them at the clinic, we had realised that our frustration at not being able to do anything to help our daughter was a problem we all shared. After so many months of not knowing what to do, we now knew exactly what to do, and had in fact so much to do that we doubted our ability to do it!

Just before our return flight was called, the scene in the departure lounge at Kennedy Airport was one I will never forget. Families who had been quiet, even withdrawn on the outward journey were now talking and joking freely with one another. Many of the children, despite their twisted limbs, were lying face down on the floor. Several wheelchairs and buggies were lying discarded, and, for the time being, superfluous, in a corner. Some children were breathing into plastic masks. Everywhere, there was a feeling of optimism, and to the casual onlooker, we must all have appeared slightly insane.

We returned home to Stafford on a Saturday, and I went straight round to see our local vicar, the Rev. Harry Myers. I didn't know him very well, but it turned out that we were both Geordies, which helped. He listened thoughtfully as I explained about our trip to the Institutes, about Alison's new home programme, and that we needed to find two volunteers to help us, each morning and afternoon. I later heard that, after my visit, he had torn up his sermon already prepared for the following day, and instead had preached on the theme of The Good Samaritan, linking the parable to our own need for help. Immediately after the service, he rang to ask if 47 people would be enough!

As all these volunteers lived in our neighbourhood, everyone was willing to come to our house, on a weekly rota, to assist in carrying out some of the repetitive routines which had been prescribed. We immediately began those parts of Alison's programme which didn't require special equipment, and, over the next two weeks, I made almost all of the recommended devices and gadgets myself. As he was also Chaplain to Stafford Prison, Harry arranged for some of the inmates to construct Alison's patterning table – an item of furniture that was to last for many years. Fifteen days after we had returned from America, Alison's programme was in full swing, and we were achieving 12 sequences of activities each day.

Within six months, we began to see improvements. She was no longer *allowed* to stagger about, and spent all her time on the floor. Yet her balance and co-ordination became more controlled. She started to respond to more sounds. She began to learn how to creep on her tummy. She became much more aware of her hands, and started to use them. Her fits became less frequent.

A team of American staff flew over to England in June 1970 to see English children on the programme, and we travelled to Cheltenham for Alison's first reassessment.

After another very thorough series of examinations, and many more questions for us to answer, the team gave us further advice, re-designed her daily routine, and confirmed our own feelings that at last we, and Alison, were beginning to get somewhere.

When we had returned from the States, we had thought that 12 sequences of activities each day were almost impossible to accomplish. Now, we had 18 to do, but we were beginning to win, and, when you are winning, everything is possible!

CHAPTER 3
The Staffordshire Society For Brain Damaged Children

In August 1970 a lady who had heard of the efforts we were all making to give Alison a real chance to improve, came to our home. She handed me a cheque for £30, which had been raised during a Charity Football match by the people with whom she worked. She then said, 'It is to help children like yours.' This was a generous gesture, and was to have far-reaching consequences.

We did not know any 'children like ours', but there had to be other Alisons, whose parents were just as desperate as we had been. This donation, and perhaps others, could give them the same help that we had been so lucky to find. I decided to consult our vicar again, and, following his advice, called a public meeting in St Bertelin's Church Hall, Stafford. Many of Alison's helpers came; well-wishers came; and, much to our delight, so did a number of parents of brain injured children.

I had not spoken in public since my schooldays, but such was the empathy and interest of the audience that I found myself explaining in detail, and with some confidence, what we were doing for our daughter, and how much she had improved. At the end of the evening there was a unanimous vote to set up a new organisation to help children like Alison, and that night, September 15th, 1970, the Staffordshire Society for Brain Damaged Children was launched, a committee was formed, and I was asked to be Chairman.

We immediately wrote to the Charity Commissioners in London, applying for registration. This took six weeks to obtain, and in the meantime, we planned several events to raise money for our new cause.

Within a matter of weeks four families had asked for our help to go to Philadelphia. I contacted the Cheltenham organisation, and they agreed to allocate places for 'our' families on a second group flight they were planning to send to America.

Valerie and I took Alison down to Cheltenham in the October, to keep our appointment for her next reassessment, and were pleased to hear from the American staff how well they felt she was progressing. She was now allowed up on to her feet, and showed us that, far from forgetting how to walk, she could do so with much better balance and purpose.

At the end of that day, I was able to explain to Wendy Middleton, secretary of the Cheltenham organisation, what our new Society had so far succeeded in doing, and confirmed our places on their next group flight.

As we drove home, I felt elated. Alison was beginning to achieve her goals, and so was our new Society.

In the months that followed, we found ourselves busier than we had ever been before. During the day, I was out at work, while Valerie, supported by our helpers, carried out Alison's programme, and looked after our other two children. In the evenings we both somehow found the energy to attend committee meetings, and to lend a hand with fund raising.

We saw the visiting American staff again in January 1971. They continued to be very pleased with Alison's progress, made several changes in her programme, and kept our workload at the same level – 18 sequences per day. Her hyperactivity was reduced, she could creep on her tummy independently, and her crawling on hands and knees was much more co-ordinated. Best of all, she could now walk with confidence, and staggering was a thing of the past.

Arrangements had been completed for our Society's four families, who duly flew to Philadelphia for their initial assessment week in February 1971. We thought about them all through that week, knowing what they would be doing, and what would be happening.

Counting Alison, our fledgling Charity was now responsible for a total of five children. We secured places for two more on another group flight due to depart in May 1971, and pressed on with the paperwork and the fund raising.

In April, a major problem arose. We heard from Wendy Middleton that their May flight had been cancelled, and what was worse, the American staff would not be coming to England again to reassess the children already following the Institute's programme. The Cheltenham organisation was in disarray, and could offer no immediate solution.

It is bad enough not knowing what to do to help a child whom you love. It is worse knowing what to do, and not being allowed to do it. I placed another call to the States, and asked if the American staff would consider making fresh arrangements with our own Society. Their positive response triggered a flurry of activity in our very small, local and entirely voluntary committee, which now found itself running what amounted to a national organisation, with a new responsibility for all the children in Britain whose parents had enough to do in just getting on with their home programmes.

From that moment on, all new contacts from families in Britain were routed by the Institutes to us. Local press coverage of the efforts of the families we had already sent to America generated more interest, and we were flooded with enquiries and appeals for help from parents all over the country. We decided to organise a flight of sixteen new families, and also arranged to take three children already following the programme, including Alison, back to the Institutes for reassessment. This decision relieved some pressure, but created even more in other directions. Funds had to be raised. Information had to be sought from doctors. Visa arrangements had to be made with the American embassy in London, and we had to solemnly promise that we were not planning to permanently dump a group of 'handicapped kids' on our American cousins, but that we would bring them home again after *only one week* in the States.

The flight was planned for November 1971, but owing to problems at the Institutes, it was rescheduled for February 1972.

We hit other snags, and as fast as one was solved, another arose. Then we heard that the two airlines we had contacted were not prepared to accept our children as passengers. They had never carried brain injured children before, and were unwilling to accept responsibility for their safety at high altitudes. We tried a third, and this time got a very different reaction. Aer Lingus, the Irish airline, were not only prepared to help, but promised to pull out all the stops to make sure our families were treated as VIPs.

Our own first visit to Philadelphia had taught us several practical lessons about how to fly long distances with brain injured children, and we resolved to organise this third trip as carefully as we could, in order to avoid as much stress as possible for everyone involved. The airline agreed to include two trained nurses in the cabin crew. Specially prepared foods were promised for the children. A bus was chartered to take the whole party from Kennedy airport, New York, to specifically booked accommodation at a motel near the clinic.

Five weeks before the date of departure, we were told that our flight could not take place. Under IATA regulations, to qualify for special charter rates an organisation had to have been in existence for at least two years, and our own Society was not old enough! We quickly enrolled all our parents and children as temporary members of the Stafford Rugby Club (founded in 1885), and re-booked the tickets!!

During the week at the Institutes, and completely out of the blue, I was faced with a major decision. Glenn Doman was indeed willing to work with us, to see children we sent from England, and to send his staff regularly across the Atlantic to review their progress. But what was needed in England was a British Institute. Was I prepared to create such a body, and was I prepared to run it?

Up to this point, the Chairmanship of the Society, the fund raising, the talks and the problem-solving had been almost a reflex response to a challenge, and an interest sparked off through our own search for a solution to an insoluble problem. Now, I was being asked if I was prepared to commit to a course of action, the results of which I couldn't possibly determine. A British Institute, able in time to do so much not only for Alison, but also for many, many other children, was a concept which challenged the imagination, and could only bring a welcome stability for future families. Yet I already had a full-time, responsible job with an excellent employer, and for me to go off at a tangent would not only cause problems within the Company, but might also put my family at risk.

That night Valerie and I talked it over into the small hours. She felt it had to be my decision, but would support me whatever choice I made.

'There is a tide in the affairs of men . . .'. I agreed.

If we had had problems in organising the trip to America, they were as nothing compared to those which now had to be overcome. Yet, the biggest log-jam had been shifted: at least we had something positive to offer to all the British families.

In June 1972, Glenn Doman accompanied by Raymundo Veras, an ophthalmic surgeon who had founded several similar Institutes for brain injured and Down's Syndrome children in his native Brazil, flew to England with a staff team to re-assess all the British children on the programme. We arranged for them to stay at the Seighford Hall Hotel, a beautiful Tudor manor house near Stafford, and the hotel was temporarily transformed into a clinic, with the staff using their bedrooms in the daytime as clinical offices.

On June 3rd 1972 a dinner was held at the North Staffs Hotel, Stoke on Trent, to celebrate the foundation of the British Institute for the Achievement of Human Potential. We were off!

CHAPTER 4
The British Institute for the Achievement of Human Potential

Usually a new organisation is allowed to pace itself, and grows from small beginnings. We had already had our beginnings, and were swimming in the deep end from the word 'go' – without staff, or premises. But at least we knew how to start a Charity, and a new application was soon on its way to the Charity Commissioners, enclosing a Constitution which must have been a masterpiece, as it has survived the test of time, and has since been used by the Commissioners as a model for other new Charities!

Our schedule for the rest of 1972 and all of 1973 was, in hindsight, ridiculous, but we achieved it, nevertheless.

It was

Sep	1972	children's reassessments in Stafford
Nov	1972	a 30 family group flight to USA
Dec	1972	children's reassessments in Stafford
Jan	1973	a 15 family group flight to USA
Mar	1973	children's reassessments in Stafford
Mar	1973	a 15 family group flight to USA
Apr	1973	a 15 family group flight to U.S.A
May	1973	a 15 family group flight to USA
Jun	1973	children's reassessments in Stafford
Jul	1973	a 15 family group flight to USA
Sep	1973	a 16 family group flight to USA
Oct	1973	children's reassessments in Stafford
Nov	1973	a 15 family group flight to USA

Frank Cvitanovich, a film director working for Thames TV, and the father of a little boy on the Institute's treatment programme, had been asked to make a series of documentaries of his own choice, and had decided that one should be the story of his son, Bunny. The finished film was shown in late 1972 in all ITV regions, with my home address as a contact for any interested families! We received over 400 letters, which explains why so many flights were organised in 1973.

It was obvious, even at the beginning of that year, that the new Institute needed full-time direction. Our Board acknowledged this fact, and I agreed to resign my job, and take on the post of Director from April 1st. Much to my surprise and gratitude, my employers were very understanding, and gave their blessing to my decision.

The Welsh Society for Brain Damaged Children, one of our support groups which had come into existence following the initial success of the Staffordshire Society, offered to arrange guarantors for a bank loan to provide my salary for the first year. After that, the problem of raising the funds to keep the Institute and its staff going was to be entirely mine!

We leased two rooms in a large private house, and employed a secretary. More space was soon needed, so we moved into a three-roomed office suite – with more decorating and furnishing to be done.

As our schedule for 1972/73 indicates, we were extremely successful at the task of sending children and parents to Philadelphia for their Initial Assessment weeks. In fact, we were so successful that, by the summer of 1973, it was obvious that to regularly reassess all the children, the American staff would need to be based almost permanently in England, to the detriment of their own centre.

A decision was therefore taken to set up a locally based reassessment team, comprising an American clinician on rotation, the Directors of the British and Irish Institutes, and Mary Kett, an Irish staff member who was shortly to complete her training at the Philadelphia clinic. The team would work alternately in Ireland and England, seeing parents and children, spending two weeks at a time in each country, and a 'hot line' would be permanently maintained with IAHP to ensure that the best possible advice would be given to each family.

The Irish Institute had been founded, in the same year as our own Institute, and for very similar reasons, by Eugene Campbell, whose daughter, Keelin, was also brain injured. Eugene was most willing to co-operate, and there then followed another hectic four months on both sides of the Irish Channel. Temporary accommodation was found for our new team in a house in south Dublin. In England, we located and purchased a fifteen-room town house – Lanrick House – at Rugeley, nine miles from Stafford.

Eugene and I had already experienced one rapid transition, from being simply the fathers of children on the programme to becoming Directors of Institutes. Now, we were to experience another. During the last four months of 1973, we both attended an intensive training course in clinical work at IAHP. It was a major advantage to us that we had both *done* the programme with our own children, and already had a basic understanding of the philosophies involved.

Christmas 1973 was a nail-biting period for everyone. The day after the completion of purchase of Lanrick House the builders moved in and plumbing, partitioning, electrification and decorating began at a great rate.

There were many who doubted that we would be ready in time, but on January 3rd 1974 the American-Anglo-Irish team began reassessing children in Rugeley, and on schedule.

Over the next two years we flew from England to Ireland, and Ireland to England, until we were nearly dizzy. When at Lanrick House, I looked after administration and fund raising, whilst the other three concentrated on the families. In Dublin, Eugene ran the Institute, and the rest of us reassessed the children. And all the time we were flying more parents and children to the Institutes in Philadelphia for initial assessment.

Sometimes, curious things happen for which there is no apparent explanation. In 1974, a family wrote to BIAHP asking us to help their son, who had been hurt in a car accident several years before. The handwriting on their letter seemed familiar to me, but as their name did not 'ring any bells', I made the normal arrangements for them, and filed the letter. In due course we took the family to Philadelphia, they began a programme with their son, Martin, and, as the years went by, saw him develop into a fine young man, with an 'O' level in English and the Duke of Edinburgh Gold Award to his credit.

When, in 1980, we decided to appoint our first 'Home Visitor', his mother, now released from the daily pressures of the programme, was the obvious choice, and Marguerite Walker joined the staff.

Two years later, I was looking through some old correspondence, and came across a letter Valerie and I had received back in 1968, long before we had ever heard of the Institutes. It was an encouraging letter, at a time when we needed encouragement. It was from the acquaintance of a mutual friend, and it was signed 'Marguerite Walker'!

Each of us had been anxious to help the other, without either of us knowing who the other was. And we had continued in ignorance for several years after the event!

*

The retarding effects of poor breathing in some of the children had been on Glenn Doman's mind for several months. In early 1974 a

Respiratory Department was set up in Philadelphia, using respirators to reinforce proper breathing rhythms, and not long after we created mini-Respiratory Units at both the British and Irish Institutes.

The previous year had been a very bad one for Alison. After all the gains she had made, she had suddenly developed a toxic reaction to her anticonvulsant drugs, which had by now been increased to **five** per day by her English paediatric specialist. After everyone's hard work, she had not only lost the ability to walk, but was deteriorating almost before our eyes. The June 1973 visiting team from the Institutes had included Dr Edward LeWinn, a physician of considerable standing in the USA, and one of the most kind and reassuring doctors I have ever met. After examining Alison, he had at once telephoned our own GP, and gained his agreement for a medication elimination programme to be started immediately. Three months later, when she next saw the American staff, Alison had hardly regained any of her abilities, and they felt that her breathing was so shallow and irregular that her life was at risk. It was therefore decided that as soon as it could be arranged, she should attend our respiratory unit on a regular basis. As every child attending the unit had to be supervised at all times by an adult, my wife began to spend each day with Alison at Lanrick House. Soon, however, Valerie became responsible for the daily supervision of the whole department, and we had to train a local girl to be with Alison all the time that she was 'hooked up' to her machine.

At the end of May, 1974, a meeting of the World Organisation for Human Potential was held at Kilkea Castle, County Kildare, in Ireland. Eugene, as the Irish Director, was wholly responsible for arranging this prestigious conference, but of course all four of us became heavily involved, both in the preparations, and in the events themselves. It was fun, it was fascinating, it was terrifying, and, most of all, it was exhausting. All four of us breathed a sigh of relief when the last delegate flew home from Shannon Airport, and we could get back to 'normal'.

It is interesting that during this period, Northern Ireland was in turmoil, with Catholics and Protestants at each other's throats. Yet, on our flights, and during the reassessment weeks in Dublin, there were often families from both England and the North and South of Ireland, and they all mixed together without difficulty. This was also true at the American clinic: Arab and Jewish families helped each other's children; Irish and English parents co-operated together; and any political and religious differences seemed unimportant as compared with the many problems of the children, and the faith each family placed in Glenn Doman and his staff.

Each weekday, in either country, we saw three families. Starting at 9 am, we worked through, stopping only for a quick lunch, until the last family had departed with their new programme. A late meal was invariably followed by bed, unless there was a fund raising event or a committee or Board meeting to attend. Each morning the families would arrive, burdened with problems and, at the end of the day, they would return home refreshed and re-enthused for another four months, leaving their burdens on our shoulders. No wonder that when the weekends came it was hard for us to relax!

By 1976, our team was tiring. Both Eugene and I felt that it was time for us to concentrate independently on the development of our individual Institutes. The Irish Institute had already moved into a beautiful country mansion in Port Arlington, County Laoise, and was well placed to see children from both the north and south of Ireland. Lanrick House, which had seemed so big to us only two years before, had already 'shrunk', and with an expanding patient list, we needed to find a larger centre.

By good fortune, we heard of the availability of Knowle Hall, a 44-roomed country house in thirteen acres of land near Bridgwater in Somerset. Built in the early years of the nineteenth century, it had been in its turn a private residence, a boys' school, and a property development prospect that had not worked out. It had lain idle for the previous six years, and was in a poor state of repair and decoration, but with imagination and effort, it was capable of providing the Institute with a great deal of scope for future development. We bought it!

We were sad to leave Staffordshire. It was not easy to say goodbye to my secretary, Tess Dean, and the other staff who had served us well for three years, and to supporters who had done so much to put the Institute on its feet. Of the forty-seven helpers who had originally offered to assist us with Alison's programme, twenty-nine were still involved, and by this time were responsible for a great many of the improvements she was once again continuing to make. We, and she, were going to miss them. Nevertheless, our future, and the future of the Institute, now lay in Somerset and in June 1976 we moved the entire clinic – lock, stock and barrel – to its new home.

CHAPTER 5
Our Permanent Home

We had bought a new clinic, but the initial list of defects and alterations was formidable. We appealed for help, and were astonished at the response. The local Round Table club arrived with paint, ladders and members, and set to work with a will. Many of the fathers of our children brought their specialist skills to bear on the problems, and, armed with tools and sleeping bags, spent several weekends partitioning, plumbing, electrifying and painting. Those Saturday nights will never be forgotten by the regulars at our local pub, 'The Knowle Inn'. The 'foreign' accents of Liverpudlians, Londoners and others brought new interest and colour to the scene – and the singsongs . . .!

On June 14th, 1976, Jo Sherwood and Mary Coulson, later to become respectively our Clinic Manager and our Administrator, joined the Institute, and well remember having to share the one functional office available with our bookkeeper and me. Gradually more rooms became serviceable. Only two weeks after we moved in, reassessments of children on our programme re-commenced, despite the rubble!

The same month, we opened an English branch of the IAHP School for Development Education. This unique school, begun at IAHP two years before, offered a special curriculum to brain injured young people over the age of eighteen, whether or not they had previously been on a home stimulation programme. It sought for physical, intellectual and social excellence in its students, and combined a very rigorous outdoor 'course', involving all the techniques successfully pioneered by the Institutes to improve balance, co-ordination and mobility skills, with reading, writing and mathematics. A very full programme of social activities including visits to the theatre, the ballet, concerts and sporting events was also included.

A term in England was seen as an excellent addition to the school's prospectus, and as Knowle Hall could provide enough space and accommodation for both visiting staff and students, our newly acquired centre found itself with an additional set of responsibilities and pressures.

The first group of young people from the American school arrived at Gatwick airport in the early hours of the morning, while we were still tiling their showers on the top floor of Knowle Hall!

Our close association with the American Institutes had already led many people in the local community to think that we, too, were American. Several rumours circulated about us in those early days. Whilst carrying out their five hour physical programme each day on the field in front of Knowle Hall, the school students were dressed in ex-army fatigues – an attempt to keep them reasonably clean! Before long, we were investigated by the local police, following up a complaint that we were 'training recruits for the IRA'!

Once our explanation had been accepted, we issued a challenge to the local police and fire brigade, to compete against our students in completing the outdoor course. The local lads did their best, but were no match for a group of severely brain injured youngsters who were expert at rolling over and over, hanging upside down, swinging hand over hand along ladders, and completing twenty forward rolls, one after the other. Still, there were no further complaints!

Most people will remember the famous summer of '76, when for week after week there was no rain, and the Government appointed a Minister for Drought. For us, that summer was memorable for three reasons. Firstly, we were creating a much larger clinic, and writing the rules as we went along, whilst the school was providing us with a simultaneous and parallel, but very different set of challenges.

Secondly, we had inherited a large, open-air swimming pool, which – so legend had it – was built during detention periods by the boys of St. Andrew's School, a previous owner of Knowle Hall. Unfortunately, it was out of commission, and needed professional attention before being used for swimming. Of course, we had other, more urgent priorities to attend to, and every day the students in our school had to walk past the empty pool on their way to and from a very dry, dusty and hot outdoor course. Eventually, we were able to fill the pool, and put the youngsters out of their misery!

Thirdly, the American staff in charge of the students decided that it would be an excellent idea to take their charges on a tour of Britain. A mini-bus was duly purchased, and, after a lot of poring over maps, a route was arranged which not only included many of the more famous landmarks, but also passed close to the homes of several of our families on the programme. The parents concerned were wonderful and provided hospitality and even accommodation whenever they could. It is one thing to cope with your own brain injured child; it is quite another to open your house to a dozen of them, and we were overwhelmed, yet again, at the generosity of our families.

It had been decided that my family and I should live in the main building, so that I could be close to the day-to-day operations of the clinic, and could oversee the renovations. Our initial accommodation was one big room, with three single beds on one side, and two plus a cot on the other. Local volunteers had painted the walls and ceiling before we arrived, and the oak floorboards had been polished. There was no central heating, and I was deeply grateful that we had decided to move in June, and not November!

Making our home at Knowle Hall turned out to be a two-edged sword. My four daughters (the latest edition, Heather, had arrived in 1974, and was only two years old) found themselves with the biggest 'garden' they were ever likely to enjoy; Alison was able to join the students on their daily coverage of the outdoor course, accompanied by Carolyn Vowles, a very enthusiastic and very fit local girl who had almost become 'one of the family'; and we could all use the pool in the evenings and weekends. On the other hand, we were all living on the job; we were in a self-created goldfish bowl, visible to all, with no real privacy; and we were on call twenty-four hours per day, and seven days per week. I was not only Director of the Institute, but its care-taker as well!

Between 1976 and 1978, the school was a regular feature in the life of the British Institute. Our patient list kept on growing, as we continued to organise regular flights to the USA. Our reassessment clinic, under the direction of Mary Kett, who had opted to stay for the time being with the British Institute, and who was to serve as our Clinical Director for the next two years, was seeing children and parents every day. Our fund raising was also gaining momentum, as it had to, now that the number of staff employed by the Institute had expanded. We sent two staff members to IAHP to undertake a full two-year clinical training, and, as a member of the American Board of Directors, I regularly attended Board Meetings, conferences and additional periods of clinical training in Philadelphia.

There were other trips too, some of them even longer. In January 1977 I was asked to join an international staff team which reassessed all the children on the programme in Australia. In May of the same year, I represented BIAHP at a conference held in Rio de Janeiro, which was followed by a tour of the Brazilian clinics originally set up by Dr Veras. Twice, in 1976 and 1977, I was included in staff teams who flew to Lake Maggiore to reassess the Italian children. In 1978, Valerie and I were invited, together with Alison, to attend the official opening of the new Italian Institute. Later that year, in the company of our Board chairman, I attended a 'two-city' conference held in San Francisco and New Orleans.

On April 1st 1977, a spectacular charity fund raising concert was held at the Royal Albert Hall in London, with the carefully selected title of – 'Nobody's Fools'. The proceeds were to be shared between BIAHP and 'MIND', the National Association for Mental Health.

At the end of a very successful evening, I went on stage to receive a cheque from John Cleese. After the show, he asked me what the Institute was all about, and became so intrigued that a few weeks later, he visited Knowle Hall to see everything at first hand. John became a friend and supporter from that day on.

In the autumn of the same year, a young reporter visited Knowle Hall from our local paper, the Bridgwater Mercury. Starting off with the usual question – 'Well, what *do* you do here?' – she became more and more interested, and decided to write an article about our work. As this was a golden opportunity for us to explain in detail to our local community who we were, and what we actually did, I suggested that she should do the job properly, and come along on our next flight of new families to IAHP.

Jointly sponsored by her editor and by ourselves, she did come, spent the full week observing and learning, and on her return wrote an excellent feature, which was duly published. One person who read it was a senior executive at the BBC, who called her in for interview, and asked her if she had ever thought about a career in television. The reporter's name was Anne Diamond, and she has been a close friend of mine, and of the children ever since.

A series of lectures was given at Knowle Hall in September 1977. Glenn Doman, accompanied by his wife, Katie; Dr Ralph Pelligra of NASA; and other members of staff from IAHP, spoke at length to the British families on the programme, outlining and explaining the techniques involved in growing their children's intelligence.

On September 10th, after the lectures were concluded, many of our parents and children, our staff, our Board members, several distinguished guests, and colleagues from America and Ireland, assembled at the Institute to witness Glenn Doman officially open Knowle Hall as a Clinic for Brain Injured Children. Those of us who had been involved since the early days felt that we were also witnessing, in the words of Sir Winston Churchill, 'the end of the beginning'.

Little has so far been said about the Board of Directors of the British Institute. Our Board consisted of men and women who, in an entirely voluntary capacity, had offered their services to help the development of our venture. Their time, that most precious of commodities, was freely given, and in addition to attending Board meetings, several members frequently accompanied the families on our group flights, 'riding shotgun' during the long and tiring week in Philadelphia to make sure that everything went as planned. Marsden Proctor, the Aer Lingus representative who had assisted us so effectively when we were organising the Staffordshire Society flight in 1972, had agreed to join our Board from the outset, and in his subsequent capacity as Chairman, he helped to steer BIAHP round many of the problems which arose during these years.

Our relationship with Glenn Doman, the American Board and the American Institutes' staff was excellent. Whilst there was never any time to relax, we all felt we were doing something really worthwhile, and the morale of our own staff was very high. The children were, in the main, making good progress, and we were seeing a particularly good response from a small number who were regularly attending our Respiratory Patterning Department, now enlarged from the Lanrick House days, and in full-time operation.

As part of our improvements to the structure of the main building, we had created five 'family-size' bedrooms, and parents and children were therefore able to stay with us for a week at a time, whilst attending the Respiratory Unit.

Each Christmas, a fancy dress party gave everyone a chance to enjoy themselves, and both staff and students entered thoroughly into the spirit of things. We did not have the funds available to give each of our staff a Christmas bonus, although they richly deserved one, so instead we gave them extra time off. (This long Christmas break became a tradition, which was still followed, up until my departure in 1995). The 'family' of the Institute, albeit international in make-up, was very much united in a common purpose.

A second lecture series was held for our parents in June 1978, and, as on the previous occasion, Glenn Doman gave a full presentation of the Intelligence Programme. Now, however, there was a new ingredient. IAHP had decided to expand its activities into the field of well children, and there was much discussion about the creation of 'Better Babies'. It was suggested that we might offer a regular instruction course to expectant and new parents, using our facilities to show them how to make their well children 'even more well'.

CHAPTER 6
Crisis!

Suddenly, we had a problem. All the funds we had raised over the years, had been specifically donated to help brain injured children. Our Constitution did not allow for such a major switch of policy, and, surrounded by hurt youngsters, we could not morally divert our meagre resources away from them, and towards children for whom our support would represent merely the 'icing on the cake', and who *could* survive in any event without help.

From the end of 1978, the attitudes of the staff of IAHP towards the British Institute began to cool. Correspondence became more peremptory; communication more difficult; we were no longer, if we ever had been, the 'blue-eyed girls and boys'.

This total change of attitude was not confined to BIAHP alone. The Irish, Australian and Italian Institutes were also put under pressure, and we learned the exact meaning of the phrase – 'it's all or nothing'. What had begun as a small problem relating to the principle of offering our help to well children, had now magnified to the point that we were virtually beyond the pale. To the Americans, everything was suddenly wrong at BIAHP, and we could do nothing right.

Several years before, Glenn Doman had emphasised to me that without the support and help of the Philadelphia Institutes, we had nothing and were nothing. I am sure this infectious thought was present in the minds of many of my staff, our families and even our Board members during the summer of 1979. It was in part my own fault. For nine years I had been telling everyone just how wonderful Glenn Doman was. I had praised the Institutes, and with good reason – Alison was a totally changed girl as a result of their advice. In 1973, they had, quite literally, saved her life.

Now, at the centre of the storm, I could see that the original concept, of the British Institute eventually becoming able to stand on its own feet, make its own decisions, but take its place alongside other national clinics in an interdependent role, had changed beyond recognition. Our future now depended on our making one of three possible choices. We could remain an American satellite, with no authority, but total financial and moral responsibility. We could become independent, and exercise full control over the future of the British Institute, and its children. Or we could close down.

The rest of 1979 was grim for everyone involved with the British Institute. We had built up, over the years, eighteen Affiliated Societies for Brain Injured Children spread far and wide around the country. I visited each committee, explaining what had happened, the three choices open to us, and my recommendation that the Institute should become independent. I am sure that many committee members were bemused by my apparent U-turn.

One of our trainees had just returned from Philadelphia to continue his clinical career at BIAHP. A further complication arose: he did not wish to work for an independent British Institute, preferring to set up a small unit of his own and continuing to liaise with the American clinic.

I was in regular contact with both the Irish and Australian Institutes, and was grateful for the optimism and support which were forthcoming from Eugene and from Tim and Claire Timmermans, the Australian Directors. Our Board decided that all our parents should be notified of the options open to them, and asked to make a choice. They could work directly with Philadelphia; they could stay with the British Institute; they could transfer to the new unit. It was felt that the parents' decisions would clearly establish whether or not there was to be any future role for the British Institute and its staff; if no-one wanted their children to remain in its care, then there would be no point in its continuation.

On November 17, 1979, we held a meeting at Knowle Hall of all interested parties. A substantial majority of both families and Societies voted to stay with BIAHP, and the die was cast.

We were lucky to have enjoyed such a long and happy relationship with Glenn Doman and his staff. We had learned a great deal, and although our paths were now to diverge, we knew that the principles of the therapy we had so thoroughly absorbed were sound. Nor were we alone. The Irish and Australian Institutes had decided to take the same decision as ourselves, and, like us, they were now free to develop further their own ideas and techniques. Sadly, the Italian Institute was unable to survive independently, and despite the enormous amount of work which had been done by its Director, Germano Caine, his staff member, Rosa Collodel, and the Italian parents, it was forced to close its beautiful villa in Varese, and cease operations.

CHAPTER 7
An Independent Institute

January 1st, 1980, became a very significant date. This is the date from which all our computer records commenced. This was 'the first day of the rest of our lives'.

The previous month, we had almost broken all our records in terms of achievement. We had had only that one month to change our name, our constitution, to arrange reassessment appointments for our families, and to construct a lecture theatre in which we could teach new parents. Several families who had originally expected to join one of our group flights to Philadelphia, had been forced to wait until we knew where the future of the British Institute lay, before beginning the programme with their children. They were one of our highest priorities, and on January 28th, we held our first Initial Assessment Week at the new **British Institute for Brain Injured Children**.

Now that clinical staff training, which had previously been available only in the USA, could be carried out at Knowle Hall, and at a fraction of the cost, we were able to recruit several additional staff. Our new name made it considerably easier to explain our objectives and to attract financial support, and by the end of our first year, forty-four new families had joined our programme. Freedom can be a heady sensation, and in making those changes which were necessary to suit the needs of British families, we had to be constantly on our guard not to 'throw the baby out with the bathwater'.

Over the next two years, we both gained and lost staff members and families. Our Board chairman, Marsden Proctor, who had supported us through 'the first ten', retired, and his place was taken by Chris Spencer, a local solicitor. Yet, as a constant and encouraging thread running through the whole period, we continued to see exciting changes taking place in many of the children. Our skills, experience and confidence were growing, and a previously unattained level of stability was reached.

As more space was needed for clinical work at Knowle Hall, my family and I moved to a house of our own. It was only two minutes drive from the Institute, but it was far enough away for us to be able to 'shut the door' at the end of each day, and to regain some measure of privacy.

One of the greatest assets of any organisation involved in training, is a standardised 'operations' manual. We had learned literally hundreds of different techniques for improving the functional abilities of brain injured children. Passing this information on to new staff, and teaching them precisely what to look for when assessing the children's abilities demanded a specific set of rules. We therefore compiled a comprehensive clinical manual, which ensured that whichever staff member assessed a child, the results would be the same, and whoever taught a family a new technique, the correct information would be given. However well parents are taught, it is always possible for misunderstandings to occur. When a family might be working at home for four months at a time, unseen by our staff, variations and errors could easily creep in to their daily routines. Britain is a relatively small country, and in theory, if a family could get to the Institute, then we could also get to them. To give on-the-spot support, and to avoid the possibility of inadvertent mistakes, we therefore created, as I have already mentioned, the new post of 'Home Visitor', and offered this extra service to all our families.

In the fight to rescue our children from the catastrophic effects of brain injury, and in the absence of any Government support, an income sufficient to meet immediate needs was always of vital importance to us. Money isn't everything, but without it, we could have done very little. In 1980, and again in 1981, we were given donations of £25,000 by the student Rag committee of the University College of Aberystwyth, in Wales. These gifts did wonders for our financial position, just at the times when they were most badly needed, and we were proud to name a Wing of the Institute after ABER RAG. For the next fifteen years, the Institute's work was supported by an ever-growing number of Rag committees in Universities and Colleges throughout the country, and we, in our turn, gave the students all the help we could. They taught us a valuable lesson – to be successful, there should always be some fun in FUNd raising.

In 1983, much to my relief, our efforts to raise cash were given a new impetus with the appointment of Roger Holyoake, an ex-marketing specialist, as our Appeals Director.

For several years, we had been asked by other professionals to produce some scientific evidence of the effectiveness of our programme. This had been difficult to do, since we were all fully occupied, on a daily basis, seeing to the needs of parents and children. The opportunity now arose for us to collaborate with the University of Surrey in a control study. The initial condition and subsequent progress of thirty-six children were carefully recorded throughout 1983, and the findings – which were an exciting endorsement of our methods and stated results – were subsequently published in the journal of the Royal Society of Health (See Appendix 2). The national media began to take a serious interest in our progress.

At the same time, another significant step forward also occurred. We entered the world of computers. I became persuaded by another neighbour, Ian Luckman, that our system for recording and updating the extensive data which we had by now amassed on our children was antiquated, and I suddenly found myself learning yet another new and different skill. We obtained the appropriate hardware, Ian wrote a unique program to process our information, and after several weeks of processing existing data, we had access to every child's Development Profile at the touch of a button. By 1995, 5,500 profiles had been accurately and permanently stored in our computer's memory banks, and more are doubtless being added every day.

Late in 1985, several distinguished people from the worlds of Science and the Arts became closely associated with the Institute's work, either as Board Members or Vice-Presidents. Professor John Dickerson, the Bishop of Bath and Wells and Dr Miriam Stoppard all agreed to lend their aid, and their considerable reputations, in endorsing our activities. At a later date, other distinguished men and women, well known in their various fields, agreed to support our work publicly, and the list of Vice-Presidents grew to include Dr George Carey, the Archbishop of Canterbury; Rabbi Lionel Blue; Anthony Brett; Lady Elizabeth Cavendish; Paddy Garratt; Roy Hudd; Lady (Maurice) Laing; Ruth Madoc and Dame Ninette de Valois.

During 1984 and 1985, families living abroad began to show a lot of interest in our programme, and several parents brought their children to us from as far away as Hong Kong, Singapore and Russia. Their efforts on behalf of their children led to an increase in public awareness about our work. More overseas families applied for help, and we began to hold a series of discussions with interested people in Singapore, Greece, Holland, Switzerland, and West Germany. In some of these countries, there was a strong possibility that similar Institutes might, in time, be created, and Lorna Whiston (Singapore), Mas and Marien Verhulst (Holland) and Theo Wollweber (West Germany) became regular visitors.

At the time of our disassociation from IAHP in 1980, we had agreed to avoid being linked in any future way with the Institutes in Philadelphia. In Britain, we had successfully achieved this objective, and BIBIC was now beginning to gain a reputation in its own right amongst families and other professionals for its good results.

On the continent, however, we discovered that our work was being referred to as the 'Doman therapy' – a description which was as inaccurate as it was unfair, both to Glenn Doman and to us. Old habits die hard, and despite our best efforts to avoid this confusion, it still exists today, *eighteen years* since my last contact of any kind with IAHP!

Early in 1986, the British Institute re-launched its newsletter under the new title of 'LEVEL 8'. During our search for a suitable name for this small but important publication, we remembered that every child on our programme is regularly assessed against our own standard – the Developmental Profile. Since there are eight levels on the Profile, then the eventual goal for every child and adult should be LEVEL 8, and this seemed a very appropriate title for the regular record of achievement which the newsletter in time became.

In March and April of the same year opportunities arose for the Institute to be nationally featured both in the press and on television. An article in the new daily paper 'Today' was followed up by both the BBC and TV-am. Since this was by no means the first time we had attracted the interest of the national media, the immediate result caught us unawares. Within a few weeks, over 700 families had written to us asking for more details! We knew that if only one third of them applied to join our programme, we would be very quickly swamped. The alternative would be to create a very long waiting list, which was out of the question.

An immediate expansion programme was agreed upon by our Board of Directors, involving the building of a new clinical wing, and a further increase in staff. A nation-wide 'Birthday Appeal' for £110,000 was conceived by our Appeals team and directed by Roger Holyoake, to highlight the forthcoming 15th anniversary of the original founding of the Institute, and to provide the finance needed to support our new plans. Anne Diamond and John Cleese agreed to spearhead our campaign, and we all got busy.

One month later, in May 1986, we held our first International Conference at Knowle Hall, to celebrate our tenth year in Bridgwater. Representatives came from Ireland, Australia, West Germany, and from the newly formed Institutes in Holland, Switzerland and Greece. Papers were read by several distinguished guests, and a considerable amount of fresh information was gained by everyone who attended.

The response to our Birthday Appeal was magnificent! Help came from all corners of Britain and from several overseas sources as well.

Sponsored events, a round-Britain rally, contributions from our local Societies for Brain Injured Children, gifts from large Trusts and small companies all helped to swell the kitty. Donations came from old friends and brand new ones. By January 1987 we had raised enough to allow building work to begin and from then on, despite some early bad weather, everything went to plan. In fact, progress was so good that we were able to set a date in July for the official opening. Once again, painting, plumbing and electrifying was the order of the day – only this time, we were able to rely on professionals to do it for us!

The climax to the whole venture came on July 1st, when Her Royal Highness, the Duchess of York visited the British Institute, and opened the new Wing.

After seventeen years; after an incredible amount of hard work by a great many people; after storms and periods of tranquillity, her visit was, as one of our mothers said, 'a dream come true'. BIBIC had finally 'arrived', under its own steam!

It became a tradition, almost since the Institute began, to frame the largest cheque we had ever received. Happily, this was a dynamic process, and from time to time new cheques were placed on the top of a growing pile. In 1987, Tony Brett, a London estate agent who had been impressed by our work, chose BIBIC to be the recipients of the proceeds of a large raffle, which he was in the habit of organising every two years. When the cheque was handed over, it was by far and away the largest single sum we had ever received – £31,040.

We thought that it would be a very long time before we received a donation larger than this. We were wrong. At the beginning of 1990, Tony did it again, only this time he succeeded in raising £61,140. I often wondered how long it would be before someone beat this record!

From time to time, the progress of all the children was reviewed, and this exercise was a measurement not only of their success, but also of the staff's skill. We had grown sufficiently confident that we *expected* progress to occur, and were delighted, but not necessarily surprised, when an eight-year-old boy walked for the first time, or a four-year-old girl learned to read for the first time, as a result of our programme. This review, however, not only measured our successes. It also measured our failures.

In 1988, just such a review pointed to the fact that there were a group of children who were not making progress, because they were too stiff. They could not move their own limbs, and we couldn't move them either.

During our International Conference in 1986, the Director of the Australian Institute, Tim Timmermans who, together with his wife,

Claire, had pioneered in his own country the teaching of babies and young children to swim, had spoken of the efficacy of warm water in relaxing the spastic muscles of brain injured children. Having held some trials of our own to confirm these findings, we decided to build a special Very Warm Water Pool, which would not only provide a means of reducing the stiffness, and remove the normally retarding effects of friction and gravity, but would also give us an opportunity to develop new techniques to encourage mobility in the children, while they were relaxed. To the best of our knowledge, no-one had ever previously attempted to carry out a programme of neurological stimulation similar to our own in warm water, and we were once again, almost literally, in at the deep end!

Our Fund Raising Department launched another National Appeal, which this time was the responsibility of Rita Hodder, our Appeals Organiser, to raise the £95,000 needed. In addition to all the Friends of the Institute (by now a large and growing number), we contacted all the Swimming Clubs in England and Wales, explaining why the money was needed, and asking for help.

If the response to our Appeal for funds to build the New Wing had been magnificent, the public reaction to our Pool Appeal was fantastic! Within sixteen months, our target had been exceeded, and the Pool was completed.

It was with a tremendous feeling of pride, in our families, in our staff, and in our abilities, that on November 14th, 1989, I welcomed for the second time Her Royal Highness, the Duchess of York to Knowle Hall. It was, at the same time, a very humbling thought that so many people, both in Britain and abroad, should have such faith in us.

After this second visit, Her Royal Highness continued to take a keen interest in our work, and in the progress of our children. On June 3rd, 1993, to celebrate the Institute's 21st Birthday, we organised a 'Fête Champêtre' – a large open-air picnic and concert in the grounds of Knowle Hall. The English Philharmonic Orchestra, conducted by Neil Moore, presented a programme of Classic Rock. Our Board Members, staff, and some of our families with their children were joined by more than 2,000 music lovers who came to help us celebrate. Her Royal Highness was our special guest, and spoke to us all of the importance of our efforts on behalf of the children, and of her pride in being associated with BIBIC, as we were now inevitably becoming known.

At the end of the evening, as the orchestra played 'Sweet Caroline', the full moon hovered over us, and fireworks brought their own extra excitement to the finale, I had to pinch myself to be sure that it really was not all another dream!

As our successes with the children became more widely known, and more families found us, it became more and more obvious that apart from their enthusiasm to help their children, many of them shared another emotion. They were angry. Angry to realise that their children could have been helped much earlier, had someone only told them that there was an alternative to their despair.

To this day, I believe that parents have the right to be informed about **all** the options available for their child, as soon as they discover that he or she is brain injured. So, as a first step to achieving this, it was decided in September, 1993 to initiate the first-ever national *Brain Injury Awareness Week*. Our press and PR activities produced over three hundred enquiries from families who had never heard of BIBIC before.

In October, 1994, we repeated the exercise, and this time linked our campaign with a new mascot, originated and developed by Rita Hodder. Everyone knows the nursery rhyme 'Humpty Dumpty'. We had used it for many years to accompany one of our best known techniques: 'Patterning'. Traditionally, all the King's horses and all the King's men couldn't put Humpty together again. So WE did! We put him back on his wall, with cracks in his head, but a smile on his face, and linked it to the slogan *'Putting Children Together Again'*. BIBIC's Humpty badges proved very popular, not just with children, but with adults too, and the donations received for them made it possible for still more children to be helped.

Enormous political changes have taken place in the last ten years, changes which most of us never thought we would live to see. The Berlin Wall; the Iron Curtain; the Warsaw Pact; all have crumbled. Compared to these momentous events, I suppose it is hardly surprising that families from Eastern Europe should have sought us out. What is amazing, however, is the determination which these parents showed in raising the funds to make the trip.

In 1991, we began to see one or two children from Poland, where the weakness of the zloty meant that it cost the equivalent of three months wages for a family just to fly to the UK. These one or two became a flood, and it soon became obvious that for Polish families to be able to follow our programme for the length of time necessary to make real inroads into their children's problems, an Institute would have to be set up in Poland itself.

The newly formed Polish Association ('Daj Szanse') selected two potential staff members: Dr Anna Grochal, and Angelika Murowska, and in 1993, they both came to England to carry out a full initial training with us. Simultaneously, a Polish edition of this book was published, so that families could read this information in their own language. By 1995, one hundred Polish children had come with their parents to Knowle Hall, through reading the book, or hearing about us from other families.

In May, 1995, the Unit in Poland began seeing children, at a fraction of the cost of bringing them to the UK, and I am sure their progress will justify the enormous faith which has been shown in this project by Polish people, from all over the world.

Poland was the first country to pioneer this new approach. Others may, in time, follow suit.

On February 22nd, 1998, the twenty-eighth anniversary of our first flight to Philadelphia, I quietly reviewed in my mind all that had happened to Alison, to me, to the rest of my family, and to the 1,425 children who had followed up to that time, with their parents, in our footsteps.

Alison is now thirty-one years old. She can run faster than I can. She can balance better on a trampoline than I can. Her vision is acute, at both long and short range. She can understand a great deal of what is said to her, and although she cannot talk, she can make herself understood with sounds and gestures. She knows where her hands are now, and can feed herself. Best of all, she can make some decisions for herself. We have given her options, when in the beginning, she had none. She is now a young lady, much loved by her family . . . and she is still improving! She followed the programme for a total of thirteen years, and whilst by our present standards her progress was not by any means the most remarkable we have known, it was steady and it was worth the effort.

All of our daughters have moved away from home. Susie is a staff nurse, now working in one of the London hospitals. Judy has gained a degree in European studies and French at Nottingham Trent University, has a qualification in Linguistics, and is now working with her mother and father as part of the Brain-Net team. Heather has qualified as a veterinary nurse in Shropshire and has produced Tolli, our first grandchild! Alison has also left the 'nest', and lives at Ashbury in Taunton. She attends Bridgwater Enterprise and Resource Centre two days each week, and Peperill Road Centre at Highbridge on another two days. She spends the remaining week-day with her key-worker, concentrating on activities of daily living. She comes home most weekends. She is lucky to be in the company of very caring staff, who are dedicated to bringing out the best in her at all times. She is a cheerful and loveable young lady, with a real personality of her own – a far cry from the frenetic, sad little child whose future seemed so bleak, all those years ago.

They all come home at various times, and Susie, Judy and Heather think the world of their elder sister. So do her mother and father.

As for all the other children, I only wish I had known, back in 1972, what I know now. Every year the results get better and better, and today we know so much more. Our clinical achievements are most encouraging, and are shown in detail in Part 6.

We started with a £30 cheque. In 1995, the Institute's annual turnover was more than £600,000. In the beginning, I was on my own. At the time I left BIBIC, it had a staff of 34.

Once, we only had five children to worry about. At the beginning of 1996 I was responsible for a patient list of over 240 children, not only from England, Scotland and Wales, but also from 17 overseas countries.

Now, my new consultancy, Brain-Net, has begun to grow, and as long as there are children who need its help, it will continue to devise better ways to give them that help.

. . . And me? Twenty-eight years is a large part of one's life.

In the beginning, my only aim ·was to help our little girl. Then, a few others like her. I never dreamed that I would ever visit America other than perhaps once, one day, for a holiday. There are thirty-nine American immigration stamps in my old passport! I never thought that as the Institute grew and became better known I would meet members of the Royal Family; Nobel prizewinners like Linus Pauling; academics like Prof. Raymond Dart, Prof. John Dickerson, and Prof. Adri Vermeer; industrialists like Dr Masaru Ibuka, the chairman of Sony Corporation; well-known personalities like Liza Minelli, David Frost, John Cleese, Anne Diamond, Roy Hudd, Ruth Madoc, Jimmy Tarbuck, and the late Leslie Crowther; and politicians like the late James Dunn, and the late George Thomas, ex-speaker of the House of Commons and later Lord Tonypandy. It never occurred to me that I would go to Brazil, Australia, Singapore, Italy, Germany, Holland, Poland, Malta, and other European countries to help children. Or that when the time came, I would have to stop riding someone else's coat tails, stand up for what I thought was right, even if others were sure I was wrong, and keep faith with an ideal.

Although, to this day, Alison has never spoken any recognisable words, she has taught me an enormous amount. So have all those other children who followed in her footsteps.

Thomas Edison once said that genius is one per cent inspiration, and ninety-nine per cent perspiration. We are still learning, every day, and the more we learn, the more it seems to me that, like genius, our results depend on similar proportions of those same two ingredients.

CHAPTER 8
A Step in the Dark:
the Founding of Brain-Net

Right from the time that I first sat down to write this book, I had begun to realise that although BIBIC could contribute much towards the treatment of brain injuries, it could never hope to reach all the children who might benefit from its skills. Apart from the obvious limitations which geography imposed, travel costs and, in some cases, the sheer inability of patients to travel at all, meant that thousands of youngsters all over the world would have to live with their problems, unless a different approach was attempted.

They couldn't travel . . . but I could. The knowledge we had gained in these twenty-six years wasn't available in their countries . . . but it could be taken there. The British Institute was established, and no longer needed a Founder, or a 'trouble-shooter'. At the beginning of 1996, I took another giant step into the unknown, and resigned my position as Chief Executive of the Institute.

Within a month, Brain-Net was created, a consultancy which could help to develop Institutes for Brain Injured Children anywhere in the world. Local staff could be trained; families need not go outside their own countries; funds could be sought locally, and invested locally. Staff from one Centre could, on occasion, assist and back up staff in another; an 'Internet' of expertise could gradually be created, and many, many more families, irrespective of colour, creed, nationality or language could find help. Brain-Net could offer mobile knowledge, and a window of opportunity for any organised group, anywhere, to develop its own Centre of Excellence for brain injured children.

Its motto states its objective very simply

'Rescuing Brain Injured Children Around the World'

This was another leap into the darkness, but within a matter of days, I was approached by Edgar Borg, Chief Executive of the Institute for Brain Injured Children (Malta). Could I help him and his Board to create and develop their own Unit to serve both Maltese children, and those of the Mediterranean basin?

For six years, beginning with Edgar himself, his wife Marika, and their daughter Maria, Maltese families had been regularly bringing their children to BIBIC. The expense was enormous, and the travelling involved often produced tired children and tired parents, just at the time when they needed to be bright and alert. There was a nucleus of children following the programme on the island, and their parents had clearly indicated their willingness to support their own Centre; Christa Bonello and Kenneth Cremona, two Maltese professionals, wanted to be trained; the Maltese Board was confident that sufficient funds could be raised to support the venture.

Brain-Net could do the job – of this I had no doubt, but at this point my wife, Valerie offered to join me. This made an enormous difference to our plans, since she could not only contribute her own extensive experience as a physiotherapist, and as a mother who had carried out a home programme with Alison for thirteen years, but she could also provide me with a Research and Development backup. Then, much to our delight, our daughter Judy asked if she could also join Brain-Net. Judy had been part of the family team working with Alison all the time she was growing up, and was already very familiar with our work; she had a strong affinity with children and had a degree in European Studies and French, and a qualification in Linguistics.

I signed a two-year contract with the Maltese Institute, or IBIC(M) as it soon became known, which would require us to work in Malta for three weeks in every six, and at the end of May, 1996, we flew there to begin.

The Maltese Board had found a beautiful villa on the coast, six miles north of Valletta, in a village called Bahar ic-Caghaq (pronounced Bahar ichar, and meaning 'Sea of Stones'). But when we arrived, there was not even a paper clip! This was soon rectified, and after a week of dawn-to-dusk typing, and magnificent scrounging on the part of our hosts, we saw our first Maltese patient.

The creation of IBIC(M) felt to me like a constant experience of déjà vu. For every problem that arose, we had an answer. We had 'been there before'. Our first Initial Assessment week, for new Maltese families, was an exercise in improvisation, but it worked, and both we and the families thoroughly enjoyed it.

For so many years we had faced an uphill struggle to gain acceptance for our work with the children by the medical establishment. Then, in December 1996, I was invited to become a Knight of Honour of the Maltese Order of Knights Hospitallers of St John of Jerusalem – an honour which belonged not just to me, but to Valerie, Judy, and to all those Maltese families, staff and Board Members who had together created the Maltese Institute.

When our Maltese venture began, and we started to implement the principles upon which Brain-Net had been created, it never occurred to me for one moment that we would ever be working again in the UK Our future seemed to be solidly linked with overseas countries, because that was the way we had thought of it. But destiny has many strange and devious twists and turns, and in the autumn of 1996, we were approached by several families in Britain who wished us to treat their children. One of these, Una Nunan and her daughter Brigid, we had known for 25 years. My first thought was, obviously, 'But our time is fully taken up with our Malta contract', but of course this wasn't true. Half our time, that spent in the UK, *was* available. The requests were insistent, and demanded a positive response.

We had no centre of our own in the UK. We had no equipment. But we had twenty-seven years experience of working with brain injured children. And if we could create a British Institute, and a Maltese Institute, we could certainly create a Brain-Net Unit.

We soon found our centre. When she died, in 1991, my mother had left me her house in our village. It was large – large enough to provide us with Consulting Rooms, and a big area in which to work with children and parents. We sought planning permission for change of use, and it was granted. Equipment was no problem. Our equipment has always been simple, so that it could easily be constructed by parents in their own homes. All we really needed was a good carpenter, and one was soon found.

Our new Unit needed a name, and this was perhaps the easiest decision of all. Brain-Net's new base in the UK would be called

THE ALISON CENTRE.

From the moment that we began to turn our latest idea into reality, I was amazed at how many people were ready and willing to help us. John Williams, who had joined BIBIC as a bookkeeper, and had in due course been promoted, on my recommendation, first to Comptroller, and then to Finance Manager, had decided to leave the Institute, and to start his own business. Brain-Net became his first customer, and it is a measure of his confidence in our future, and our friendship, that many of the hours of work which John spent helping to set up our consultancy were never charged for. His wife, Irene, was also always willing to lend a hand whenever she could.

We needed funds. We approached the bank, and their response was immediate, positive and helpful. Their only question was, 'How much do you want?'

Our local newspaper, the Bridgwater Mercury, ran an article on the start of our new venture, and followed it up by publishing our own editorial, supported by advertisements paid for by local businesses who had helped us.

The North Devon Society for Brain Injured Children, for many years a supporter of our work, announced that it wished to mark my 23 years service at BIBIC by providing the Alison Centre with a gift. This gift turned out to be a complete set of measuring tools, imported from Switzerland, and the very best available. Our children's future physical growth would be most accurately recorded.

The 'Internet' of Clinics was also becoming a reality. We had direct contact with similar units in Ireland, Australia, Poland, and of course, Malta. We were beginning to share data. The Maltese Board had readily agreed to lend us staff, as and when we had need of them, and in all these places, the children were beginning to benefit from our combined knowledge. Thanks to good friends of ours in Holland, Machteld Linschoten and Dieter van Werkum, we had our own web-site on the Internet. And, to complete the circle, we received a request to help a brain injured child in .... the United States!

On 2nd April 1997, we saw Brigid Nunan for re-assessment at our new unit. Five days later, on 7th April, we saw our first *new* children at the Alison Centre. Our second Brain-Net venture was up and running.

We have learned many lessons. We have successfully started three Centres for Brain Injured Children. We have treated over 1,400 children, whose quality of life has been greatly improved as a result. There are still many more questions to address. But now is a good time to put some of the lessons already learned on paper, in the hope that others may read them and come to realise that many of the problems created in children by brain injury can often be alleviated, and sometimes even eliminated.

PART TWO

Why?

CHAPTER 9

What is Wrong with your Child, and What Isn't?

Ever since the first child was born 'different' from the rest, human beings have tried to find appropriate language to describe these differences, and the more that has been learned, the more the vocabulary has grown.

Cerebral palsied, spastic, autistic, mentally retarded, handicapped, dyspraxic, Aspergers Syndrome, backward, ADHD, hyperactive, Down's Syndrome, epileptic, dyslexic, . . . the list goes on and on, and these words have become a lingua franca amongst both parents and professionals, although their meaning is not always fully understood by either group. Yet it is apparently possible for one child to be simultaneously suffering from several of these 'diseases', and it is also possible that the number from which he is suffering is often in direct proportion to the number of specialists whom he has seen.

What are these words? They are an exercise in classification. They are a description of symptoms. They are, in fact, labels.

Unfortunately, once labelled, a child is thereafter expected to conform to experience, and if experience shows that all previously known cases of mental handicap, or whichever other label it happens to be, have not shown much improvement, then it is assumed that his future will be similarly bleak.

'Once a spastic, always a spastic' is a well-known saying. So is, 'There is no cure for mental handicap'. Yet these statements, like all statements, must surely be open to scrutiny? To say that a child is the way he is, and must always remain that way, is rather like saying 'We live in mud huts, we have always lived in mud huts, and we will always live in mud huts!' Who says so?

It would be more fair if such statements were at least followed by the words, '. . . in my experience'.

It is hardly surprising that children suffering from the 'disease' of mental handicap stand no chance of overcoming their problems, if no-one believes this to be a possibility. If no-one had believed it possible to fly, aircraft would not exist. What is worse, labels like these, and the dismal predictions which accompany them, can become self-fulfilling prophecies!

If we were to look, not at the symptom, but at the underlying cause of all these problems, then we would invariably discover that it lies, not in the arms, legs, eyes, ears, or intelligence quotient, but in the BRAIN.

The brain is the controlling mechanism for every part of the human body. It is responsible for receiving and storing information, and for sending instructions to the entire body. The arms, legs, eyes and ears are the brain's tools, by which it translates thought into action. It therefore follows that if any part of the brain sustains an injury, the result will be seen in a reduction of function somewhere in the body.

Since the brain is encased in a solid skull, and cannot be seen, whilst arms, legs, eyes and ears are readily observable, it is easy to jump to the conclusion that, if the arm or leg no longer works as it should, the problem must lie there, on the periphery. Yet BRAIN INJURY IS IN THE BRAIN, and if we want to solve the problem created by the brain injury, we must surely look at the brain, rather than at the arms or legs.

I have made mention earlier of 1976 – the British 'Year of the Drought'. It was also the year I moved, with my family, to Knowle Hall.

As we now found ourselves living in part of a large house, set in the middle of thirteen acres of parkland, and as our children had already learned how to ride a horse, it seemed a good idea to give them a regular opportunity to do so. My mother very generously bought for them a suitable pony.

One day, my second-eldest daughter, Susie, was riding the pony when, unfortunately, the animal was stung by a horsefly. It reared and threw Susie, who, having lost her riding hat on the way down, struck her head on the ground. The soil was so hard, after the prolonged period of dry weather, that she might as well have hit her head on solid concrete!

The first I knew of the incident was when I saw one of our staff hastening up to the house from the bottom of the field, carrying my daughter in his arms. I ran across, and immediately noticed that the pupil of one of Susie's eyes was a different size from the pupil of the other one – a standard symptom of concussion.

She had not hit her EYES on the ground. She had hit her HEAD on the ground, yet the pupils of her eyes were now no longer the same size. Although the symptom of concussion could be seen on the periphery, it was the brain, not the eyes, which had been concussed.

Luckily, Susie was none the worse for the mishap, and as soon as her brain recovered, the symptoms disappeared and her pupils became normal once again.

There is no disease that can be cured by treating the symptom. The common cold, if left untreated, lasts about ten days. If we treat the symptoms, it lasts about ten days Fever is a common symptom of appendicitis. Yet no-one would dream of treating the fever, in the expectation that the appendicitis would 'go away'. Only by operating to remove the offending appendix, would we be sure to rid the patient of the fever.

The words 'cerebral palsy' are very commonly used to describe a child with a physical handicap, or motor disorder. **Cerebral** sounds like something to do with the brain. So far, so good. **Palsy**, however, means either 'paralysed' or 'shaking', and since the brain can neither be paralysed, nor can it 'shake', the whole label is clearly inaccurate and archaic. What is worse, there appear nowadays to be over 100 different types of 'cerebral palsy' – not very helpful to the enquiring parent.

What does 'mentally handicapped' mean? Are you, the reader, mentally handicapped? It depends, doesn't it? If we compare you to a severely sub-normal patient in the locked ward of a mental hospital, you will doubtless say 'No! Of course not.' But, what will you say if we compare you to Einstein? The term 'mental handicap' is not the description of a disease. It is rather the result of a social comparison.

Suppose I had a 'spastic' arm. I couldn't lift it, or move it. To all intents and purposes, it was useless to me. Suppose you were feeling particularly philanthropic, and decided, out of the goodness of your heart, to give me your perfectly good right arm. Suppose such a transplant could be efficiently carried out.

On you, my 'spastic' arm would function (given a certain amount of physiotherapy). On me, your perfectly good right arm would very rapidly become 'spastic'. The reason? The problem does not lie in my arm – nor in my fingers, my wrist, my elbow, or my shoulder. The problem is IN MY BRAIN, and until it has been successfully treated IN MY BRAIN, I will continue to show the symptoms in my arm.

If all these labels are not the problem, and only lead to more and more confusion, and if brain injury is the real culprit, then why don't we stop using all the labels, and refer to the problem by its real name – BRAIN INJURY?

The probable answer is that people are scared of brain injury. They don't understand it, and feel the words to carry some form of stigma. There should be no stigma relating to 'brain injury', any more than there is to 'leg injury' or 'back injury'. But we all understand the other two disabilities. We can see legs and backs. We cannot see the brain, we don't understand the brain, and we often link the brain with some sort of mental aberration or unpredictable behaviour.

Would we still do this if everyone in the world was brain injured?

It is amazing how many people stick doggedly to the old terms, as if they can somehow live comfortably with the thought that their child is mentally retarded, but cannot cope with the awesome prospect that he might be 'brain injured'.

There are, in fact, only three descriptions of hurt children which attempt to describe the real problem, rather than its symptoms. These are:

CONGENITALLY MALFORMED

PSYCHOTIC

BRAIN INJURED

When we speak of a congenital malformation of the brain, we mean an aberration which occurred at conception. A child with this problem could not have developed a whole, normal brain in any event.

Were we to take a biopsy or sample of certain areas of a normal child's brain, and look at it under a microscope, we would see plump, healthy, spaghetti-like tissue. A biopsy from the same areas of a child's brain which was malformed from conception would show tiny, shrunken, hairpin-like distortions, which are known as macro- or micro-gyro. Sometimes the tissue of the brain is badly formed, and its quality is poor. On other occasions, parts of the brain never developed at all, and the result is an organ which is quantitatively inferior. This usually leads to a qualitative deficiency.

Thomas came to us in June, 1984, when he was eighteen months old. He had already been diagnosed as having an 'agenesis of the corpus callosum', meaning that this particular area of his brain, which is responsible for the co-ordination of information between the two hemispheres, had not developed. His parents were told that he would never walk, and faced a 'wheel-bound' future. After six years following our programme, Thomas had begun to read and talk; had learned to creep on his tummy, crawl on his hands and knees and to walk, all despite the fact that his brain was congenitally malformed!

There are some children whose brains show no evidence of malformation, but whose behaviour is markedly different from that of normal children. They are thought to be suffering from a severe form of mental disturbance, and, are called psychotic. In our experience, they do not respond positively to our programme.

. . . Then there are BRAIN INJURED children.

CHAPTER 10
What is Brain Injury?

We define a brain injured person as someone who, from the time of their conception, began to develop a perfectly whole, perfectly normal brain, but who, seconds, minutes, hours, days, weeks, months or years later, suffered an insult to the brain which resulted in the loss of one or more brain cells.

CHAPTER 11

Who is Brain Injured and Who Isn't?

This is a good question! By our definition, EVERYONE is to some degree brain injured, a fact which should bring the whole problem back into perspective. Unfortunately, it usually doesn't.

To the parent of a brain injured child, the following story might sound familiar.

You are pushing your brain injured child, in her pram, along the High Street, and a neighbour, with whom you are barely acquainted, comes up to you and declares, 'Oh, do let me see the baby!'

A look then passes across her face. I call it the 'There, but for the grace of God' look, or the 'Thank God my child's not like hers' look. What the neighbour doesn't realise is that the only difference, neurologically, between herself and your child in her pram is the number of functional brain cells which have been destroyed.

It has been estimated that a new-born baby has, within his skull, approximately one hundred thousand million brain cells (100,000,000,000). Of these, ten thousand million (10,000,000,000) are thought to be neurons, or nerve cells capable of function.

From birth, the death process begins, and every day we lose cells from areas all over the body. The less complex the organ, the more regenerative power it has, which is why the skin – that clever but relatively uncomplicated outer layer of our bodies – is able to completely regenerate itself each month.

The brain itself is not excluded from this very slow and gradual process of decay, and, being the most complex of all our organs, it has no known ability to regrow cells. Therefore, we are all losing brain cells at a gradually increasing rate. It has been calculated that, by the time he reaches the age of thirty-five, a normal human being is probably losing 100,000 brain cells PER DAY! And this rate of attrition excludes any untoward accidents.

Of course, there are ways of accelerating our losses. When you bend down in the kitchen, or in the garage, to pick up something you dropped, and bang your head on the cupboard door during the return trip, you lose more brain cells. When you go to a party, and have a few drinks with friends, you lose a few more: alcohol kills brain cells. When you succumb to a virus, particularly during childhood, and suffer an unusually high fever, you can suffer the loss of quite a few brain cells which are killed by the high body temperature.

In fact anyone who has ever banged his head hard, or who has taken a drink of alcohol, or who has suffered a high fever, has probably increased the extent of his brain injury.

And yet, you say, 'I can function perfectly well. How can you possibly compare me with those poor children who cannot move, or see or hear?'

Ten thousand million is a large number. We know it is possible for the brain to lose, literally, millions of brain cells without there being any obvious functional impairment as a result.

In the case of our children, something overwhelming has obviously occurred in addition to the normally expected loss rate of brain cells. What?

CHAPTER 12
What Causes Brain Injury?

I have so far mentioned three ways by which any one of us can suffer a degree of brain injury: a blow to the head, the intake of alcohol, and high fever. There are, however, hundreds of ways the brain can be insulted, and any attempt to catalogue all the possibilities would become tedious both to read, and to compile. It should also be remembered that the relationship between the cause of a brain injury and the eventual outcome is largely academic. So is the timing. Whether it occurred before, during or after birth is like saying, 'Did the child's head go through the windscreen of the car in the morning, at lunchtime, or in the afternoon?' When it happened is scarcely relevant. The important fact is that her head went through the car windscreen AND SHE IS NOW BRAIN INJURED. Nevertheless, there is always a tendency in parents to compare the history of their child with other children's, particularly when other children have made good progress in overcoming their problems. They are also anxious to avoid, if possible, the same thing happening to their next child. So let us look at some examples of how brain injury can occur.

Dominik's mother caught a viral infection within the first three months of her pregnancy, and he become severely affected. Although in this example Dominik suffered from the effects of the Rubella, or 'German Measles' virus, any virus can be damaging.

If a mother-to-be indulges in smoking or alcohol during her pregnancy, or is given drugs, or if she suffers a physical accident, any of these insults can cause brain injury in her child. Drugs, in this context, can include the 'Pill', and a conception immediately following the discontinuation of an oral contraceptive can be hazardous to the embryo. Rosemary's mother was given Thalidomide, which resulted in Rosemary suffering a severe brain injury.

Christine's mother suffered toxaemia, which caused severe damage to the baby's brain.

At the time of delivery, an over-swift labour can also cause problems. During the passage of the baby's head through the birth canal, several positive and negative pressures are experienced which are held to be important to proper brain development. A very fast delivery can negate the effects of some of these pressures, and brain injury can result. Diane's mother experienced her first labour pains 40 minutes after a surgical induction. Ten minutes later, she felt the onset of the second stage, and the baby was born 10 minutes after that – a total labour time of 20 minutes. Diane suffered brain injury.

On the other hand, a very long labour can also produce problems. Craig's mum was allowed to undergo an extended labour of 21 hours, which brought about severe injuries to Craig's brain.

Prematurity is often a cause of brain injury. Whilst by no means all premature babies are, of necessity, brain injured, a higher percentage of premature babies exists within our population of brain injured children than is the case in the total population. Of a sample of 613 children whom we have treated, prematurity can be cited as the primary cause of brain injury in 38, and as a secondary cause in 93. Meghan was born at 31 weeks, and still could not walk when she came to us at the age of three.

The converse – babies who go over term and are post-mature – also run a higher than average risk of being born brain injured. Philipp was finally born after his mother's pregnancy had been allowed to continue a full three weeks beyond full term.

It is possible for a child to be hurt if delivered by Caesarean section. One of the first such recorded cases was that of Julius Caesar, from whose name the procedure derives, and he was brain injured. (He suffered from epileptic fits, one of the symptoms of brain injury.) Of course, not every child born in this way is automatically brain injured, far from it. But, again, we have had a much higher percentage of children born by Caesarean section amongst our patients than exists in the total population.

Brain injury can occur if there is a pre-existing obstetrical problem, such as placenta previa, where the placenta has developed close to, or across, the exit from the womb, or placenta abruptia, where the placenta becomes prematurely detached from the wall of the uterus. Edward suffered brain injury from the first condition, and Jeroen from the second.

Occasionally, and regrettably, a baby can become hurt during the final stages of labour as a result of professional incompetency. Paul's mum was left without assistance for 29 hours, over a bank-holiday weekend, and during this time, he developed symptoms of foetal distress. By the time help came, he had been starved of oxygen for too long, and was severely brain injured.

When Nicola was born, the umbilical cord was very tightly wrapped round her neck, preventing the intake of oxygen, and the flow of blood to her brain. This caused widespread brain injury.

Once a baby is born, the risks do not diminish.

When only six hours old, Jonathan suffered a cardiac arrest, and was starved of oxygen for too long. The result: brain injury.

When seventeen weeks old, Ross was given the triple vaccine to protect him from whooping cough, diphtheria and tetanus. Unfortunately, he was allergic to the vaccine, and developed an encephalitis, or brain inflammation, resulting in brain injury.

At the age of eight months, Guy was being pushed along the pavement by his father when a car mounted the kerb and carried the pram and baby through a plate-glass shop window. Guy suffered instant injury to his brain.

One of the primary requirements of all brain cells is a regular and sufficient supply of oxygen. If the brain is deprived of oxygen for more than three minutes, cells begin to die. At a year and a half, Jake was toddling around the edge of the pond in his own back garden, and fell in. By the time he was discovered, taken from the water and re-suscitated, he had been starved of oxygen for too long, and millions of brain cells had died.

When he was three years one month old, Jim went into hospital. His only problem was that his left ear 'stuck out', and his parents felt he would suffer less teasing at school if it was pinned back. Whilst under general anaesthetic, his heart stopped. The surgical team took immediate action, but by the time they had succeeded in restoring normal heart function, Jim had been deprived of oxygen for too long, and was now severely brain injured.

Lucille, who did not receive the appropriate vaccine, caught measles when she was 14 months old. She was allergic to the virus, and developed encephalitis, resulting in brain injury.

Paula, a lively ten-year-old girl, was attacked by a man with an axe on her way home from school. She received twelve blows to the head, and was left lying in a ditch, unconscious, bleeding and severely brain injured.

At thirteen, Astrid fell from the bars whilst climbing in the gymnasium, and suffered a severe trauma to her brain . . .

Lisa caught meningitis . . .

Trevor fell off the back of a motor bike . . .

All these examples, and many, many more, are of children and young people whose conception was in no way unusual, and who had every expectation of becoming fully functional, normal human beings. They sustained brain injury seconds, minutes, hours, days, weeks, months, and even years later. What happened to them could happen to anyone, and suddenly, the future for both them and their parents became a nightmare.

CHAPTER 13
Neurological Organisation

Dr Edward B. LeWinn, who was for many years Director of Clinical Investigation at IAHP in Philadelphia, defined the concept of 'Neurological Organisation' as being 'the process whereby an organism, subject to environmental forces, achieves the potential inherent in its genetic endowment'.

Human beings are intended to be able to see, hear, understand, creep, crawl, walk, run, talk and write. Every human egg or sperm contains a genetic blueprint which, once the egg becomes fertilised, begins to produce human physical and neurological characteristics. Provided this blueprint is not interfered with, and is allowed faithfully to reproduce its information, a baby will be born with arms and hands, eyes and ears, legs, a whole body, and a brain capable in time of controlling the fantastically complicated systems and subsystems which are needed in order to sustain and promote life and function.

This blueprint not only carries instructions relating to physical growth and development, it also contains information relating to neurological growth, and during the first six years of life, a child's brain slowly develops within this predetermined framework, until he or she is able to function like all other normal human beings,
provided this blueprint is not interfered with.
There are two obvious ways in which interference can occur. If a child is exposed to a very high level of sensory stimulation, coupled with a greatly enhanced opportunity for motor activity, his development can be speeded. If a child is deprived of the opportunity to take in very much information through his senses, and has no chance to practise what little information he has been able to absorb, then his development will be slowed, or even stopped. This deprivation can be of two kinds: environmental or pathological.

In our culture, it is considered quite acceptable to allow a young child to spend time on the floor. As the famous educator, Arnold Gesell wrote, 'The floor is nature's playground for the infant.' Normal children learn to roll over, lift their heads, creep, crawl, walk, run, hop, skip, jump, perform cartwheels and somersaults *on the floor*. As we will see later on, it is also on the floor where they first learn to focus their eyes, a necessary precursor to the skill of being able to read.

There are, however, other cultures in the world that view the floor very differently. In South America, for instance, some Indian tribes would not dream of placing a baby on the floor. Their 'floor' is the earth itself, and it is inhabited by snakes, spiders and other creatures whose very existence would threaten the life of a precious child. Instead, mothers carry their babies on their backs until they are old enough to fend for themselves, and these children never have the opportunity to creep or crawl.

Since the 'floor' does not play any part in their early development, it is hardly surprising that whilst the adults in these tribes develop extraordinarily good long sight, they have no ability to focus their eyes at near point. Nor is it strange that in these cultures, there is no written language, and that no-one can read.

In this example, the hostile environment has prevented the development of a basic neurological function – the ability to read.

Of course, non-readers exist in our own culture too, where the floor is 'friendly'. Their lack of ability to focus can very often be traced to the presence of **brain injury**. In fact, I have never seen a child whose history revealed that the presence of brain injury was incontrovertible, who did not have a visual problem. Of all the senses, vision is the most fragile, and the first to be affected when an injury occurs to the brain.

Brain function can be graded. Children can be mildly hurt, moderately hurt, severely hurt, profoundly hurt or completely hurt, and it is possible to define each of these conditions in terms of loss of function. If we were to invent a scale, from 0 to 10, and apply it to the organisational abilities of the brain, then it would cover all conditions from death, where neurological organisation would be zero, to ideal, where we would have to describe a child so far advanced physically, intellectually and socially that he does not yet exist except in our imagination.

Since the beginning of this century, the definition of death has changed several times. Of course, everyone knew what death meant, but the question was, 'When is someone actually dead?'

It was thought that death was connected with respiration, and a person was dead when he stopped breathing. But, once it became possible to restart the body's breathing mechanisms by means of artificial respiration, this was no longer an adequate definition. Then,

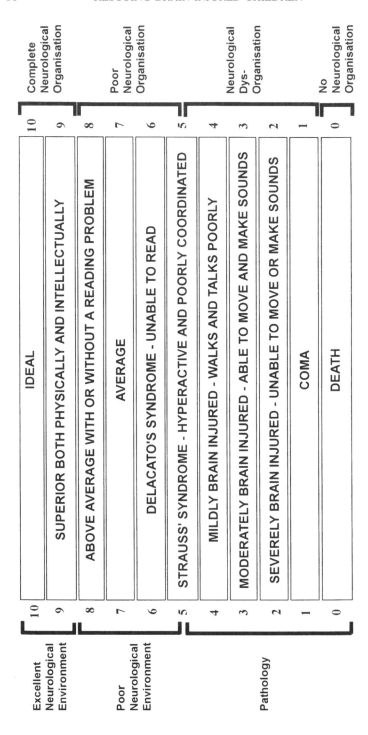

Figure 1   Neurological Organisation Chart

death was held to be a cardiological fact, and once the heart stopped beating, its owner had died. The advent of improved cardiological techniques, including defibrillation equipment and more recently the advances in transplant surgery, soon discounted this view. Now, it is generally held that death is a neurological state, in which the brain has ceased to function.

If we put that another way, death can be defined as a condition where there is NO neurological organisation, and as such can be regarded as the lowest point on our scale.

At the next level, scoring only 1, must be the child who cannot see, hear, feel, taste or smell, and whose breathing is so shallow and irregular that it cannot be easily detected or monitored. This condition, which is referred to as coma, is close to death, and represents a very poor level of neurological organisation.

Having seen children who, following the success of our coma programme (see Part 5), had recovered from coma, but although once more conscious were unable to move any of their limbs, and/or produce any sounds, it seems reasonable to assume that this is the next level, rating a 2, and demonstrating a slightly improved degree of neurological organisation.

I have seen children who, having been in coma and having regained consciousness, have then begun to respond to an appropriately increased amount of sensory stimulation coupled with plenty of opportunity for motor activity. Some of these children have in time begun to move independently. Some have begun to develop communicative sounds. Some have achieved both of these skills. Their degree of organisation must be regarded as better than level 2, and we can score them at level 3.

A child whose mobility is limited to forward movement on his tummy, and who can only make a few meaningful noises, may after some time respond sufficiently well to his daily home programme to begin to take some independent steps, and to speak a few simple words. Obviously, this youngster's brain has learned more advanced skills, and his neurological organisation is higher up the scale – at level 4.

Whilst all brain injured children are a challenge both to their parents and to us, the child at level 5 is particularly difficult to cope with. He is at one and the same time hyperactive and poorly co-ordinated. His brain has developed enough organisation to enable him to walk, and even to run – albeit badly – yet not enough to prevent the frenetic behaviour typical of this developmental stage.

Hyperactivity can be calmed and co-ordination can be improved. Yet we may still be left with a child who can walk, and talk, and appears to be normal until we ask him to read. We may then find that he cannot focus his eyes, or has mixed dominance (see Part 4), or reverses words, or generally appears to be intellectually very mixed up. His level of organisation, whilst higher than the other levels already described, is still below normal, and we would rate it as 6.

The vast majority of children probably fall into the next category, as do those children who respond to our programme and learn to read. They are called average – a word which is difficult to define when talking about human beings. Everyone is good at something. All of us do some things better than other people, and some things worse than other people, and no-one is truly 'average'. But, as everyone understands, or thinks they understand the word, let us use it. These children are 'averagely' organised, and we place them at level 7.

We know that, given a sufficiently stimulating environment, some children function at above average levels. Strangely, they may nevertheless experience problems when asked to read, yet are still good enough to come out top of the batting averages, or can produce a superb, hand-crafted piece of furniture. In their case, only one function of the brain is disorganised, whilst all the others are of a high standard. This child merits a score of 8.

Some children develop so well that they achieve high honours both physically and intellectually. They become Rhodes Scholars and Olympic Stars. They put the rest of us to shame, and personify human achievement at its highest level. On our scale, at level 9, they represent the best present performance of homo sapiens.

Level 10 children do not yet exist. But I suspect that one day they will. I also hope that they will, since their extraordinary abilities are going to be badly needed if man is ever going to overcome the ecological and survival problems already beginning to threaten his existence on this planet. We call these children 'ideal' although, as I suspect their emergence will be gradual rather than immediate, it may be that a new scale will one day be required to measure the various levels of 'ideal'!

The scale is now complete, and every human being alive has a place on it somewhere. The top two levels represent as complete a picture of neurological organisation as we can imagine. The very fact that they exist, or could exist, has the effect of downgrading the next three, so that what would otherwise be acceptable must be regarded as relatively poor. The next five demonstrate increasing levels of disorganisation, and the last, level 0, indicates no organisation at all.

There is little difference in function between a child who has absorbed information into his brain, and then lost it as the result of brain injury, and a child who, because of environmental deprivation, has never absorbed it in the first place. Between levels 0 and 5, tests can reveal positive evidence of brain injury, and the presence of pathology is therefore provable. Between levels 6 and 8, relatively poor neurological abilities can be the result of insufficient stimulation, or a poor neurological environment. Levels 9 and 10 require, and are the product of, a comparatively excellent neurological environment.

Now we can measure children in terms of their function, and relate them to other children whose abilities may be greater or lesser than their own. We can also measure the progress of well children, since our scale mirrors very clearly the early stages of their development, too.

We could say that a new-born baby is somewhere between levels 2 and 3, in that he can move his limbs, although only at random, and can produce a few sounds although these lack any meaning. By the time he is six months old, he has learned to creep on his tummy, to crawl on his hands and knees and to make communicative sounds, and has moved firmly into level 3. At twelve months, he is beginning to walk, using his arms for balance, can say a few words, and is at level 4. At two, he is learning at a mile a minute, and is so busy that to keep up with him would quickly exhaust the strongest athlete. This hyperactivity is coupled with a degree of clumsiness, as he has not yet learned how to fully control his hands, feet and body movements. He is now at level 5. Then, from the age of three, as his physical abilities become fully established, and he progresses to running, hopping, and kicking a ball, he moves up to level 6. If the opportunities present themselves, or if his parents are keen, he may well move rapidly on to level 7, reading before he enters primary school.

The well child does not start at levels 2 and 3 because he is brain injured. He begins there because at birth his brain has not yet developed higher skills. His upward progression from level to level is not only predictable; it is also expected, and if it does not happen, then we face the probability that he is either brain injured, or is suffering from severe environmental deprivation.

Children can also move down the scale. Sadly, while you have been reading this chapter, a child somewhere in this country will have travelled very rapidly indeed down the scale, accompanied by a screech of brakes. Depending on the speed of the car that hit him, and the force of the blow to his skull, this youngster, who was probably at level 7 a few moments ago, may well now be anywhere between levels 0 and 4.

It is also possible for people to forsake their normal level temporarily, and to travel gradually or swiftly to much lower positions.

Imagine a fighter pilot flying overhead at 65,000 feet. If a problem occurs in his oxygen supply, he will quite quickly begin to descend the scale, as the organisational ability of his brain begins to deteriorate. He will become unable to read the aircraft's instruments. He will no longer be able to co-ordinate his movements on the controls. His speech over the radio will become slurred, then incomprehensible. He will lose all ability to move, and will become comatose. Finally he will die – unless his supply of oxygen is restored, when he will gradually regain his original skills, and move back up the scale to his starting point.

We aren't all fighter pilots, but most of us enjoy a drink now and again. Whenever someone drinks too much, his neurological organisation deteriorates. He finds it harder and harder to read notices and posters behind the bar. He spills his drink as his co-ordination worsens, and he may become belligerent. He can no longer walk normally or talk coherently and before long falls down, and stays down. Were it possible for him to continue to take in more alcohol, he would become comatose, with death just around the corner.

Yet if we were to cut off the supply of alcohol, and allow time for his blood alcohol level to return to normal, his neurological abilities would be restored, and he would once more be able to function at his normal level.

Most of us, at one time or another, have had to go into hospital for an operation involving a general anaesthetic. This is usually preceded by a pre-med injection, and once the drug begins to take effect, we slowly begin to descend the scale. In the space of a few seconds, after breathing into a mask or feeling a second prick in the arm, we lose consciousness, and are now down at level 1.

Once the operation is over, we are put in a RECOVERY room, since we are expected to recover, or regain completely our normal capabilities. A nurse will regularly check to see if we 'have come round yet'. WE ARE EXPECTED TO RECOVER. WE ARE EXPECTED TO TRAVEL BACK UP THE SCALE TO NORMALITY.

Earlier, I discussed the confusion which regularly occurs in parents' minds as a result of the use of labels. Suppose we were to apply some of the labels to our scale. Describing a child at level 1, we might find the American term 'vegetable', or even worse the more specific British word 'cabbage'. At level 2 might be 'severe spastic', and at level 3, 'moderate cerebral palsy'. 'mentally handicapped' could be used to describe level 4, and 'having autistic tendencies', level 5. The old word for level 6 used to be 'stupid', but this has now been supplanted by the modern term 'dyslexic'.

There are also words for the other levels. 'Strange' is applied to level 8: 'Isn't it *strange* how he is so good at sport, yet so bad at reading'. Level 9, with its connotations of superiority and the master race concept, is downright 'threatening'.

As we have seen, our scale is dynamic. It allows for movement, in both directions. But whilst it makes a great deal of sense for a child to rise gradually up the scale as his neurological organisation improves in response to intensive stimulation, it makes no sense that the day he overcomes the condition called 'severe spasticity' he should immediately begin to suffer from a new condition called 'moderate cerebral palsy'! etc., etc.

I wish we knew how to restore brain injured children to a full level of function as speedily as we can bring a pilot round from anoxia, a drunk round from overindulgence, or a patient round from a general anaesthetic. We don't. It takes far, far longer. But it can be done. As you read this page, several hundred children in several different countries – our children – whose brain injuries vary from level 1 to level 6 on our scale of neurological organisation, are very slowly progressing upwards, despite all the negative prophecies, despite the pessimistic opinions, and despite all those who insist that it cannot be done.

CHAPTER 14

The Potential of the Brain

Very occasionally, neurosurgeons have to perform an operation known as a hemispherectomy. When a patient suffers from strong and uncontrollable convulsions, coupled with the paralysis of one side of the body, and also exhibits wildly aberrant behaviour, there may be no alternative to the removal of one hemisphere of the brain.

I know of a child who underwent such an operation. Today, that little girl can walk, talk, read, write, and is virtually indistinguishable from her peer group. Yet, she only has half a brain.

Of course, this could lead us into the exploration of two entirely different questions: 'If she can function as well as I can with only half a brain, whatever is wrong with me? Should I not be able to achieve more, with my whole brain, than she does with only half a brain?' They are both interesting philosophical questions, but as we are concerned with raising the functional levels of brain injured children, rather than 'moving the goal posts' further away from them, let us avoid this red herring, and proceed!

Some years ago, the BBC broadcast a programme with a challenging title. It was 'Is the brain really necessary?' The story it told was of a young man who had been killed in a car accident. The usual post-mortem had been carried out, and he had been found to have only one-third of the normally expected three centimetres of cerebral cortex. The first reaction of the police had been to wonder how he had managed to obtain a driving licence in the first place, but on enquiring further, they had found that he had not only gained a driving licence, he also possessed a first-class honours degree in mathematics from one of our old-established Universities!

It turned out that, as a child, he had contracted hydrocephalus, or 'water on the brain', and the excessive pressure to which his brain had been subjected had destroyed two-thirds of his cortex. Yet he had lived an above average life.

The conclusion therefore drawn was: 'So who needs the rest?' If he could achieve all that with a fraction of the brain which the rest of us have, then surely large areas of our brains must be redundant.

For the vast majority of us, this is, in fact, true. At the present stage of development of mankind, our brains have an enormous, built-in redundancy factor. Even if we were all to live to the age of 100, none of us would use more than perhaps 10% of our available brain capacity, and the rest – 90% of the neurons with which we were born – would have lived, remained dormant and died, without ever having being called upon to function.

But remember, ten thousand years ago man probably used very much less of his brain than is the case today, and the very fact that we still have so much, not redundant brain, but *potential* brain, would indicate that homo sapiens still has a long way to go before he reaches his full capability.

I did say 'for the vast majority of us'. There is one group of human beings for whom this vast potential resource is significant: brain injured children. If a way could be found to utilise some of the dormant neurons, in effect to teach them how to perform the functions of those millions of other brain cells which have been destroyed, then perhaps it might be possible to restore lost function, and provide these children with a real future. But how?

CHAPTER 15
How the Brain Learns

Each of us has five senses: vision, hearing, touch, taste and smell. Every piece of information we have ever learned about anything has reached our brains through one or more of these five pathways. Whenever a new bit of data is picked up by one or other of our senses, it is transmitted to the brain, and, if retained, then a single dormant neuron becomes activated, and stores the information for future use.

The process of acquiring and storing information is continuous, throughout our lives. When we are young, we take in and store a great deal of information very rapidly. We activate new neurons far more quickly than we lose them, and the equation is very heavily weighted in favour of development, rather than deterioration. In our middle years, the pendulum begins to swing in the other direction, and in old age, we lose cells faster than we activate new ones, which accounts for the gradual slowing down of our thought processes, and recall.

The 'learning curve' often referred to by educationalists is steep in childhood, but flattens out in our middle years and begins to dip as we grow old. This is why it is so much easier for a young child to learn a foreign language than for someone in their fifties.

When brain injury occurs, and millions of neurons are wiped out, unselectively, then a great deal of stored information is lost. This loss may show in the brain itself, if the injury is sufficiently great, and may be visible on a brain scan. But it is much more readily detectable in terms of lost function. An example of this is what can happen after someone has had a stroke. A blood vessel in the brain becomes blocked by a clot, or bursts. Oxygen, carried in the blood, can no longer reach a group of cells, and they die. The data they contained is also lost, a fact we cannot see. But what we can establish is that the patient has lost the use of one eye, or can no longer move one side of his body, or can no longer speak.

The cells which have died cannot be restored. But the information can, and successful rehabilitation depends on how well the patient can re-learn the lost information or, in our terms, how successfully we can speed up central nervous system transmission in order to restore the data bank.

CHAPTER 16

How Do We Treat the Brain?

If someone was to hit you on the head – just hard enough and not too hard – and provided they hit you in just the right place, you could lose your sight, or your hearing, or become paralysed. There would be nothing wrong with your eyes, ears or limbs. The problem would be in the brain, yet because the effect would be seen on the periphery, you would either be offered treatment aimed at the periphery, or told that it is impossible to cure the brain, and that nothing could be done.

I would agree that it is impossible to cure the brain, if by 'cure' you mean returning it to its uninjured condition before the blow was struck. The affected brain cells are not just dead, they are dead and gone: absorbed into the bloodstream or incorporated into scar tissue. Yet, suppose it *were* possible to restore lost function? Would it matter that a child had lost several million brain cells if he could perform as well as any other child of the same age, and could keep up with his peers? We so-called well people live out *our* lives gradually losing more and more neurons, and take completely for granted the fact that, as we grow older, our memory deteriorates, or our reaction time can become less immediate.

Yet no-one regards us as being odd, or strange. We are not segregated from our fellows.

We all possess far more brain than we will ever use. Remembering this fact, let us now look again at the brain injured child, and consider the various possible methods open to us in treating the brain.

Firstly, we could employ surgery. Sometimes, as in the case of a tumour, this may be the only available approach. Yet, whether the knife or the more modern laser is used, neither of these tools can alter the *condition* of individual cells, or groups of cells. They can cause live cells to be destroyed, but they cannot turn a dormant neuron into a functional one. Surgery can alter the quantity of cells in the brain, but it cannot directly affect their quality, or their ability to perform.

The second treatment approach is chemical in nature: the use of drugs. Sometimes this method can produce dramatic improvements, especially in speeding up the transmission of information within the central nervous system. However, sometimes the use of drugs can produce the most alarming side effects, and these can in fact be worse than the original condition.

Mankind has known about these two approaches for hundreds of years. Successful neurosurgery of a primitive kind was carried out as far back in history as the days of Neanderthal man. Tribal 'medicine-men' employed herbal concoctions to treat neurological conditions in prehistoric times.

But there is a third method: STIMULATION.

As I have already said, every human being has five senses: sight, hearing, touch, taste and smell. All the information you have ever learned about any subject has reached your brain through one of these, and has been stored in one or more of the millions of neurons which actually make up your brain.

When brain injury occurs, and millions of brain cells die, the information contained in some of those cells dies too, and a loss of function results. But it is most unlikely that every cell relating to a particular function has been destroyed. What would happen if we exposed your senses to a very high level of fresh information? Provided they were still intact, could these pathways gradually begin to work again, as undamaged but dormant neurons became stimulated, and began to interact with one another?

The brain develops, from birth, in a very regimented way. Before we learn to see details, we first become aware of outlines. Before we gain the ability to run, we first have to learn to walk. It therefore follows that the re-development of the brain, following brain injury, would have to be a careful reconstruction of the normal process by which data is assimilated. A child who suffered brain injury before birth would need to be carefully taught, in the right order, all the information which an unhurt child learns for himself. A child who had become brain injured at a later stage would need to re-learn all the information he had lost, step by step, and in a totally co-ordinated way.

But could this proposition ever work? Could a child, blinded by brain injury, ever regain his sight? Could a 'spastic' baby ever lose the tightness, or the lack of co-ordination, which prevents him from moving or controlling his limbs?

CHAPTER 17
Frequency, Intensity and Duration

We have already examined the ways by which the brain takes in information, and how the information is processed. But it is not enough simply to present the brain with new data once and expect it to be permanently stored. Of course, there are people who are proud of the fact that they only have to see a face once, and they never forget it; or hear a piece of music only one time and have total recall. They are rare.

For most of us, the learning process involves being exposed to a fact or facts several times, until, as we say, 'it has sunk in'.

If this is true for most of us well people, how much more true is it for the brain injured child, whose ability to detect, and to retain information is so severely limited. He cannot see very well, and most probably does not see our world in the way that we do. He cannot hear very well and his hearing may be very limited, or too acute. His sensation can vary in different parts of his body, ranging from hypo- to hyper-sensitive. His senses of smell and taste may be dulled, or overactive.

It is not enough to present him with new information in the same way we would anyone else. He needs to see it, hear it, feel it, taste it, or smell it over and over and over again.

It is a basic principle of neurophysiology that if you want to increase central nervous system transmission, you must increase the stimulus in terms of its FREQUENCY, its INTENSITY and its DURATION. A proper understanding of these three words is crucially important, if we are to establish, or re-establish function following brain injury, and they deserve a full explanation.

If I was to ask you the meaning of the word 'NOCTIVAGENT', you may not know the word, and would be unable to give me an answer. This isn't surprising. It is not a commonly used word. If I was then to tell you that it means 'to walk at night', you might remember this for a few minutes, or, if you have an exceptional memory, for an hour or two. But, certainly, you would not remember the meaning of the word six months later, having only been told it once.

If, on the other hand, I told you its meaning every day, or even four times a day, for six months, there is no doubt that you *would* remember it, without difficulty. I would simply have ensured that the data I wanted you to know had been permanently stored in your brain by increasing the FREQUENCY of the message.

When you have a conversation with someone who is hard of hearing, you have to speak louder, if you want to be sure that they can hear what you are saying. If your eyesight is poor, you have to increase the brightness of the light in the room, to make it easier to see more clearly. In both these cases, the INTENSITY of the data reaching the brain has been increased, to make sure that it is correctly received.

Both these principles form the bedrock upon which our stimulation programme for brain injured children is based. However effective any individual technique might be, it depends for its success on the number of times it is carried out, and whether it is a strong enough message to overcome the resistance created by the brain injury itself.

There is, however, a third factor, one which became increasingly apparent as we published, each quarter, the achievements of the children. In the September 1988 issue of BIBIC's Newsletter, LEVEL 8, the following item was printed:

'**Andrew Collins** started our programme in July, 1985, when he was 11 years old. Now, after 36 months of very hard work, he has finally begun to *walk* unaided. Andrew lives in Plymouth, Devon.'

Andrew was seriously hurt in a road traffic accident in May 1984. When he first came to us, 14 months later, his only independent forward movement consisted of creeping on his tummy. He had lost all his other mobility skills, and his parents knew that it would require something extraordinary if he was ever to walk again.

I could not promise them that he would walk. All I could do was to teach them how they could stimulate his brain, each day, and how to give him the best opportunity to develop.

It took three years. That was the DURATION required. Perhaps other words for duration are courage, persistence, perseverance, or even 'guts'. Yet, we know from long experience that if the right stimulus is presented with sufficient frequency, intensity and for a long enough duration, the brain will in the end accept new information and process it correctly.

Let us look at two examples of Frequency, Intensity and Duration being used in a practical way.

During the Second World War, members of the Royal Observer Corps had to be trained to identify many different types of aircraft. It was crucial that they should be able to make an instant decision whether a moving shape in the air was friendly or hostile. They were therefore shown brightly lit pictures of aircraft which were projected on to a screen. At first, they had up to ten seconds to make an identification. Then, gradually, the time was shortened and the intensity of the light was reduced until they had less than a second to determine what the image represented. This procedure was repeated, over and over again until they could instantly, and correctly recognise not only the nationality of the plane, but its make and type.

Let us suppose that there is a leak in the plumbing in your house. As water begins to collect, and finds its way to the nearest join in the plasterboard ceiling in your lounge, a tiny drip falls, and lands on the top of your hair. You are sitting in your armchair in front of the fire, dozing, and you do not feel the first drip. Nor the second. The third drip falls, and now, for the first time, you feel it. The fourth one, of course goes in your eye, as you look up to locate the source of the drip.

If I want you to learn more quickly that you have a leak in the plumbing, I have three ways of teaching you.

Firstly, I can increase the rate of the drips, so they will fall on your hair more often: FREQUENCY. Secondly, I can increase the size of each drip. The ultimate drip is a bucket of water, and if I throw that over you, you will very quickly learn about the plumbing problem: INTENSITY.

Thirdly, I can keep on dripping and dripping and dripping. As the sensory effect is cumulative, you will begin to think that it is not a drip of water landing on your hair, but the head of a hammer: DURATION.

When trying to improve the abilities of brain injured children, many people nowadays employ the general principles of sensory/motor stimulation. However, they often regard the Frequency, Intensity and Duration of the stimuli as always being of equal value, and they are not.

If a child is in coma, and is therefore functionally blind, functionally deaf, and functionally insensate, he needs regular stimulation, and he needs it to continue consistently for a lengthy period of time. But, the most important thing he needs is the INTENSITY of the stimuli. He needs a *very bright* light, a *very loud* noise, and *very strong* tactile information: bright enough, loud enough and strong enough to get through the very dense blockage between his brain and his environment. I shall return to the particular subject of coma later.

It is a very different case with a child whose mid-brain injury has not affected his intelligence, but who cannot control his limbs and is constantly writhing. Whilst he needs a sufficient intensity of stimulation to make an impression, and he needs it on a consistent basis, it is the FREQUENCY of the message which is the most important element for him. We need to say to him, 'Not like that, like this! Not like that, like this!' over and over again.

CHAPTER 18

Does the Severity of the Brain Injury Matter?

The most severe form of brain injury is probably 'profound coma'. The least severe is probably a child with mild reading and learning difficulties. Yet, to those most closely involved, all conditions give cause for worry.

However severe the injury, it is self evident that a very large number of functioning brain cells must still be intact, or life could not be sustained. It is not unreasonable to assume that an even larger number of dormant neurons must also have survived, and it is the PHYSIOLOGY OF these, rather than the PATHOLOGY relating to the dead cells, that should be of most concern.

Suppose there was a family: mother, father, and two children. Suppose one child was involved in an accident, and died. Suppose the parents then spent the rest of their lives mourning the dead child, and totally ignoring the living one. Surely, we would think this strange? Would we not condemn the parents for wasting the potential of their living son or daughter?

This is just as true of brain cells as it is of people. We can do nothing about the dead cells. They are DEAD and GONE, long since absorbed into the blood stream and disposed of. So why mourn them, when there are so many living cells remaining which deserve and demand our attention?

In theory, the less brain injured a child is, the easier it should be for him to catch up the ground he has lost. In practice, I have known some very severely involved children make excellent progress, whilst others, only mildly hurt, have failed to respond. The converse is also true, and leads me to the conclusion that it is impossible to forecast how well a child will respond to extra stimulation. Each child must therefore be regarded as unique, and his future progress as entirely unpredictable.

Some people wonder how we arrive at the God-like decision whether or not to accept a patient on to our programme.

In fact, there is no God-like decision to be made. However severe his injury, we are prepared to offer our help to any child, no matter what his colour, creed, nationality, social or financial status may be. The only exception is in the case of a youngster who is suffering from some form of on-going pathology, such as an active brain tumour, or a progressive neurological disease.

Since the objective of our work is to stimulate dormant brain cells, there would be little point in attempting to do this if, in all probability, brain cells were being destroyed by the tumour or the disease at a faster rate than any significant gains which our programme might achieve. This situation, graphically described as the 'hole in the bath' problem, would be totally unreasonable, and would make all our work, and that of the child's family and friends, a total waste of time. Happily, we very rarely come across such children, although we carefully screen every child in order to eliminate this possibility.

CHAPTER 19
Function and Structure

If you were to ask an architect to build you a building, his first question would be: 'What is its function?' Obviously, there is a vast difference in the structural design of a house, for living in, as opposed to a warehouse, for storing things. The function of the building would therefore determine its structure.

It is one of the functions of a human being to walk fully upright, on two legs. We therefore possess a structure which allows us to stand, and walk erect. However, if we were never to exercise this functional ability, the structure of our bodies would become distorted, and would in the end prohibit us from being able to walk.

Following an injury to the brain, abnormal impulses may be sent out from the brain to voluntary muscles, which can create an abnormal state in these muscles. If spasticity and flaccidity is created in opposing muscle groups, contractures will result. The inability of a person to move his limbs can lead to the formation of calcium deposits in the joints, and in time these become rigid. Abnormal function or a total lack of function causes the formation of an abnormal structure.

New-born babies do not possess fully-fashioned hip sockets. If they creep on their tummies, crawl on hands and knees and then walk, the constant movement and pressure of the head of each femur or thighbone against the surface of the lower pelvis or acetabulum gradually helps to create effective sockets by stimulating bone growth. If a child is brain injured, and cannot move, then his hip sockets will remain immature, and partial dislocation (subluxation), or full dislocation will sometimes be apparent.

This natural law – Function Determines Structure – can be observed at work in all of us. Lumberjacks are not lumberjacks because they have big muscles. They have big muscles because they are lumberjacks. Pearl divers don't dive for pearls because they happen to have well-developed lungs. Their function – being pearl divers – determines or creates their lung capacity. It is not a pre-requisite of desk-bound executives to have middle-age spread! Paunches develop through a lack of exercise. An insufficiency of function promotes a weakening of structure.

This law applies just as much to the brain as it does to the body. When one of our children learns to see, hear, feel, read, write, walk and talk, the sensory and motor pathways leading into, and out of the brain have sufficiently matured to control these functions. As we will see in more detail in Part 6, this maturation involves a process known as myelination, and every time this process occurs, brain growth takes place. As the brain becomes more able, its structure changes and develops.

We will come across other examples of this natural law when we look at the reasons for the use of many of our techniques in Parts 3, 4 and 5. Some will be of a physical nature. Others will be concerned with brain growth and neurological maturation. All of them will demonstrate that, if we improve a child's abilities, we cannot avoid improving his physiology.

CHAPTER 20
The Size of the Problem

Before we can begin to solve a problem, it is first necessary to define it. As I have already stated, every child is different. Nevertheless, there are some common denominators in all children – well or hurt – which can help to determine the degree of injury.

Unfortunately, no-one has yet invented a machine capable of counting precisely how many cells have been destroyed, (since they are no longer there to be counted); or even how many cells which relate to a particular function still remain. For this reason, it is not possible to stimulate a specific area of the brain, and instead we must use a broad-spectrum approach.

Since we cannot, with any precision, discover the information we need by looking at the brain, we rely instead on an assessment of each child's individual abilities. This we call a Functional Evaluation, and it is based on a very important tool – the Developmental Profile.

From the time he is born, every normal child follows a very clearly defined series of steps within the six most important areas of function present in human beings. These areas are Vision, Hearing, the Sense of Touch, Mobility, Speech and Manual Dexterity.

There are eight distinct and separate stages which normal youngsters go through in their progress towards adulthood, and these occur at reasonably well-defined times. This is true in each of the six functions, and the Profile therefore shows a total of 48 different 'boxes', eight for each function, representing abilities which a child should be able to perform, depending on his age. I have described each of these compartments later, in Part 3.

There are specific tests for each of these 'boxes', and very specific criteria which must be met before a child is awarded credit for a given ability. The tests are standardised, so that no matter who carries out the developmental evaluation, the findings will be the same.

Since the Profile reflects the abilities of well children, it provides a standard against which brain injured children can also be measured.

When we first assess a child, part of that assessment involves a

BRAIN - NET
DEVELOPMENT PROFILE

NAME OF CHILD _____

AGE AT INITIAL EVALUATION _____ AGE TODAY _____

RE-ASSESSMENT NUMBER _____ EVALUATED BY _____

INDEX NUMBER _____

PRESENT DATE _____

DATE OF INITIAL EVALUATION _____

MONTHS SINCE LAST ASSESSMENT _____

	SENSORY						MOTOR	
VISUAL DEVELOPMENT	AUDITORY DEVELOPMENT	TACTILE DEVELOPMENT (L / R)	TIME FRAME	LEVEL	MOBILITY	LANGUAGE	MANUAL COMPETENCE (L / R)
Able to read fluently with appropriate visual dominance	Understanding of complete vocabulary consistent with age level using appropriate dominant ear	Able to identify by touch using appropriate dominant hand	PEER LEVEL IF OVER 6 YEARS	8	Able to move with coordination of age level consistent with appropriate dominant foot	Able to converse appropriately at age level	Able to write at age level using appropriate dominant hand
Able to read single words	Able to understand complex sentences	Able to identify tiny objects by touch	6 YEARS	7	Able to hop, skip, jump and kick a ball	Able to speak in complete sentences	Able to write single words
Able to recognise symbols and letters within experience	Able to understand two-step commands and simple time concepts	Able to differentiate between similar objects	3 YEARS	6	Able to run in cross pattern	Able to speak in short sentences	Able to use both hands together purposefully
Able to recognise pictures within experience	Able to understand simple commands	Able to differentiate between dissimilar objects	18 MONTHS	5	Able to walk with arms no longer required for balance	Able to say two words together	Able to simultaneously oppose index finger and thumb of both hands
Able to focus both eyes simultaneously, and to perceive depth	Able to understand single words	Awareness of the third dimension	12 MONTHS	4	Able to walk with arms used for balance	Able to say single words	Able to oppose index finger and thumb of either hand
Able to see details within an outline	Able to recognise meaningful sounds	Able to react to light touch	6 MONTHS	3	Able to crawl in cross pattern on hands and knees	Able to make sounds culminating in communicative sounds	Able to grasp objects purposefully
Able to see outline	Vital response to threatening sounds	Awareness of vital sensation	3 MONTHS	2	Able to creep on tummy in cross pattern	Able to respond by crying to vital threats	Able to release in response to a vital stimulus
Reflexive response to light	Reflexive response to loud noise	Babinski reflex	BIRTH	1	Free voluntary movement of limbs	Able to cry	Reflexive grasping with hands

Profile Copyright Brain-Net 1996

Figure 2   Development Profile (Results)

very thorough investigation of his abilities, and the Profile is used to help determine exactly what he can and cannot do. It shows how he compares with well children of the same chronological age, and highlights those areas where he has some ability but needs further reinforcement.

Each time he is seen again, his abilities are re-assessed, and the Profile is re-marked. Significant progress can therefore be readily determined, and specific objectives can be much more easily decided upon.

The Profile is a very useful tool, but it is only a tool. In the end, the most important indicator of progress is the child himself, and, for this reason, we always listen very carefully to the observations reported to us by his parents. They see their child every day, whilst we only see him every four to six months, and they are usually a very reliable source of information.

Level 6 on the Profile indicates the expected abilities of an average three-year-old; Level 7 shows the comparative skills of a six-year-old. It takes three years for a normal three-year-old to become a six-year-old. In this same time span we might well see a brain injured child at least six times, and on each of these occasions, he might not show any change in function on the scale. Yet, there is a vast difference in ability between a three-year-old and a six-year-old, so at this stage it is far more important to watch the child, than to become a slave to a document!

Although a single line is drawn between each Level, that single line represents possibly a thousand tiny lines, each signifying a very small, but important functional gain.

I have never seen a brain injured child who had only one problem. Some problems directly result from the injury – blindness, deafness or paralysis are good examples. Others can be caused by deficiencies in the brain's environment: poor breathing leading to an insufficiency of oxygen, or inadequate nutrition. Still more can be traced to the larger environment in which the child lives: overprotection on the part of the parents (understandable, in the circumstances, but no less inhibiting to progress), or the lack of consistent social rules within the family.

Even in his functional abilities, the typical brain injured child varies considerably, and this can be explained by the type of injury which almost always occurs.

If someone took a hammer, and hit you very hard on the head with it, every brain cell in the direct path of the hammer would be destroyed, but those present in all the unaffected areas of the brain would be unharmed, and would continue to function normally. This we refer to as a FOCAL injury, where a relatively localised area of the brain is affected, and, generally speaking, such an injury would create a specific number of problems.

If, on the other hand, someone was to fire at you with a shotgun, the pellets would begin to spread out even before they reached you, and were they to penetrate your skull, would cause widespread damage in many different areas of the brain. Some abilities would be greatly affected, others only mildly so, and others would show little if any sign of interference. This type of injury is DIFFUSE in nature.

The vast majority of the children whom I have seen, over the years, have suffered diffuse injuries. In some of the six basic functions which the Profile measures, they have reasonable levels of ability. In others, they are far behind, with many of the basic skills lacking.

CHAPTER 21
Other Investigations

Although the main thrust of our work is developmental in nature, the functional abilities of a child are only one of several considerations which we take into account in assessing the full scope of his problems.

He will probably have been given a number of different clinical tests by those initially responsible for reaching a diagnosis. These may have included brain scans, EEG measurements, blood tests, and other examinations. This information can be of great importance to us in deciding whether or not any child is a suitable candidate for our programme, and one of the responsibilities of our medical officer is to make and retain contact with each child's GP and specialist, so that all the available data can be shared.

In addition to assessing neurological difficulties, careful note is also taken of physiological problems. Lack of musculature, degrees of spasticity, contractures, joint dislocations, and other orthopaedic problems cannot be ignored, and the advice of our medical officer is vital to us in designing a safe and pain-free programme for a child.

Many children experience regular, and sometimes severe fits. Not only are they distressing to watch, but they can be totally exhausting for the sufferer. On the other hand, most children who are prone to seizures tend to be in receipt of anti-convulsant medication, and the side effects of some drugs prescribed for this purpose can include drowsiness and reduced awareness. If we are to **increase** a child's ability to take in information, medical expertise is needed to find a sensible balance between the effects of fits, and the effects of medication: another challenging problem for our doctor.

There are so many, apparently disconnected items of information which we must glean before we can begin to design an effective programme for a child. What size of house does the family have? Is there enough space to carry out various activities, and to accommodate equipment? How good is the child's diet? Is he physically under- or over-weight for his age? What metal are the family's cooking utensils made of? How many helpers might be available? How well does he breathe? Does he appear to suffer from any allergies? What are his biggest problems? How does he react to other people, both inside and outside the family circle? The list seems endless.

Yet, if we are to succeed, we have to know everything possible about each child, and, thankfully, we have the advantage that we can talk directly to the world's leading experts: his mother and father. They know more about him than anyone else, and are always more than willing to share their expert knowledge.

1a Alison – 1997.

1b   Alison – 1980.

2   Lanrick House, Rugeley, Stafordshire – our first home.

3 Anne Diamond ready to leave for Philadelphia, USA with a group of families – March 1978.

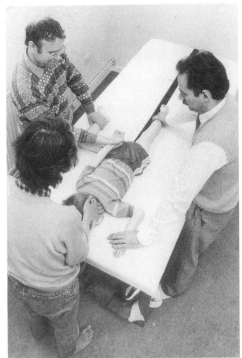

4 'Cross Patterning'. (Photo by Keith Palmer).

5 Alison in her creep-tunnel 1970. (Courtesy of *Stafford Newsletter*).

6 Creeping in warm water – 1990. (Photo by Jennie Painter).

7 'Masking'.

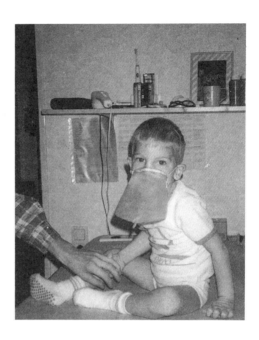

8 'Positive Respiratory Patterning'. (Photo by Douglas Allen).

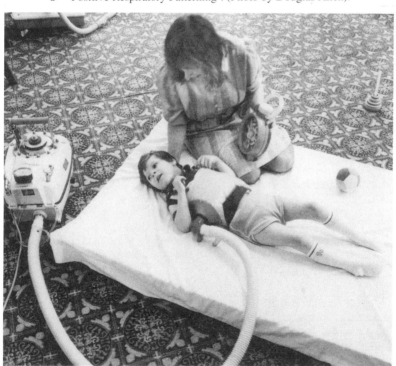

9 Above. 'Stepping
Stones' (Photo by Jennie
Painter).

10 Below left.
Using a 'D-Ring'.

11 Below right.
'Brachiation' – Swinging along
an overhead ladder (Courtesy of
Daily Telegraph).

12 Time off for an important meeting.

13 Right. 'Suspended Inverted Rotation'. (Courtesy of *Daily Telegraph*).

14 The Prestrim. (Photo by Jennie Painter).

15 Above. Dr Anton, Christa, Edgar, Kenneth and Freddy: stalwarts of the Maltese Institute.

16 Below. April 1998, graduation day for the first two Maltese staff, Christa and Kenneth.

CHAPTER 22
Our Objectives

Many people still believe that there are no answers to the problems created by brain injury. Parents are still advised to take their child home, to give him a lot of love and affection, and, in my own words, 'to learn to live with the problem'.

They are still advised to put their child in a 'special' school, so that, in the majority of cases, and again in my own words, '*he* (or *she*) can learn to live with the problem'.

They are still advised to 'put him in a home, and have another one', or, once again in my own words, 'to get rid of him before they have learned to love him'.

Is this really the best we can do? In the 1990s? Can it really be true that we can put a man on the moon, dive safely to the bottom of the ocean floor, and successfully harness the power of the atom for peaceful means, yet not have any more inspired objectives than these for brain injured children?

Why is it that we can repeatedly transplant human hearts, yet still insist that it is impossible to provide a brain injured child with sight, hearing, mobility or speech?

Why (which is even more strange) do we refuse to believe in the possibility of real improvements, even when we see them in front of our eyes?

There is another odd thing about the subject of brain injury. No one ever sits on the fence. They either heartily approve of what we are doing, or they utterly condemn it. No-one ever thinks to ask those young people who went through the programme, and succeeded, whether *they* think it was worth it! I have. Perhaps the others should.

Time and time again I have heard the four criticisms:-

1. 'There is no scientific proof to support these theories. Control studies are not encouraged, and visitors to the Alison Centre are not welcomed.'
2. 'Any improvements made in the children are the result of natural maturation and development, and would have happened anyway.'

3. 'Any child would improve if given the amount of individual attention which Keith Pennock advocates.'
4. 'There is no need to go to the Alison Centre. We can offer you just as good facilities here.'

It has to be said that all of these comments are invariably made by experts who are too busy to come and see what we are doing! Busy doing what?

To each of the above criticisms there is a short answer.

1. See Appendix 1. And, by the way, we enjoy having visitors!
2. When one of our children walks for the first time, at the age of ten, and after three years of hard work on our programme, I doubt if it would have happened anyway, and if it would have, then why did it take so long, so much work, and why wasn't the final outcome *predicted* in the first place?
3. Isn't this more a commentary on the lack of resources presently deployed within the system by those in authority, than a criticism of our own efforts?
4. If this is true, why have so many families, from so many different areas of Britain, and from fifteen overseas countries, travelled to Bridgwater to see us?

It is so easy to get side-tracked into the morass of argument and counter-argument that, if we are not careful, it can become more important to win the debate than to win with the children.

I believe that if we can consistently win with the children, then *they* are the ones who will win the argument for us! So, let me turn away from the temptation to become embroiled in controversy, and instead state our objectives, since it is the achieving of these which is far more important to our children, our parents, and to our own future.

We have four objectives for each brain injured child whom we try to help.

PHYSICAL GROWTH
INTELLECTUAL GROWTH
SOCIAL GROWTH

Each of these aims is reasonably self evident. Each of these aims, if achieved, will have the effect of bringing our children closer to the one primary goal for which every parent strives, and about which every parent dreams.

SURVIVAL or INDEPENDENCE

It is the task of every mother and father to ensure that their children 'leave the nest' and make their own way in the world. This task becomes ever more difficult as the pressures of modern life increase, and youngsters seek solace in drugs, alcohol, smoking and other destructive habits.

For our families there is a different nightmare. 'Whatever will happen to her when I die?'

It is our job to improve the quality of life of all our children. It is our job to create as great a level of independence as possible in each child, because until we succeed in this aim, the nightmare will persist.

Now that our objectives are stated, in black and white, please don't confuse this statement of objective with any kind of guarantee that they will always be achieved. *No-one* can offer such a guarantee.

There are only three things that we *can* guarantee. We can guarantee a lot of hard work. We can guarantee a more positive series of objectives for a brain injured child than may have been previously suggested. We can guarantee our support to a family for as long as they want it. These things we can control. We can control nothing else.

Without any question, our programme is a difficult one to carry out. It is tiring, it is demanding, but most of all it is repetitive. It is, of course, this regular repetition of the information which a child needs that produces results, and until we find a way to achieve just as good results with less repetition, we have no choice but to offer our families a programme which many people regard as being very hard. And it is very hard . . . unless you are winning! If you are winning, and seeing positive improvements, it is amazing how much less difficult it seems.

Some people say, 'But surely an hour a day is better than nothing?'

In my experience it is possible to do enough of the programme in an hour to cause chaos in the family, but not enough to do any good.

How much is enough to do any good? I don't know.

But I do know this. The chances of solving a problem improve in direct proportion to the amount of effort, time and resource which is brought to bear on it. And, as it is impossible to guarantee results, I would prefer to throw EVERYTHING into the fight, than to try to gauge exactly how much or how little to do, and find at the end of the day that my estimate was inaccurate, and that it wasn't enough.

So what about those families who can only work with their children for two or three hours a day? Are they wasting their time?

No, providing they accept the fact that they must tailor their objectives accordingly.

There are no easy answers to difficult problems, and problems as difficult to solve as the problems created by brain injury are going to require difficult solutions. Especially when many people still believe that there are no answers to the problems created by brain injury . . .

CHAPTER 23

When is a Child too Old
to Respond to Extra Stimulation?

In theory, no-one is ever too old to respond to a fresh stimulus. It is a well known fact that the stimulation provided to senior citizens by Over 60s Clubs can help to prevent intellectual deterioration. However, in the case of brain injured children, TIME is the greatest enemy. Every day a hurt child is not a day better, he is a day worse, since the gap between himself and the well child, with whom he is in direct competition, is a day wider. Gradually, this gap broadens to the point where it is no longer bridgeable.

There are, of course, exceptions. Where an accident has robbed a teenager or young adult of previously acquired skills, it may be possible to restore these, since some of the data involved may still be stored in undamaged areas of the brain. There may have been severe bruising of tissue, and probably some swelling (or cerebral oedema), which can take up to 3 months to subside fully. Once these have had time to disappear, some neurons may begin to function once again. Stroke patients may, for this reason, begin to respond positively after a time to specific stimuli, provided care is taken not to overstress them physically or mentally.

Because time, or more precisely delay, can so swiftly compound the difficulties involved in creating or restoring function in brain injured children, in an ideal world every child who suffers brain injury should begin to receive extra stimulation from the day his difficulties have been established. Let us look at an example of an extreme case of delay.

Several years ago, I received a telephone call from a family in Pembroke, South Wales. They asked me if I would see their daughter. When I asked for more details, they said she was eighteen years old.

At that time, we did not accept patients over the age of sixteen, preferring to specialise in brain injured *children*. I explained this, as gently as I could.

They said, 'You don't understand. Kathryn weighs twenty-four pounds!'

I suggested that in the circumstances they ought to bring her to see us as soon as possible, and a day or so later, they did. And Kathryn *did* weigh twenty-four pounds. She was also only *thirty-six inches* long!

We discovered that she had been starved of oxygen immediately after her birth, and had suffered severe brain injury. One of the areas affected had been the pituitary gland responsible for growth. As a result, each year Kathryn's mother had bought a new calendar, and Kathryn had become a year older, but had stayed the same.

Gradually, all the other children in her peer group had developed, gone to school, and some had even married. But Kathryn had just stayed the same. The gap caused by this developmental delay was such that she was only eighteen years old 'in theory'. In practice, her abilities were:

Vision	3 months old	**Mobility**	Birth Level
Understanding	6 months old	**Language**	6 months old
Tactile	6 months old	**Manual**	3 months old

From a developmental point of view, her brain was functioning at no more than a six month old level in any area. Her brain injury had not merely slowed her down, as is true in so many brain injured children who are six years old *chronologically* but function like typical one or two year-olds; it had brought Kathryn's neurological and physical development to a complete standstill.

In her case, it would have been as ridiculous for us to enforce our (then) rule about not treating children once they reached sixteen, as it would have been had we refused to help a six-month-old child, and Kathryn's story only serves to underline the point that each child should and must always be looked at as an individual.

CHAPTER 24

What About Down's Syndrome?

So far, I have referred at all times to children who are brain injured. That is to say to children in whom an enormous barrier has been created between their brains and their environment, as a result of injuries sustained by the brain.

There is not a great deal of difference between a child whose 'data banks' have been destroyed by a virus, or a blow to the head, and a child who has never possessed the data in the first place. Nor is there much to choose between the effects of severe brain injury and the effects of severe environmental deprivation.

Children with Down's Syndrome used to be called 'mongols', another label, but one which is very much harder to live with. Presumably they were given this unpleasant title because their features appeared oriental. Perhaps the term was originally chosen because, at the time, few people knew very much about Mongolia, or its inhabitants, and cared less; perhaps few people knew very much about these children either, and cared less.

Until 1971, even IAHP in Philadelphia thought that children with Down's Syndrome had a congenital defect which produced *deficient* brains, and could not be regarded in the same way as brain injured children. Until Dr Raymundo Veras, a Brazilian disciple of Glenn Doman, disproved this notion and demonstrated that Down's Syndrome children, given an appropriately enriched environment, could rapidly develop and even catch up with their normal peer group.

Our experience with these children has certainly borne out Dr Veras's findings. We are used to seeing *brain injured children* make excellent progress, once they are given the right amount of stimulation. These improvements occur quite frequently. But even after twenty-five years, I am still filled with amazement when I observe the very dramatic response to our programme shown by many ***Down's kids***. In some cases, it is almost as instant as the sudden releasing of a seized tap!

Several years ago, Ruth was brought to us by her parents. Her mother had been the first to realise that Ruth had problems, and despite the fact that neither she nor her husband had been given any formal diagnosis of their daughter's condition, they had both been very strongly advised to institutionalise Ruth as soon as possible.

Instead, they had attempted to give her what stimulation they had been able to devise themselves, basing their efforts on what they had read in books or gleaned from other families. She did not become able to hold up her head with any steadiness until she was a year old; did not begin to move forwards on her tummy until she was 16 months old; and only started crawling on her hands and knees when she was 18 months old.

When we saw her for the first time, only three weeks after she had begun to crawl, her understanding had already caught up with her age level; she babbled a lot, but had only a two-word vocabulary; she could oppose the finger and thumb of either hand successfully, but not at one and the same time.

In company with most Down's Syndrome children, Ruth tended to breathe through her mouth. Her nose was stubby, and had little bridge development. Her breathing was fast, shallow and irregular.

In view of this, we included respiratory reinforcement in her programme, hoping that by overriding the chaos of Ruth's own breathing pattern, we might increase the availability of oxygen for her brain.

Ruth began to walk just before her third birthday. Her understanding began to accelerate, and, before she was five, she had begun to put words together spontaneously. She had also begun to run.

All these changes had been hoped for. What we had not expected, however, were the dramatic changes brought about by our respiratory intervention. As air began, for the first time, to pass through Ruth's nose, she became aware that she had a nose. She began to breathe through her nose, and, as this functional ability increased, the structure of her nose began to change. The bridge began to develop, and the folds of skin under her eyes, which gave her the appearance of being 'oriental', began to disappear.

It is nice when something you hope for happens. It is even nicer when you find out something interesting and valuable *by chance*. I believe this is called serendipity!

From that time on, many of our Down's Syndrome children have been given respiratory reinforcement as part of their overall programme, and similar results have occurred.

Today, Ruth is twenty-two. She is a very attractive young lady, can achieve anything she sets her mind to, and looks very much like her father. She has not yet reached her FULL potential, but can read, write, spell, talk, run, handle money, and cope with the real world.

Ruth now has a future. What has changed? The four basic ingredients: attitude, a will to succeed, the right approach, and a very deep-seated parental determination are, I think, the keys which released this little girl from the prison in which she was supposed to remain for the rest of her life.

Attitude

If you treat a human being like an idiot, he will become an idiot. If you believe he has potential, however inaccessible it may appear, then at least he has the chance to blossom. Perhaps the concept of 'high-grade and low-grade mongols', nauseating though the words sound, is really the product of high-grade and low-grade attitudes to these children by those in authority.

The Will to Succeed

Ruth's programme was designed by staff and carried out by parents who shared an abundance of this basic motivation.

The Right Approach

This can only be judged in hindsight, as far as Ruth is concerned. But when one hundred, five hundred or even one thousand 'Ruths', in many different parts of the world, also show similar responses, something in the approach must be right!

A Very Deep-Seated Parental Determination

Most of us, faced with the carefully-considered opinion of a highly experienced and qualified professional, tend to follow the advice given. It takes extraordinary parents to reject such advice, and even more extraordinary parents to keep on looking, in the face of official disapproval, until they find an answer. It takes *most* extraordinary parents to possess enough personal energy to bring about the solution themselves.

CHAPTER 25

How Do We Stimulate One of Our Children?

Once all the information which we need has been gathered together, we can begin to design a programme of activities to suit the needs of each child. We will need to incorporate activities which will help to reinforce and strengthen poor abilities. We will need to encourage the development of missing skills, which may well have been by-passed in the struggle just to survive. And, we will need to promote new abilities.

We must carefully consider the FREQUENCY of each activity, and its INTENSITY. Giving a family a list of activities so long that each one can only be completed once a day is not likely to produce the desired result. Nor is a short sequence of events, lasting five or ten minutes, however many times it is done, each day, if it does not contain enough of the right stimuli.

Each technique we use has its own rationale. There is a right way and a wrong way to do everything. When we are sending a family home to carry out each day for four months a carefully drawn-up schedule of activities, they need to know not only how to carry out each one correctly, but why each is necessary. When they are asked by helpers or friends why they are doing something, it is not good enough for them to say, 'Because he said so!'

There are good reasons for every one of the recommendations which we make, and in the following pages I shall explain some of these basic techniques, what they are expected to achieve, and how they are married together to form a 'Programme'.

PART THREE

How? – The Six Functions

TIME FRAME	PROFILE LEVEL	BRAIN LEVEL	VISUAL DEVELOPMENT
PEER LEVEL IF OVER SIX YEARS	8	*Superior Cortex*	Able to read fluently with appropriate visual dominance
6 YEARS	7	*Advanced Cortex*	Able to read single words
3 YEARS	6	*Developed Cortex*	Able to recognise symbols and letters within experience
18 MONTHS	5	*Early Cortex*	Able to recognise pictures within experience
12 MONTHS	4	*Initial Cortex*	Able to focus both eyes simultaneously and to perceive depth
6 MONTHS	3	*Midbrain*	Able to see details within an outline
3 MONTHS	2	*Pons*	Able to see outline
BIRTH	1	*Medulla and Cord*	Reflexive response to light

Figure 3   Visual Development

CHAPTER 26

The Sensory Pathways
(VISUAL)

At birth a normal baby can respond to light and darkness. In the presence of a bright light, his pupils will contract reflexively, and conversely will open wider when in poorly lit surroundings. Within a few weeks, he develops the ability to see shapes and outlines, and before long he learns to recognise the details which distinguish one face from another, or one object from another. By the time the average youngster is a year old, he is no longer relying on the information supplied by one eye at a time, and is beginning to use both eyes together – a complicated process which gives him the ability to perceive depth and distance.

Once a child can control his eye muscles to converge and diverge his eyes, he begins to see things three-dimensionally. He now has all the equipment needed to see, and can begin the life-long process of learning to interpret correctly what it is he is looking at. This ability begins at the level of being able to recognise in two-dimensions (pictures), familiar objects which he has previously seen in the reality of all three dimensions. It develops to more complicated 'pictures', such as shapes and symbols. Finally, the correct identification of very special 'pictures', which we call words, gives a child the high level visual skill of being able to read.

Most brain injured children have visual difficulties. These problems can range from the neurological blindness of a child in coma to the mild disorders associated with learning and reading problems.

One of the standard neurological tests associated with vision is to shine a bright light into a patient's eyes, and to note the pupil response. If the response is normal in both eyes, this fact is recorded. If not, a note is made of any inadequacy observed. However, it is rare that any action is taken to correct or improve the response.

If we find the pupil reflex to be in any way immature, we incorporate into the child's stimulation programme a technique called 'Basic Vision', in which we recommend that a bright light be shone into each of the child's eyes for a recommended length of time. This exposure to light is repeated several times, and sessions of Basic Vision are carried out regularly throughout each day.

We have very often found that repeated stimulation of the visual pathways to the brain can lead to a marked improvement in the pupil reflex response – an important step along the road towards normal sight.

A bright flashlight is not by any means the only tool available to us. Disco lights, Christmas tree lights, brightly coloured mobiles, lights set to flash briefly at regular intervals throughout the night – all these and more are recommended to our families when necessary.

Once light and darkness become part of a child's conscious awareness, and not just a reflexive response, we introduce coloured lights and moving lights, which help to maintain interest and to develop binocular control. Fluorescent paints, when used with properly shaded ultra-violet light, can be much easier to see than daylight colours. Toys, pictures and shapes can be more interesting, and much more visual to the partially-sighted child, when presented under these conditions.

Conscious visual awareness is often a transient thing with our children. They find it very hard to concentrate on anything for more than a second or two. Therefore, we have to increase the INTENSITY of the stimulus, and even more importantly its FREQUENCY, in order to make any impression.

'Tracking', or the ability to follow a moving object with one's eyes, can be improved if a pencil flashlight is slowly moved in different directions while the child is encouraged to keep looking at it. Near-point convergence can be reinforced by slowly bringing a small object from a distance of about three feet in to the bridge of the nose. The reverse of this procedure helps to improve far-point convergence. These activities, unlike so many techniques that we employ to influence the brain itself, are truly 'exercises', as their use strengthens the eye muscles.

Reading can be introduced as soon as a child can see detail. Simple words, made up of large letters, painted in bright red on white card, can be shown as flash cards. It is no more difficult for a child to see, learn and recognise these than it is for him to identify a teddy bear or a toy truck. Very often, children learn to read some words long before they receive any formal teaching.

Modern advertising depends for its success on the customer hearing a slogan, seeing a slogan and thus recognising a product. This principle holds good even when used with foreign languages, and many people who do not speak a word of English nevertheless recognise and understand the word 'Coca-cola'.

As a child becomes more able to recognise words, the size of the letters can be slowly reduced. Red is a very easy colour to see, especially when it is presented on a white background. As soon as small red-on-white words are readily identifiable, black letters can be introduced; couplets, phrases and short sentences follow; and the reading vocabulary can be further challenged by the addition of home-made books.

From this point onwards, the basic neurological foundations required for reading are established, and it is purely a matter of practice and exposure for a child to improve his skills, and gradually to expand his horizons into magazines, newspapers and books.

Of the 721 children whom I have seen on more than one occasion since January 1st, 1980, 126 were neurologically blind, which is to say that their visual problems lay not in their eyes, but in the brain itself.

Of these 'blind' children, 52 have gained at least the ability to see detail. Seven of these children can now not only see, but can read at least at the level of single words.

Each one has gradually progressed from simple light and dark stimulation, through the visual levels described above, until they are now able to use their eyes to learn about their world.

Of the 337 children who came to me sighted but unable to read, 220 can now read at least at the level of several single words. Fifty have achieved this ability ahead of the majority of their chronological peers.

For them, the future includes the opportunity to gain knowledge through a new and fascinating medium: the world of books.

TIME FRAME	PROFILE LEVEL	BRAIN LEVEL	AUDITORY DEVELOPMENT
PEER LEVEL IF OVER SIX YEARS	8	*Superior Cortex*	Understanding of complete vocabulary consistent with age level, using the appropriate dominant ear
6 YEARS	7	*Advanced Cortex*	Able to understand complex sentences
3 YEARS	6	*Developed Cortex*	Able to understand two-step commands and simple time concepts
18 MONTHS	5	*Early Cortex*	Able to understand simple commands
12 MONTHS	4	*Initial Cortex*	Able to understand single words
6 MONTHS	3	*Midbrain*	Able to recognise meaningful sounds
3 MONTHS	2	*Pons*	Vital response to threatening sounds
BIRTH	1	*Medulla and Cord*	Reflexive response to loud noise

Figure 4   Auditory Development

CHAPTER 27

The Sensory Pathways
(AUDITORY)

Many people think that, of all the senses, hearing is the most crucial. To lose one's hearing is to lose easy communication with other people. To be cut off from sound is to suffer a loss of understanding of the world around, to be unable to appreciate a lot of what is going on. Deafness is often equated with loneliness.

Even a new-born baby can react to noise. The initial, reflexive response to a sharp sound is to blink, and a very young child, exposed to repeated sharp sounds, will blink each time he hears the noise. This 'startle reflex' matures as he learns to control his reaction, until the point is reached where he may blink the first and second times, and then cease blinking, once he has become accustomed to the noise.

Babies very rapidly learn to tell the difference between sounds. They become able to recognise their mothers' voices, and to enjoy soothing noises, which they associate with warmth and comfort. Nursery experiments have shown that babies are soon pacified when exposed to a tape recording of a heart rhythm – a memory of the time *in utero* and the constant presence of sound in the form of their mothers' heartbeats.

Before they are a month old, many babies will react adversely to a loud, threatening sound, and although the reaction changes as they grow older, children, and even adults, will show initial fear at the onset of a frightening, unexpected noise. How many of us have 'jumped' when the driver of an articulated lorry applies his air brakes; don't we all show apprehension when exposed to the immediate noise of a low-flying jet plane? Our first reaction is one of fear – which is rapidly followed by embarrassment when we realise what the noise related to, and that we are not in fact under threat.

A young child is constantly exposed to sounds. He hears the noise of water running when it is time for his bath; he begins to associate the clatter of pans in the kitchen with meal-times; the door-bell and telephone attract his attention. He gradually learns to link the noises that he hears with their meanings, and to differentiate between which sounds accompany pleasant and which unpleasant events.

A word is a sophisticated series of sounds. In just the same way that the repeated sight of a number of linked hieroglyphics (making words) teaches a child how to read, the opportunity to hear a group of specific sounds, related to a clear meaning, teaches a child how to understand language. The first word understood by many children is 'Mummy'. The second is most probably 'No!'

Once the principle of relating words to meanings has been established, a child begins to build his auditory vocabulary in direct proportion to the amount of speech he hears. He learns to understand phrases and sentences and, if exposed to them, is just as able to relate, for example, French or German words to their meanings as words in English. At first, he is in much the same position as an adult listening to a discussion in a foreign language, who does not understand every word, and is desperately waiting for a clue word to indicate what the conversation is about. The child may hear and understand the words 'teddy bear', and immediately want the bear, without understanding that the full sentence was, 'We are going to put your teddy bear to bed now, and you will see him again tomorrow.'

By the time a child is eighteen months old, he should be able to understand several simple commands: 'Look at Mummy', 'Give me a kiss', 'Hold my hand'. Time now begins to have a meaning, and from 'yesterday', 'today', 'tomorrow', 'now' and 'later', he progresses to clock time. Abstract concepts – love, anger, jealousy – become more understandable, and he can now hold conversations.

From this point onwards, his understanding is totally experiential. Sentence comprehension grows with a gradually increasing vocabulary. At first, any words he is not intended to hear can be spelled, e.g. i..c..e..c..r..e..a..m., but soon even this parental ploy fails to work, as he is alert not only to the words themselves, but even to the tone in which they are spoken.

Interaction with his peer group, both inside and outside the school environment; television and films; daily conversations with adults: all these stimuli help to expand word recognition and provide an opportunity for the further development of auditory competence.

As with all our senses, the development of hearing and understanding is a progressive process. If early steps are missed out, owing to the presence of brain injury, then more advanced levels will be less efficient, or may not be reached at all. We therefore design our programme of activities to include particular techniques aimed at establishing proper function in whichever area is weak or non-existent.

Some of our children come to us with a complete absence of any startle reflex. They simply do not respond in any way to sounds. Others over-react. For both conditions our response is to expose the children to a variety of short, sharp sounds. This 'square wave' stimulation, so-called because of the square tracing which it produces on an oscilloscope, is only effective if it is carried out many times each day, and the sound must be sufficiently loud for a child to be aware of it. Where there is any risk of annoying other people, we suggest where possible the use of pre-recorded material and headphones.

The same type of technique applies where children either under-or-over-react to threatening sounds. Now, instead of random sharp sounds, we employ very loud sounds, such as air horns or cymbals, to create a sudden, alarming noise. Some children who live near ports are not disturbed by the noise of ships' sirens; others who are often exposed to the sounds of jets flying overhead are not worried by the noise of jet engines, and it is important to ensure that the recommended noises do pose an auditory threat to the child.

A more sophisticated tape recording is useful for the child whose range of meaningful sounds is limited.

Nowadays, many different sound effects are available on both record and tape, and a selection of these, preceded by a statement of what the sound is, can be very helpful in expanding this range. Some children have frequency limitations; they respond eagerly to Dad's voice, yet appear to ignore anything Mum says. Our answer to this difficulty is to expose the child, many times each day, to a special tape recording of all the frequencies from 10 cycles per second to 4 kilocycles. The tape is played, once again, through headphones, and at a prescribed volume.

It is terribly easy to forget to talk to a child, if that child is brain injured. The BBC radio programme about the disabled aptly chose as its title *Does He Take Sugar?*

Yet it is *our* children who *need* to be talked to – to hear words, phrases and sentences, and to have the opportunity, over and over again, to be exposed to language. An ideal time for talking to a child on our programme is during patterning. Some patterning teams sing songs or nursery rhymes; others choose topics of interest to the child concerned, and each participant speaks for one or two minutes on their subject. Just because there is no verbal response from the child, it should not be assumed that he cannot hear, or does not understand.

One of the essential ingredients of our programme is a one-to-one relationship between the child and a caring adult. The undivided attention which this promotes also gives a golden opportunity for verbal instruction. Whether this apparently one-way conversation consists of saying words over and over again, teaching the correct responses to single-step or multiple-step commands, giving a careful briefing before a trip to a place of interest, or holding a debriefing session after returning home, it is a chance to reinforce auditory comprehension.

The programme itself provides another way of strengthening auditory knowledge. We always advise our families to tell their brain injured child what is going to happen next, at each stage of their day. 'I'm rubbing your hands with velvet, Johnny,' or 'Now we are going to do some crawling,' provides the child with the security of consistency, whilst at the same time giving him, for perhaps the thousandth time, auditory clues to match the activity.

To believe that because someone does not appear to understand what we have said to him, he must clearly be deaf, is a trap only too easy to fall into. We English people are particularly bad at this. We don't tend in general to excel in foreign languages, perhaps believing that it is somehow the foreigner's responsibility to learn our language, and not the other way around. This accounts for our national characteristic, when abroad, to assume that because a local resident has not understood what we have said, he must be deaf! The simple solution, therefore, is merely to shout, on the principle that if we shout loud enough in English, he will be bound to understand!

The same assumption is so often made with brain injured children, yet it is very often the *frequency* of the information which is important, rather than the *intensity*.

Of the 721 children whom I have seen on more than one occasion since January 1st, 1980, 40 were deaf as a result of brain injury. 34 of these children have, whilst on the programme, become able to hear and to recognise meaningful sounds. Nineteen have gained the further ability to understand speech.

128 children began the programme able to hear sounds, but unable to understand spoken language. 109 of these now understand at the very least several single words of speech.

CHAPTER 28

The Sensory Pathways
(TACTILE)

Have you ever woken up in bed, in the middle of the night, and been unable to feel your right arm? Your initial panic was quickly controlled when you felt around with your other hand and reassured yourself that your right arm was still in place, although totally numb. Nevertheless, it was very real.

Have you ever sat on the edge of a chair for too long, and found yourself unable to stand, or to walk?

In both these instances, you temporarily lost the ability to feel, and without this tactile sense you were unable to function.

When you have read this paragraph, try a little experiment. Close your eyes, and wiggle your right big toe. How did you know where it was, if your eyes were closed?

In fact, your brain always knows where all the parts of your body are, and this ability is called proprioception. Touch sensors, spread throughout the body, constantly alert the brain to their relative positions. Without this information, you would find it extremely difficult to control your movements.

Vision and hearing are so obviously important to human beings that this does not need explanation. Yet tactility, our sense of touch, is just as important, and very many of our functions depend on it. Speech, mobility, toilet training, control of saliva, eating, whistling, manual dexterity, recognition of painful and pleasurable sensations, and much more depend on our knowing how all these activities feel.

Do you remember the last time you had to have a tooth cavity filled by the dentist? If you were given a local anaesthetic, then long after the dentistry was over, you would still have been unable to talk properly, or to control your mouth sufficiently to eat and drink. The lack of sensation produced by the anaesthetic also produced a temporary loss of function.

At birth, all babies have tactile reflexes, and one, the Babinski reflex, is present as a direct aid to future mobility. In a new-born baby,

TIME FRAME	PROFILE LEVEL	BRAIN LEVEL	TACTILE DEVELOPMENT
PEER LEVEL IF OVER SIX YEARS	8	*Superior Cortex*	Able to identify by touch, using the appropriate dominant hand
6 YEARS	7	*Advanced Cortex*	Able to identify tiny objects by touch
3 YEARS	6	*Developed Cortex*	Able to differentiate between similar objects
18 MONTHS	5	*Early Cortex*	Able to differentiate between dissimilar objects
12 MONTHS	4	*Initial Cortex*	Awareness of the third dimension
6 MONTHS	3	*Midbrain*	Able to react to light touch
3 MONTHS	2	*Pons*	Awareness of vital sensation
BIRTH	1	*Medulla and Cord*	Babinski reflex

Figure 5   Tactile Development

the big toe of either foot should rise upwards when the outer edge of the sole of that foot is stimulated. This response, which is purely tactile in nature, provides a 'toe dig' when the sole comes in contact with the floor, and is very useful as an aid to propulsion during the initial stages of creeping on the tummy. Of course, the same response would be counter-productive in an older child when he was beginning to walk, so the reflex changes after the first year of life, and the big toe curls downwards thereafter in response to the same stimulus. The presence in an older child of an immature, or upward moving big toe, is an indicator of the probable presence of tactile problems, and can often be linked with inadequate mobility.

Poor awareness of painful and pleasurable stimuli is often a source of difficulty in a brain injured child.

Some of our children have such poor tactility that they are unable to detect even severe pain. They can lie against a very hot radiator and be totally unaware that they are being burned. Others cannot bear to be hugged, because they are hypersensitive to touch.

As the brain and nervous system mature, higher levels of tactile skill become established. We become able to feel the edges of things, and to recognise different objects by touch. This skill becomes more refined, to the point where we can select one key from a bunch in the dark, or pick out one coin from a pocketful, using only tactility.

When brain injury has occurred, and the sense of touch has been impaired, we must provide sufficient stimulation to create new tactile pathways into the brain. There are many different techniques which can be employed, and the following are only a sample:

The use of hot and cold water to stimulate the sensation of temperature.
Vigorous towelling after a bath.
The all-over application of a vibratory massager.
Rubbing with a variety of different textures, to teach the different feel of rough and smooth, hard and soft.
Tickling, stroking, pinching and scratching.

In the area of the head, and particularly the face and mouth, the use of tactile stimulation can be extremely helpful in the elimination of dribbling, the encouragement of better chewing, and the promotion of speech.

As with any technique, there is a right way and a wrong way to stimulate the sense of touch. Too vigorous pressure can lead to soreness. Too light a stimulus can be a waste of time. Yet, applied correctly, tactile stimulation can restore or create function.

The next time you sit too long with one leg crossed over the other, and discover on rising that you cannot walk, think about the action you will take. You will rub your leg, or stamp it on the ground. In effect, you will attempt to send tactile information to your brain in order to try to reconfirm sensation, and to reassure the brain that all is well. In practice, our tactile techniques aim to do the same thing, by teaching our children HOW IT FEELS TO FEEL.

TASTE AND SMELL

There are two other sensory pathways which carry information to the brain – Taste and Smell. Whilst these are dominant in animals, which rely heavily on both senses for survival, they are regressive in humans.

Three groups of people rely more heavily than the rest of us on their senses of smell and taste. The first are new-born children, who use them to find a source of food. The second are older, brain injured children, who also use them to find a source of food. The third are those fantastic people who take one sip of wine, and can tell you not only from where it originates, but which year it was bottled!

The rest of us can survive despite the loss of our senses of taste or smell; it is much harder to do so if we lose sight, hearing or tactility.

Although we do incorporate some olfactory and gustatory stimulation in some of our programmes, especially when dealing with Coma and 'Autism', these two senses are not included in the Developmental Profile.

CHAPTER 29

The Motor Pathways
(MOBILITY)

The Floor

For many years, eminent educationalists and child experts have recognised the value of the floor as a safe and natural environment for
a child. In our culture, a baby is placed on the floor very early in his
development. He is encouraged to roll over, to do 'press-ups', to
creep forwards on his tummy, to crawl on hands and knees, to walk,
run, somersault, hop, skip, jump and perform other physical feats.
In fact, for all of us, the floor represents stability, solidity, and
safety.

Our brain injured children not only need to receive extra sensory
stimulation – how it feels to see, to hear, to feel things – they also
need an increased amount of opportunity to *do* things for themselves,
and to learn by repetition the same information, and in the same way,
as their well counterparts. What could be a more secure learning environment than the floor?

Lying flat in the prone position, there is no requirement for balance. The body is at rest, so no demands are made on muscles to
maintain position, and the effects of gravity can be largely ignored. It
is the safest of all positions to be in. You can't fall off the floor!

If a bomb were to be dropped, and we all had twenty seconds to
take cover, I wonder how many of us would remain standing, or lie
down on our backs, face up? We would surely fall flat on our bellies,
with arms over our ears, relying on the fact that our spines and rib
cages would act as a protection for our vital organs. This is just as true
if you happen to be a severely brain injured child, and need to be in a
position where you can enjoy Mother Nature's own maximum physical protection.

For brain injured children, the floor is not, however, just a safe
'car-park', where they can come to no harm. It provides an opportunity for movement, where they can begin to experiment, moving first

TIME FRAME	PROFILE LEVEL	BRAIN LEVEL	MOBILITY
PEER LEVEL IF OVER SIX YEARS	8	*Superior Cortex*	Able to move with the co-ordination of age level, consistent with the appropriate dominant foot
6 YEARS	7	*Advanced Cortex*	Able to hop, skip, jump and kick a ball
3 YEARS	6	*Developed Cortex*	Able to run in cross pattern
18 MONTHS	5	*Early Cortex*	Able to walk with arms no longer required for balance
12 MONTHS	4	*Initial Cortex*	Able to walk with arms used for balance
6 MONTHS	3	*Midbrain*	Able to crawl in cross pattern on hands and knees
3 MONTHS	2	*Pons*	Able to creep in cross pattern on abdomen
BIRTH	1	*Medulla and Cord*	Free voluntary movement of limbs

Figure 6   Mobility Development

one limb at a time, then two, and finally all four. To achieve these movements, which are, after all, propulsive in nature, they must be lying on their tummies – not on their backs. By the way, I never saw a Rolls Royce go very far on its roof!

Once they have begun to co-ordinate these movements, and are able to creep forwards 'under their own steam', they can progress to the far more complicated business of getting up on to all fours and achieving the quadruped, or, as we call it, the 'quad' position.

A child on all-fours needs to have learned several new skills. His muscles must be strong enough to withstand his weight, and to successfully combat gravity. He must be able to lift his head up, and to control its position. He must be aware of the relative position of all his limbs, and be able to maintain sufficient pressure against the floor with each one, simultaneously, to maintain adequate balance.

Once he is able to stay in this position without difficulty, the next step is to attempt forward movement on hands and knees, and a new set of problems has to be faced. It now becomes necessary to balance on only three limbs, whilst the fourth is being lifted and moved forwards. The weight of the body must be redistributed, and the forward movement of each limb in turn must be properly co-ordinated. Crawling on hands and knees is a much more efficient method of transportation than creeping on the tummy, as the effect of friction is now limited to those parts of the body in contact with the floor. If you have ever tried to catch a child who is crawling along the floor at speed, you will know how quickly you have had to move!

In addition to the obvious opportunities for mobility which the floor can bring to a child, there is another, less recognised advantage to be gained. The ability to converge the eyes at close range – a vital precursor to being able to read – is first achieved on the floor. As a child learns to lift and lower his head, the floor becomes a visual target. As it moves closer or further away, he must learn to control the muscles of his eyes in order to keep it in focus. For this reason, creeping and crawling are important activities for children, however mobile they might otherwise be, in helping to eliminate reading problems, and in improving visual concentration.

The floor can take more than one form, and can consist of a variety of different textures. For the totally immobile youngster it can be an inclined plane, or slide, which allows gravity to become a friend instead of an enemy. Even the slightest movement becomes exaggerated, and the child begins to experience how it feels to move forwards. As these movements become more controlled, and less of an effort, the slide can be gradually lowered, until it can be replaced by the floor itself.

The easiest surface on which to attempt to creep forwards on the tummy is a smooth one. Shiny hardboard, or vinyl produce the least amount of drag, but allow feet to gain some purchase in trying to push the body forwards. A more challenging covering is a nylon carpet, whilst the most difficult is sorbo-rubber. Unsealed cork tiles can also be hard to negotiate. As a child develops his skills, the effect of friction can be increased, and provided the level of difficulty is never greater than he can accomplish, the effort required to move forwards will serve to strengthen muscles, and to improve functional ability.

If one of our children is totally immobile, he is required to spend all his free time on the floor, in the prone position. For this reason, his world – the floor – must be always clean, warm and safe.

One of the first things any of our visitors learns is that outdoor shoes are never worn in any of the rooms where children spend time on the floor. This 'law' is not only strictly enforced at the Alison Centre, but is also recommended in the homes of all our families. It is an easy way to keep the floor relatively clean, and makes for a much more wholesome environment for our children. And it is worth remembering that, in Japan, no self-respecting householder or visitor would dream of wearing outdoor shoes inside the house!

A floor which is carpeted is much warmer than one made up of quarry tiles or stone slabs. Cold air at ground level can be reduced by fitting draught excluders to doors and windows.

Mains electricity sockets should be blanked off and made safe from questing little fingers. Any valuable ornaments or reading lamps should be removed, and, obviously, adequate guards should be fitted wherever there is a fire of any kind. The easiest way to check if a floor area is safe is to pretend to be your child, and to creep around it yourself. Anything which could hurt you could most certainly hurt him, so leave nothing to chance.

Many of our older children sleep on the floor. Of course, they are wrapped in blankets, and may lie on a thin (3 inch) mattress, but if they decide to begin to move forwards for the first time, and it happens to be 3 am, then at least they can do so without restriction.

Several years ago, I advised a family whose child had no mobility to arrange for him to sleep on the floor. Two months after starting our programme, the mother rang up to tell me that her son had broken his hip. Since it is very difficult for a totally immobile child to break a hip, I asked what on earth had happened. She replied, 'Well, you know you told us to have him sleep on the floor. We didn't think you really meant it, so we had been letting him sleep in his bed, just like he has always done. And last night, he must have tried to move forwards on his own, fallen out of bed, and broken his hip!'

If we recommend that a child sleeps on the floor, we DO mean it!

Of all the techniques that we use in giving our children opportunity for improvement, potentially the most effective is the floor. All our parents have a floor. It is the one piece of equipment they don't have to go out and buy, and to place a child on it, in the prone position, requires no skill.

It is the first step along the road to mobility.

Patterning

'Patterning' is a term we use to describe a series of physical movements carried out regularly on many of our children, by teams of up to five people. There are several different movement patterns, and each is aimed at stimulating a different brain area, in order to encourage different levels of co-ordinated movement. The choice of a specific patterning technique depends on the needs of each individual child, and is a primary tool in teaching the brain a particular function where this has not yet developed or has been by-passed.

Roll Patterning

Where a child is so hurt that he is unable to move his own limbs voluntarily, this simple activity, which normally requires only one person to carry out, gives him very basic information about simple co-ordination. The effect of the technique is to roll him over, from side to side, slowly and gently, and we believe that this rolling motion recapitulates in the brain the very early movements experienced by a child in the womb, and helps to reinforce the child's awareness of his body and limbs.

As voluntary limb control is present in new-born babies, the absence of this ability places a brain injured child 'below birth level' in mobility. We believe the stimulus of the pattern is aimed at the medulla, the brain area most concerned with function at this very early stage.

Trunkal Patterning

This technique is normally carried out by two people, working in co-ordination with one another. One moves the child's arms, the other

Homolateral Pattern
3-man team

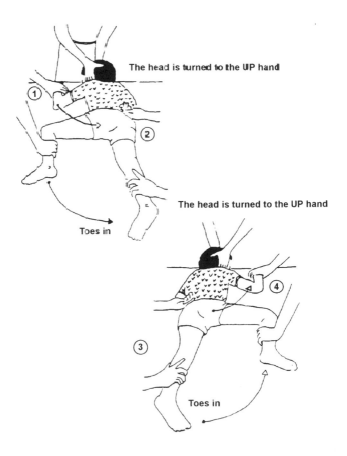

The head is turned to the UP hand

The head is turned to the UP hand

Toes in

Toes in

Before starting, the head should be turned to one side. The arm and leg on that side should be in the UP positions (1). The opposite arm and leg should be in the DOWN positions (2).

As the head is turned in the opposite direction, the arm and leg which were UP are moved into the DOWN positions (3), and the arm and leg which were DOWN are simultaneously moved into the UP positions (4).

These movements are then rhythmically repeated. The head should always be turned towards the rising hand.

Figure 7   Homolateral Patterning

his legs, and the movements again recapitulate some of the pre-birth activities of a baby, the first controlled attempts by the brain to co-ordinate activity in arms and legs simultaneously.

Trunkal Patterning is used where a child is very stiff, or very floppy; where co-ordination is very poor, or non-existent; and where a child's ability to breathe is inadequate.

Homolateral Patterning

If a child has sufficient movement in his limbs, but cannot creep forwards on his tummy, then Homolateral Patterning is used to teach him how it *feels* to do so.

In a small patient, this technique requires the use of three helpers, in a larger one, five. With him lying face down on a suitable padded surface, the head, arms and legs are moved in a slow, steady and good rhythm. If viewed from above during Homolateral Patterning, the child appears to be creeping forwards, in a movement pattern similar to that of the amphibian, using one side of his body to propel himself forwards, then the other. It is the pons area of the brain which is responsible for controlling the ability to creep on the tummy. It is interesting that, although the input pattern is homolateral, or one-sided, in nature, the response from the child, once he begins to move forwards unaided, is very often a cross pattern movement, using the opposite arm and leg to propel himself.

Cross Patterning

The highest brain levels which we believe can be stimulated by patterning are the mid-brain and cerebral cortex, and these control, respectively, crawling on hands and knees, and walking. Cross Patterning represents a more sophisticated form of prone patterning where, instead of moving one whole side of his body at a time, helpers move opposite arms and legs in synchronisation with the head.

The brain is now able to co-ordinate each individual limb, rather than just one side of the body at a time, and has developed sufficient awareness of space to be able to control balance with the body held away from the ground by arms and legs, or legs alone. The cross pattern of movement, which most of us use in walking with a good arm swing, distinguishes us from those less fortunate people who are the bane of the drill-sergeant's life; those who cannot march except in a poor homolateral pattern!

All patterning is passive in nature. The child is not required to do

Cross Pattern
3-man team

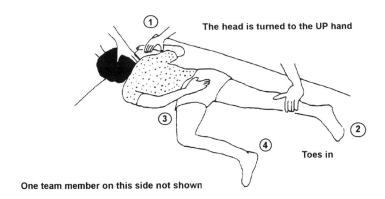

The head is turned to the UP hand

Toes in

One team member on this side not shown

Limb positions 1 & 2 change to 5 & 6
Limb positions 3 & 4 change to 7 & 8

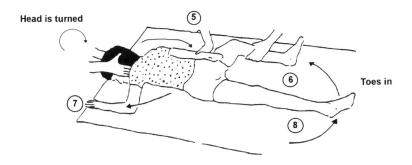

Head is turned

Toes in

One team member on this side not shown

Before starting, the head should be turned to one side. The arm on that side should be in the UP position (1). The leg should be in the DOWN position (2). The other arm should be in the DOWN position (3) and the other leg in the UP position (4).

As the head is turned in the opposite direction, the position of each limb is simultaneously reversed.

These movements are then rhythmically repeated. The head should always be turned towards the rising hand.

Figure 8 Cross Patterning

anything, as the whole principle of the activity is to present a series of related bits of information to his brain for storage. For this reason, it should not be considered an exercise; the only muscles which will grow as a result of patterning are those belonging to the helpers! It is certainly true that the regular movement of limbs can help to prevent stiffness in the joints, but this should be considered a helpful bonus, rather than a goal for the technique.

I have already talked about 'the Floor', and its role in creating mobility. Patterning is the precursor of the Floor, as it provides a child with information about basic movement, which he can then try to imitate himself when on the Floor.

As a technique, Patterning offers several additional benefits which are extremely important to some of our children.

It enhances tactility, and thus body and limb awareness. At higher levels, it improves balance through the regular stimulation given to the inner ear by the turning of the head. It can give visual stimulation, when targets are placed on each side of the table, at different focal lengths from the child.

Auditory stimulation, which often goes by unrecognised, is also provided by the helpers, without whose daily or weekly involvement regular patterning could not be carried out. Talking to the child is important, and many patterning teams have weekly topics which they research before their visit, thus bringing with them not only welcome pairs of hands, but new sources of interesting information. While a child is being patterned, it is an excellent opportunity to teach him French, or another second language; poems; multiplication tables or items of general knowledge.

Because patterning has become more widely known than perhaps any of our other techniques, people sometimes, and quite incorrectly, tend to call the entire programme 'patterning'. I have seen newspaper articles which refer to families carrying out 'patterning' for four hours each day! Not so.

Patterning is designed to teach the brain 'how it feels to move', in a variety of different ways, and is normally carried out for no more than five minutes per session, as this is the length of time an average patterning team can keep up a good rhythm before becoming tired.

Hang By Hands

Some of our children, especially the younger ones, have great diffi-culty in mastering head control. This skill, which develops quite early in a well child, depends on muscle power, but motivation is also required for a child to WANT to lift his head. When vision and hearing are impaired, the absence of these stimuli can often further retard the establishment of good head control.

It is often the case that in children who cannot lift their heads, manual function is also very poor, and they have not developed the ability to grasp, using the whole hand.

In these circumstances, we have found that by making it possible for a child to hang by his hands from an overhead bar, head control and a full-hand grasp can both be encouraged. At first, two people may be needed to carry out this technique – one standing facing the child and holding his hands on to the bar, and the other supporting the child's weight from behind, whilst at the same time allowing the child's head to rest in an upright position against the helper's chest. Gradually, as the grip strengthens, this support can be reduced, until the child can hold on to the bar by himself.

Over a period of time, as his muscles strengthen and he becomes more aware of the feeling of his head being upright instead of drooping forwards, the child begins to try to keep it in that position, and control starts to develop.

The D-Ring

Once a good grip in the hands has become established, it is an obvious progression from the use of a static overhead bar to the introduction of a D-Ring.

This piece of equipment is secured to the end of a rope suspended from a pulley fixed to the ceiling, and can therefore be raised and lowered.

If a child cannot sit up, his hands can still be held on to the horizontal bar, and as the bar is raised, he can begin to take a little of his own weight. If able to stand up with support, he can steady himself by holding on to the D-Ring above his head.

Once he has a good grasp, and is strong enough to bear his own weight, the child can hold on to the bar whilst he is lifted off the ground for gradually increased periods of time.

Walking With the Overhead Ladder

Once a child has developed the ability to creep on his tummy, and to crawl on hands and knees, the next stage is walking. A normal child will encounter the edge of the sofa, or a chair, and will try to pull himself up until he is standing. After he has learned to walk holding on to furniture, he will take one or two very unsteady independent steps, before falling over; but as his confidence and his ability to balance on just two limbs improve, he takes more and more steps forward.

However, these attempts to walk do not resemble the effortless gait, and the good arm swing which you and I adopt without ever thinking about it. His hands are up at shoulder level, helping him to balance, and he takes one small step at a time. If he tries to change direction, he cannot maintain balance, and falls over.

Gradually, as his confidence and ability increase, and the brain becomes more able to interpret and control all the information flooding in from the environment, his arms drop down, until he no longer needs to use them for balance. Instead, he can hold objects in his hands as he moves forwards, or use his hands for an independent purpose, like carrying a toy, or even putting them in his pockets!

How easy and natural these developments sound. Yet, for the brain injured child, even standing up can be an insurmountable problem, unless he has had a great deal of help to learn where he is in space; where all the parts of his body are, and how to control his limbs. His muscles must be strong enough to maintain his own weight; his vision must be sufficient to see where he is going, and to want to go there; his balance centres must be able to respond to his search for equilibrium, and his breathing must be adequate enough to supply the oxygen his system needs during this stressful activity.

In the past, such patients have been encouraged to walk using parallel bars. Unfortunately, this type of equipment requires adequate strength in the arm muscles; the effect of gravity on the upright body creates a poor posture, and every forward step becomes a major feat. For these, and other reasons, we prefer to use an overhead ladder.

The ladder is supported at each end by uprights, and can be adjusted to take account of a child's physical growth. Its rungs are brightly coloured, to add visual interest, and the floor beneath the ladder can be covered in a variety of different materials, depending on the amount of friction or traction required by the soles of the feet.

As a child walks along, under the ladder, he holds on to the rungs above his head. As he stretches forward with each alternate hand towards the next rung, he can develop better eye/hand co-ordination. With his arms raised above his head, his diaphragm is expanded, thus making it easier for him to breathe. Now, the effect of gravity is to help him to straighten out. His arms are in the appropriate balance-role position required developmentally for early walking, but the stress of independent balancing is aided by his grasp on the rungs above his head.

Once he is able to walk confidently with the support of the ladder, the rungs become less vital to him. They can then be raised out of reach, and instead, a series of knotted ropes, hanging from the overhead rungs, can be provided for support. These are less firm, and present a new challenge both to his eye/hand co-ordination, and to his balance.

Brachiation

The overhead ladder offers another, different opportunity to our children.

By learning to swing hand over hand from rung to rung, with the feet off the ground, a child can begin to develop stronger arm muscles; his spine begins to straighten; his eye/hand co-ordination speeds up, and breathing is both easier and more challenged by this exertion.

As proficiency increases, he can learn to turn at the end of the ladder, and to increase the number of 'trips' which he can make, without stopping. These turns can be encouraged, until he is skilful enough to turn his body completely round several times as he negotiates a full length of the ladder.

Observers, watching some of our children swing from rung to rung, admire their ability. Yet those same observers would probably accept without comment similar skills shown by well children on a climbing frame in the local play area.

Brachiation, as we call this activity, provides every child, and particularly our children, with the opportunity to develop areas of the brain which we believe to be vital if higher levels of spatial awareness, balance and co-ordination are to be achieved.

The overhead ladder is a most useful tool, and can be constructed indoors or out; its value far outweighs its cost, and many brain injured children have, over the years, swung along it, walked along it, and even walked off the end of it!

Suspended Inverted Rotation, or Upside-Down

The planet on which we live produces gravitational forces, drawing every living creature downwards towards the centre of the earth. For mobility to be possible, one of the ingredients is the ability to cope with this gravitational pull, and to know 'which way is up'. A constant awareness of space, and our position relative to the vertical and horizontal, is a basic requirement for all human beings, since we are designed to walk upright, balancing on two relatively small surfaces (our feet).

The brain's knowledge of 'where we are' at any time, comes from a host of different bits of information. The balance centres in the inner ear advise on equilibrium. The eyes tell us whether what we are looking at is vertical or horizontal, and therefore whether our own position is upright or not. Our tactile awareness of all the different parts of our body allows us to adjust to uneven ground, or to a sloping surface, so we can maintain our perpendicular position.

All this information is based on experience, which we believe starts long before our actual birth. An unborn baby, in the womb, can sense and adjust to the movements of its mother, and is already learning how it feels to be moved. In the young child, part of the information he needs is provided by his parents, and which father hasn't picked up his offspring, and despite his wife's protests, thrown the baby up into the air and caught him again?

If we were to ask that father why he did such a strange thing, it is probable that he would have no rational explanation to offer. It simply seemed a natural thing to do. In a human family, it normally falls to the father to 'play rough' with his children, and this apparent 'roughness' is in fact an instinctive attempt to encourage them to become more aware of themselves and their environment.

Which young boy has not climbed a tree and hung upside down from a convenient branch?

How often has one seen little girls swinging upside down on the railings outside the school playground?

Isn't Granny delighted when the toddler first puts his head between his knees, and views the world the other way up?

Each September, here in Bridgwater, we have Fair Week. Every year, showmen vie with one another to provide ever more thrilling opportunities for us to hang upside down, spin round and round, turn head over heels, and 'defy' gravity. They never seem to lack customers, and the shrieks and screams are an expression of temporary terror, but deep-down delight.

If we look at the animal kingdom, our predecessors in evolutionary terms, we see the same type of activity. The young cubs run up to the adult animal, which bowls them over and over with a sweep of the paw. They then come straight back for more! It is, interestingly, the female in the cat family who takes the initiative in developing balance and equilibrium in her young. Using her teeth, she picks up her babies by the scruff of the neck, and shakes them vigorously, before letting them fall to the floor.

It would seem part of the instinctive nature of all creatures that they should learn how to cope with their environment, and this need to learn to be aware in space, and to balance, is very much a basic requirement for survival.

We all admire those human beings who have perfected this awareness to a high degree. The Olympic gymnast is honoured for her knowledge of where she is, all the time, in space. The ice dancer, the acrobat, the ballerina – so many examples exist of people who have an above average ability to cope with gravity, and who always know 'where they are in space'.

How, therefore, is this knowledge to be gained by the brain injured child, whose sources of information are often greatly reduced by his inability to see, feel, or even move his limbs? He lives in an almost wholly protected environment – he has been hurt once, and his mother has no intention of it happening again. He is cocooned by love, but also by fear, and has very little chance of learning the way a well child learns.

Our task, as we see it, is to provide him with an opportunity to discover, in a totally safe way, the same information as his well counterpart. Mother has to begin to 'open up' the world for him, and to give him the chance to learn. Therefore, we have devised a safe, stimulating and often enjoyable way to teach him where he is in space.

We hang him upside down! Using reliable equipment, we hoist him up into the air, and swing him forwards, backwards, sideways, and round in circles. The immediate adult reaction to this is one of surprise, and even alarm, yet the same activity, carried out by well youngsters within the environment of a children's playground, produces a very different reaction – approval, pleasure and perhaps even pride. Well children are positively encouraged to develop new skills, and to try new experiences which can teach them more about their world. Our *method* is different, but the philosophy and the effect are much the same.

As with every technique we use, the same criteria are always applied.

1. Is it safe?
2. Is it ethical?
3. Is it effective?

Yes, it is safe. Our medical officer examines every child before the commencement of the programme, and where any factor exists which might put a child at risk if he were to be inverted, the technique is ruled out immediately.

Each family is carefully taught how to use the correct equipment; how to build the child's confidence; and for exactly how long to hang him upside down.

Yes, it is ethical. If any child experiences pain or physical discomfort, the technique is discontinued.

Yes, it is effective – both in terms of improving physiological and neurological functions.

When one of our children has developed a spinal distortion, hanging him upside down creates traction on the spine, with his own body weight helping to straighten out the curvature.

Many children come to us already suffering from a physical condition where the spine has become curved or twisted. Scoliosis, lordosis or kyphosis often result from the inability of weak back muscles to support the spine when children are encouraged to sit up before they are ready.

Here again, gravity is the main enemy, as the weight of the head, pressing directly downwards on the insufficiently supported spine, produces a buckling effect.

Once a brain injured child has grown sufficiently to be too heavy to carry, parents are encouraged to buy a 'buggy' – or miniature wheel chair – to make it easier to transport him. Very sensible. Unfortunately, however, once he has been moved from A to B, he often stays safely strapped in the buggy, because it is easier to leave him there than to undo all the straps and get him out again, and because being able to sit up is felt to be such an important milestone. Except that HE isn't sitting up. He is being *propped up*!

The larger and heavier the child, the more time he tends to spend in his wheelchair, and his posture can only encourage spinal curvature.

On my way to work each day, I used to drive past a unit for 'physically handicapped' children, and in the summer I often saw them being parked outside in the sunshine, in their wheelchairs. Returning home, at the end of the day, I would see them being wheeled back inside, after a 'healthy day in the sun'! I wonder how much less scoliosis they would have developed, and how much more mobility, for that matter, if they had been allowed to lie prone on the grass?

Wheelchairs are fine – and sometimes essential – for transportation. They are NOT fine as sophisticated 'activity centres'. By all means use one to move Johnny from A to B. But, when you get to B, take him out of it and put him back in the land of opportunity, on the floor. If you don't, we may be faced with trying to eliminate the problem of a twisted spine which didn't have to happen in the first place!

Crossed eyes, a very common symptom of brain injury, often straighten whilst a child is inverted. The effect of gravity on the muscles of the eyes is reversed, and several of our children have actually learned to read whilst upside down, an ability which they do not have when 'the right way up'!

Some of our families live on the continent, and when it is time for their children's reassessments, they travel to Bridgwater by car. In winter, they sometimes experience a bad Channel crossing, and, by the time they reach us, the parents look not only tired but distinctly 'green'. Not so their hurt children, who have invariably enjoyed the whole thing! Nausea, whether in the form of air, sea or car sickness, is a very rare condition in those children who are regularly spun around upside down. Their ability to relate in space is enhanced, and they learn to compensate for sudden changes in equilibrium more efficiently than do the rest of us.

Bent limbs begin to straighten. Tight heels relax. Head control improves.

But perhaps one of the most important factors of all is that hanging upside down is fun! Why else do we *all* do it, at one time or another?

Some Other Spatial Activities

S.I.R. is not, of course, the only spatial technique which we can use to encourage better balance and co-ordination. There are many others, and they can be broadly divided into two groups – pre-walking and post-walking.

Pre-Walking

In the first category, our main objective is to supplement patterning with other activities which can provide the brain with a great deal of information about space. While a child is creeping on his tummy, he is only concerned with two dimensions – longitudinal and lateral movement. Once he gets up on to his hands and knees, the third dimension – depth – becomes important, and he needs to be able to judge where he is in space.

Rolls

This activity involves lying a child full length on the floor, with his arms above his head, and rolling him over and over, first in one direction, then in the other. If he has poor, or no head control, particular care must be taken to ensure that he cannot bang his head on the floor, and in severe cases, his arms should be kept down at the sides, and he should be wrapped in a rug, or put inside a cardboard tube of suitable internal diameter, before rolling commences.

Somersaults

Forward and backward somersaults, better known to gymnasts as 'forward or backward rolls', provide similar stimulation to the balance centres in the inner ear, but along a different axis. Care should be taken to cushion the child's head and neck, and the base of his spine, and this activity should be carried out on a thick foam mat.

N.B. Both Rolling and Somersaults can be hazardous for some Down's Syndrome children, where the cervical vertebrae may not be fully formed. Before attempting either of these two techniques with these particular children, we always first insist on an X-ray of their cervical spine.

Arm and Leg Swings

This technique is easy to carry out on a small child, but can be impossible with an adolescent, because of his size and weight.

With one person holding an arm and leg on each side, and the child facing upwards, he is lifted up off the floor, and swung forwards and backwards, slowly and gently.

When swinging him in the other plane, (side to side), one person holds both arms and the other, both legs.

With the larger child, one helper may be needed to hold each limb.

Where there is poor or non-existent head control, a blanket can be used to accomplish this activity safely.

Suspended Rotation

Once a child has gained head control, and can sit up on his own, we may decide to introduce suspended rotation. This is in many ways the reverse of S.I.R. Instead of spinning him round, out of contact with the ground, whilst upside down, we provide the child with the same sensations except that he is now *the right way up*.

This is best achieved by fixing a basket chair to a rope suspended from the ceiling. The child is safely strapped into the chair, which is then spun, clockwise and anticlockwise, slowly at first, then gradually faster.

Garden Swing

With the same provisos – that he has developed head control and can sit up on his own – we can also introduce a garden swing into the programme. A small child can be seated in an enclosed chair; a larger and more competent child can be allowed to sit on the traditional flat seat. The movements, as with all spatial techniques, should be gentle and slow at first, and should only be speeded up once the child has gained enough confidence to cope with the sensations which are produced.

The garden swing can also be used to encourage a stronger grip, with the hands holding on to the ropes on each side. If a mattress is placed vertically at the end of the normal travel of the swing, the youngster can learn to push against this surface with his feet, helping to strengthen his leg muscles.

Piggy In The Middle

Once a child can sit up without help, his balance can be challenged quite safely by introducing this game. He is seated in the middle of a circle of helpers, and is then pushed gently off-balance. His safety is ensured by the person in whose direction he is pushed being available to catch him if he cannot right himself. When once more upright, he is then pushed in a different direction, and so on. Many children love this game, and here is yet another example where the programme can be fun to carry out for both children and adults.

Once a child is able to stand without support, a variation of the same game can offer him further opportunities for learning how to keep his balance, and how to shift his weight from one leg to another to maintain equilibrium.

The Trampette

Whilst a child is learning to stand upright, another way of improving his balance is to encourage him to challenge his own abilities. A trampette, or small trampoline, incorporating in its design a bar which he can grasp, will allow a child to bounce up and down in safety. If he loses his balance, the elasticity of the base will cushion his fall, and he can enjoy the sensation of jumping up and down, whilst strengthening his arm and leg muscles.

Post-Walking

Balance Beam

The first time a child attempts to walk along a narrow beam of wood lying on the floor, it must seem similar to the challenge faced by a non-acrobat in trying to walk along a tight-rope.

A typical beam is 8 feet long and measures 4 inches by 3 inches. The wider faces are at the top and bottom, to give stability and to provide a reasonable width upon which to walk.

To begin with, the child will need considerable support, and this is best given by two adults walking one on each side of him whilst each is holding one of his hands. If only one adult is available, she should walk backwards, straddling the beam, holding both of his hands in hers.

As his confidence and skill improve, the child will need less and less assistance. The support of two hands can be reduced to one hand only, and, in time, our aspiring 'Blondin' will be able to walk along the beam from one end to the other without help.

Once this stage has been reached, more challenging activities can be introduced, including 'walking backwards' along the beam, and squatting on one leg in the centre. The beam itself can also be raised off the floor, up to a height of 2 feet. It is surprising how much more difficult it is, even for those with good balance and co-ordination, to negotiate a beam raised off the ground. The third dimension – depth – brings the entirely new element of danger into an otherwise straight-forward activity. This is even more the case for one of our children, and the height of the beam should therefore be increased very gradually indeed.

Stepping Stones

Anyone who has walked across a stream by stepping from one boulder to another will realise the amount of co-ordination and balance which is required to successfully accomplish this feat. The same challenges can be offered to a brain injured child with safety, indoors, through the use of 'stepping stones'.

These are strong wooden boxes, ideally with a base 18 inches square, and of heights varying between 4 inches and 18 inches. They can be placed on the floor in different patterns, but should always be close enough to each other for a child to be able to reach the next one in a single pace, without overbalancing. A non-slip surface on the top of each 'stepping stone' is recommended, and if each one is painted a different colour of the rainbow, it is easier to point out to the child which one is his next 'target'.

The support principle of 'two hands; one hand; no hands' should again be applied, so as to build confidence as well as skill.

Trampoline

In the early stages of learning how to perform on a trampoline, a child can progress through each developmental level, from prone to being on all-fours to standing upright. We know no better way of repeatedly reinforcing, in turn, each of the brain levels involved, and a trampoline, properly used, can also provide our children with a great deal of physical exercise – toning up muscles and improving respiratory function.

As with every activity, there are safety rules. There should always be a helper on each side of the mat, 'spotting', and ready to assist if balance is lost. Edges should always be covered with protective foam, to cushion a fall. A child should NEVER be allowed to use the trampoline without supervision.

When a child has no mobility, he is totally at the mercy of gravity. To get on to his hands and knees, he has to learn to press against the floor with all four limbs. Once standing up, he has refined this skill and developed his strength to the point where he needs only two limbs to defeat the pressure of gravity. But it is only when taking advantage of the elasticity of the trampoline that he has the freedom, momentarily, to compete with gravity on almost equal terms.

The Prestrim Spatial Stimulation Device

The ultimate spatial experience for a child is a Prestrim device, which combines all our other spatial techniques in one piece of equipment. The Prestrim, originally designed to help sailors, pilots and other people whose hobbies or occupations require them to have good spatial awareness, was adapted by the manufacturers at our request to accommodate brain injured children.

The device itself works on the principle of a gyroscope. An upright seat is fixed within a circular steel frame. This frame forms the innermost of three circular steel frames, and by virtue of the ability of each frame to revolve on gimbals within its own, different axis, and in a full 360 degrees, anyone sitting in the chair can be rotated three dimensionally, and at random.

This equipment can therefore provide a child with the experience of being in any position from the horizontal to the vertical, and in any plane. Since it can be rotated faster or slower by the operator, the Prestrim offers a child a constantly altering spatial environment, to which he must adjust. This is a rigorous challenge to the balance centres in the inner ear, and combines the benefits of all the other spatial techniques which we use.

Of the 721 children whom I have seen on more than one occasion since January 1st, 1980, 155 children, 44 of whom were previously immobile, have learned to creep forwards independently on their tummies. Seventy-three children have learned to crawl on their hands and knees. Sixty-two children have learned to walk, and sixty-eight can now run.

Nineteen children who were totally immobile have learned to creep on their tummies, crawl on their hands and knees, and to walk. Five of these can now also run.

CHAPTER 30

The Motor Pathways
(LANGUAGE)

One of the most upsetting problems for a family to cope with is the lack of ability in a child to communicate. To hear the voice of your child as he says his first words is always a major event, and if this does not happen, it is very hard to live with.

Like many other functions of a human being, speech is made up of a number of components, and if any of these is missing, then poor or no communication will result.

Firstly, a child has to be able to control his breathing.

As any of you who have had to make a speech in public in front of a large audience will know, breath control is vital to the proper production of words and sentences.

When 'stage fright' occurs, and a speaker loses his breath control, it is no longer possible to utter words or sentences correctly. Air must be able to flow into and out of both the mouth and nose, and a poor rhythm of breathing, breath holding, or an inadequate 'tidal flow' of air will immediately restrict or prevent speech.

If you have ever sprinted for a bus, and then immediately had to state your destination to the driver, you will understand. If you have ever been asked to speak whilst someone has been taking your temperature by thrusting a thermometer under your tongue, you will understand.

In the second place, it is essential that a proper level of tactile awareness is present in the tongue, the lips, the teeth, the mouth itself, and in all the areas which surround them.

The injection of a local anaesthetic by your dentist into your lower jaw very rapidly robs you of sensation in that part of the mouth and in half of your tongue. Speech then becomes a struggle. For those who

TIME FRAME	PROFILE LEVEL	BRAIN LEVEL	LANGUAGE
PEER LEVEL IF OVER SIX YEARS	8	*Superior Cortex*	Able to converse appropriately at age level
6 YEARS	7	*Advanced Cortex*	Able to speak in complete sentences
3 YEARS	6	*Developed Cortex*	Able to speak in short sentences
18 MONTHS	5	*Early Cortex*	Able to say two words together
12 MONTHS	4	*Initial Cortex*	Able to say single words
6 MONTHS	3	*Midbrain*	Able to make sounds, culminating in communicative sounds
3 MONTHS	2	*Pons*	Able to respond by crying to vital threats
BIRTH	1	*Medulla and Cord*	Able to cry

Figure 9   Language

have to rely on two full sets of dentures, trying to talk when these are absent is also a struggle.

Thirdly, good proprioception is important to proper diction.

The brain must know at all times where everything is and what it is doing. If, for any reason, there is a lack of contact between the brain and the tongue, the lips, or any other part of our speech equipment, then instructions cannot be sent, and speech cannot take place.

A stroke patient who has lost the power of speech may no longer be aware of what his mouth and tongue are doing. His lack of feed-back makes verbal communication impossible.

The fourth factor which must be considered is physiological. Are the muscles sufficiently strong to carry out the work required of them?

However adequately the brain itself functions, and however accurate the messages which are sent to the many, many muscles involved in producing speech, nothing will happen if these muscles are too weak, and cannot obey the commands that have been given.

So far we have looked at the physical requirements for verbal communication. There are, however, two other important areas to be considered.

Does a child have the intellectual knowledge to talk? Does he possess an auditory vocabulary? Does he know any words, and does he know their meaning?

The first 'word' a child utters is usually 'Mum', or 'Mam', or 'Mom' and because his mother is listening avidly for these first non-babbling sounds, she always ascribes that sound to herself. Because of the instant feed-back of delight and encouragement which she produces, the child repeats the sound, and very quickly learns the 'name' for his mother. Providing the child can hear himself, and also hear external sounds, he can begin to mimic these, and to build up a vocabulary of noises which have a meaning clearly understood to his companions.

But what if he is deaf? Or what if there is no-one else with whom to explore this new world of sounds.

If no-one ever spoke to a child, then he would never develop speech, because he would have no means of learning sounds or their meaning. Equally, if he cannot hear either incoming sounds, or his own outgoing sounds, how can he try to mimic? The INTENSITY of the speech he hears has a very direct bearing on whether he will try to say the word himself. If a child only hears a word once, he will be unlikely to remember it and will probably not try to say it himself. The FREQUENCY of the input is therefore also of great importance, something that the mothers of young babies all know instinctively.

This then leads to the other important requirement for speech – the social opportunity for talking, and a need to do so.

Many years ago, a boy of eight (who eventually became a surgeon), was a great worry to his parents, as he had never uttered a word in his life. One day, when the whole family was sitting at the dinner table, a voice was heard to say, 'There's no salt!'

By a process of elimination, everyone rapidly concluded that the voice they had heard belonged to the boy in question, and his mother said, excitedly, 'Why have you never said anything before?'

The boy replied, 'There's always *been* salt!'

Speech and communication are a two-way activity. If everyone ignores you, and you are never encouraged to take part in a conversation, then why bother trying to talk.

If your every need is anticipated, why bother to ask?

We have a social responsibility to our children, especially if they are brain injured, not only to listen to what they are saying, but also to respond. We must be careful to create a need for communication, without causing unnecessary frustration.

If you ask a brain injured child, 'How are you?', you must wait for a reply, however long it takes. If you don't, then the message you are giving him is: you have no interest in his reply; or, whatever *he* wishes to say is of no importance to *you*.

Normal Speech Development

The first sound which a new-born baby makes is known as the 'birth-cry', and is in fact an uncontrolled, spontaneous response to the sudden intake of air, for the first time, into the lungs. No meaning or message can be linked to this sound, or to the sounds produced by a very young baby during the first few days and weeks of his life.

By the time a child reaches two to three months of age, he has gained some degree of control over his ability to cry, and will now produce a distinctly different cry, both in pitch and intensity, in response to pain, hunger or fright.

It is important, in both these first two stages, to realise that the word 'cry' relates to the *sound* made by a child, and the presence or absence of tears have no relevance to the issue.

The next level of ability, which occurs at around six months, is when the child begins to produce other sounds, first at random, and then gradually more meaningful and goal directed. He develops a sound for hunger, for thirst, for discomfort (as opposed to pain), and starts to experiment with a whole range of different noises, which we commonly refer to as 'babbling'.

By the end of his first year of life, the child should have developed the ability to link specific sounds to specific people or objects. He will have heard his parents, or brothers and sisters 'call' something by name, and in imitating these sounds begins to gradually build up a small vocabulary of single words.

This process continues until, by the age of eighteen months, he is able to put two words together to make couplets. The grammar at this stage may be faulty, but at least he is able to convey his message. 'Mummy gone,' leaves little doubt in the mind of the listener, as does 'My Teddy,' or 'Me hungry!'

As the vocabulary increases, so does the ability to put words together, initially into phrases, then into sentences. A three-year-old will speak in short, and sometimes breathless sentences, whilst a six-year-old will converse sensibly about anything within his scope.

Speech Development – Our Approach

Where a child has no ability to cry, either spontaneously or as an 'alarm', it is crucial to investigate in depth his ability to breathe. Where any weakness is found, the introduction of Respiratory Patterning (see Chapter 34) may be of considerable assistance. Other techniques which can improve breath control include sucking through a straw, blowing out a candle, learning to blow a musical instrument (e.g. a recorder), and blowing soap bubbles.

Where tactility and proprioception are felt to be inadequate, a whole range of stimuli can be of help. Application of very light touch to the trigeminal nerve, from the forehead, down each side of the face, across the upper lip, and below the lower lip, is a broad-spectrum approach. Applying warm and cold temperatures to the tongue and to the inside of the mouth; using an electric toothbrush; massaging the inside of the lips and the gums; all these and other stimuli can be used to increase tactile awareness.

Since function determines structure, if a child can be encouraged to 'exercise' the muscles of his face, mouth and tongue, these can be strengthened. Touching the tip of the nose or the chin with the tongue; licking honey off the tip of the nose; making faces whilst looking in a mirror; poking the tongue through a hole in a piece of paper; these activities can be made into amusing games, especially if other members of the family will join in.

Our Language Development Programme aims to provide the opportunity for a child to converse. Firstly, his mother chooses a brand-new nursery rhyme which he has never heard before. She says this to him over and over again for a week. Then, she leaves out the last word of the rhyme, and NEVER says it again, since this is *his* word. When she reaches this point in the rhyme, she shows by her expression, and by her tone, that she expects him to say his word. At first, the 'word' might only be an indistinct sound. This does not matter. As soon as he has uttered it, she makes a big fuss of him, and praises him for his effort.

Once he has contributed his first sound, she leaves out the last word of the second line, and the procedure is repeated. In the end, it is possible to reach a point where the rhyme consists of alternating words from the mother and noises from the child, and however limited this may be, it is in fact the child's first conversation. The above procedure can be repeated with any number of nursery rhymes, providing each is new to the child at the onset.

Children should be talked to!

It is so easy to fall into the trap of thinking that because a child cannot talk, he cannot understand. A lack of speech is not, in itself, an indication of a lack of intelligence. Never assume that because Johnny cannot say his own name, he doesn't *know* his own name, or that because he hasn't replied to you, he doesn't understand what you have said.

This is almost as bad an error as thinking that, to be able to read, Johnny must be able to read *aloud.* Since no-one sits down alone to read the Sunday paper aloud, why should there be a different set of rules for brain injured children?

Let a child listen to his own efforts. Tape record the sounds he makes, and play them back to him. Many children love to hear themselves on tape, and will chatter away to the tape recorder, albeit in their own language!

Many of the activities which promote language are described in detail in other Chapters, and must very often be employed in combination if the best results are to be achieved. Our Respiratory Patterning, Auditory, Tactile, and Intelligence programmes all have a part to play, and each can have a significant bearing on the effectiveness of the others, and on the final result.

Since January 1st, 1980, I have seen 400 children who, at their Initial Assessment, had no speech. Of these, 111 have since become able to talk, at least at the level of single words.

CHAPTER 31

The Motor Pathways
(MANUAL COMPETENCE)

If you touch together the ends of your thumb and first finger to make a circular sign, and then hold up this sign to someone else, they will immediately understand that 'everything is fine', or that you like something. Would it surprise you to know how few of our children can make such a sign?

Can you even begin to imagine what it would be like to have no hands?

Manual dexterity is one of the abilities which, at its higher levels, distinguishes man from all other creatures. Each civilisation in history is measured by its artefacts, and all of these creations required the use of hands.

At the time a baby is born, he already possesses some manual function. If an object is placed in his hand, its presence stimulates a reflex and his hand closes over the object. This reflexive response gives rise to the old North of England tradition of placing a silver coin in the hand of a new-born baby. 'If he can hold it, he can keep it!' It is also a simple test of the presence of the reflex, and perhaps our Northern ancestors had more reason than simply generosity in maintaining the tradition!

As his brain develops, a child begins to control his hand movements, and the grasp reflex matures and disappears.

Like many other early abilities, which are present to help avoid injury, the first level of control is limited to the releasing of objects in response to a painful stimulus, or 'vital release'. Gradually, grasping and releasing toys or other playthings becomes a more conscious act, but the whole hand is employed to pick up and let go. This 'prehensile' grasp is a gross movement, and individual fingers and thumbs are not used.

It is at this point that man begins to stand out from the other creatures, which preceded him. He learns to oppose his finger and thumb and to develop a 'pincer grip'. Initially, the thumb opposes the side of

TIME FRAME	PROFILE LEVEL	BRAIN LEVEL	MANUAL DEVELOPMENT
PEER LEVEL IF OVER SIX YEARS	8	*Superior Cortex*	Able to write at age level, using the appropriate dominant hand
6 YEARS	7	*Advanced Cortex*	Able to write single words
3 YEARS	6	*Developed Cortex*	Able to use both hands together purposefully
18 MONTHS	5	*Early Cortex*	Able to simultaneously oppose the index finger and thumb of both hands
12 MONTHS	4	*Initial Cortex*	Able to oppose the index finger and thumb of either hand
6 MONTHS	3	*Midbrain*	Able to grasp objects purposefully
3 MONTHS	2	*Pons*	Able to release in response to a vital stimulus
BIRTH	1	*Medulla and Cord*	Reflexive grasping with hands

Figure 10   Manual Development

the index finger, or another finger. But eventually, the tips of the thumb and first finger meet, and with enough strength to pick up an object.

At about the age that a baby ceases to be monocular, and begins to use both eyes together, he also starts to use both hands together. His skill in picking up small objects with finger and thumb improves to the point where he can do this, simultaneously, with both hands. Then, his bi-manual expertise develops into learning to hold something with one hand, whilst manipulating it with the other.

There is still one more goal to reach. He must learn to control an object sufficiently well to be able to make marks with it on a suitable surface. The marks may initially be lines or circles, but gradually, they take the form of standardised, recognisable letters. Now, at last he has begun to communicate by WRITING.

If a child has very poor hand function, it is not enough to advise parents to 'teach him how to dress himself and feed himself.' The ability to feel has a most important role to play in the development of hand function, and a poor grasp reflex, or inadequate vital release can often be directly related to poor tactility. Inadequate sensory information invariably leads to poor motor activity, and the techniques which we use to help mature both these functions are essentially tactile in nature. We rub the hands with a variety of different textures. Starting with hard, solid objects which are the most easy to feel and to respond to, we gradually introduce softer, more yielding surfaces which help to develop discrimination.

Once a child is able to grasp objects with the whole hand, it is time to encourage fine finger skills. He should be encouraged, for example, to lift small objects such as raisins out of little pots. As the shape of the pot prevents the use of the whole hand, he can in these circumstances use only finger and thumb.

Activities which develop bi-manual function are almost endless. Screwing and unscrewing the lids on jars; zipping and unzipping; pouring from one mug to another; buttoning and unbuttoning, beginning with large buttons and gradually reducing the size; threading big beads on a string, or a wooden mouse through wooden holes in a wooden cheese; all these activities and many others encourage the use of both hands together. Toys which also help to develop these skills are easily obtainable, and provide both opportunity and amusement.

Making a mark on something is a very basic human characteristic. Daubing on paper with fingers dipped in paint is fun. Once the idea is established, and once the ability to cortically oppose the first finger and thumb is fully developed, it is a steady progression from finger painting to scribbling with crayons, and then on to pencils or felt-tip pens.

There is only one correct way to hold a pen. The proper grasp is to hold the barrel about one inch from the tip with the first finger and thumb. The underside of the barrel should rest on the second finger, with the other fingers tucked away underneath. It would clearly be impossible to do this without the ability to cortically oppose the first finger and thumb, so it is no exaggeration to say that picking raisins out of little pots is a preliminary requirement for good handwriting.

No matter how much the brain knows about hand function, it is not possible for a child to use his hands if his muscles are too weak or too tight. His physiological needs cannot be ignored, and hand and wrist manipulation, together with activities designed to improve both muscle tone and muscle power, must be regularly employed. Stiffness can also be reduced by encouraging manual activities in warm water.

One of the basic principles of our programme is to give children 'a helping hand'. The most helpful hands of all, of course, are a child's own, and a full range of manual skills is a vital component of total independence.

Since January 1st, 1980, we have seen 373 children who, at their Initial Assessment, could not write. Of these, 85 have since become able to write, at least at the level of single words. Five children have gained this skill ahead of the majority of their chronological peers.

PART FOUR

Intelligence and Dominance

CHAPTER 32
Intelligence

We see all sorts of children. We also see all sorts of problems. Some of these are obvious, like paralysis, or blindness, but other, major difficulties are only detectable when children are required to read, write or calculate.

The world does not always understand disability. As we have already seen, when someone is obviously physically or mentally handicapped, people often make assumptions which are not in fact true – the 'Does he take sugar?' syndrome. If, on the other hand, a child appears to be normal, any poor intellectual or social performance attracts little sympathy. He is thought of as being stupid or naughty, and once regarded in this light, is often given less opportunity to develop.

Either way, the child cannot win. The physical fact of brain injury is instantly related in other people's minds to a lack of mental capability, and once that assumption has been made, it governs everyone's subsequent behaviour.

In fact, there is no correlation between brain injury and intelligence. Many highly intelligent human beings have also been brain injured, and history records the exploits of such famous men as Alexander the Great, Julius Caesar and Napoleon, all of whom suffered from epilepsy – a symptom of brain injury.

There are many definitions of 'intelligence'. The one which is perhaps the closest to our philosophy is 'how much information we store in our brains, and how well we make use of it'.

We believe that every one of our children has potential intelligence. It may be latent but, given a sufficient amount of stimulation coupled with regular opportunity to use the information supplied, it is often possible to 'unlock the system', and to increase the level of functional intelligence.

In the Chapter on VISION, I discussed the use of flash cards in the development of reading skills. We have found that the same principles can be used in the amplification of 'intelligence'. As well as exposing a child to cards on which have been printed words, we show him 'pictures' – but not ordinary pictures.

These pictures have four special characteristics; they have to be

EXACT
            DISTINCT
                        SPECIFIC
                                    and *PREVIOUSLY UNSEEN.*

For a child to learn, he needs clear information. It should be accurate, and any possibility of confusion should be eliminated. The data should be precise, and there should be no chance of ambiguity. Therefore, a picture of a bucket should be of a BUCKET, and not of a bucket, spade, sea-shore, sand castle and children playing.

It is all too easy to underestimate children, and even easier to assume that a brain injured child can only take in a limited amount of information. Yet he is just as capable of learning as is his well counterpart, if the data is properly presented.

It is not enough to show a child a picture of a pig, and tell him it is a pig. He is quite able to learn to recognise a 'large white' or a 'saddleback', just as he can learn to distinguish between a corgi and a collie.

Children see things the way they are, and what they learn is what we teach them. If we teach them that a picture of a statue is 'a statue', then that is all they will know.

If we teach them that the picture is of a statue called 'David', sculpted by Michelangelo, they will have learned a great deal more about the same basic information.

We therefore encourage parents to prepare special sets of pictures, which they show to their children at recommended frequencies each day. These pictures are made to our specification and are called Cortical Visual Stimuli cards, or C.V.S. cards for short.

Having difficulty with mathematics is not restricted to brain injured children. Many of us experienced this problem at school, and it can still be a difficulty in the supermarket, or the factory.

We were taught symbols, i.e. 1,2,3,4, which represent different quantities of things, and these symbols are the shorthand for the reality. It is more convenient to talk about 20 apples than to have to produce the real thing.

However, when we have to manipulate numbers, we carry out a rather long-winded process in order to reach a correct conclusion.

To multiply 34 by 5, we first think of 34, then write, in our mind's eye, the figure 5 underneath. We then draw a line. Multiplying 4 by 5, we write down a 0, and carry 2. Then we multiply 3 by 5, add the 2, and arrive at the conclusion – 170.

. . . and we have to do all that in our heads!

Suppose we could visualise 34 as 34 things. If we simply increased our mental image fivefold, we would be able to see immediately 170 things, and would know the answer just as quickly. Unfortunately, because we have been taught the shorthand (1,2,3 & 4), we cannot think in longhand, and either have to go through the lengthy process described above, or one just as lengthy, in which we multiply 30 by 5, then 4 by 5, and then add together the two results – three calculations instead of one!

No wonder the present generation is becoming so reliant on pocket calculators!

We have found that, in just the same way that a brain injured child can recognise pictures of words, or pictures of objects, he can also recognise pictures of quantity. We therefore make up a set of 100 cards, each of which shows a different number of red dots. (On the back is written in shorthand what the number of the dots is, as we adults are not clever enough to recognise the reality!)

The child is shown groups of these cards frequently, and is told how many dots they each contain, until he can identify one card from another, or from any other in the set. This process then leads on to problem solving, using dot cards.

This method of teaching mathematics, coupled with C.V.S. cards, and reading cards, gives a brain injured child an easy route to instant calculation, and to a large quantity of data. Later, with the introduction of projects, his acquired information can be put to use, reinforcing the thinking process, and converting raw information into useful tools to solve problems.

Improved intellectual ability has obvious advantages for our children. When one of them can use his knowledge of birds, road signs, trees or cars effectively, he has a skill which not only helps him to cope with the real world, but also to compete with and, sometimes, even to outstrip his well peers.

The Learning Capability of Brain Injured Children

By no stretch of the imagination could anyone consider it to be an advantage to be brain injured. However, if a child is brain injured, then he deserves every possible advantage, and there is one which is highly significant when it comes to learning.

If we were to draw a graph of the learning curve of a typical well child, from birth onwards, we would see that in the first three years it is very steep, and then gradually begins to flatten out. By the time the child is six, he has learned almost all of the neurological lessons necessary for him to survive in our world.

Anyone who has observed a typical two-year-old will be able to verify the fact that he is constantly trying to learn – albeit in an apparently chaotic fashion – everything he can, and all the time. Don't we call this age group the 'hyperactive' ones? Yet all the time they are *learning*, at a rate which leaves older people standing.

If eight-year-old brain injured children only had the capacity to learn of typical eight-year-olds, with their relatively flat learning curve, I doubt if we would *ever* succeed in improving their abilities enough to enable them to catch up with their well peers – which, after all must be our objective for all our children.

Happily, this is not the case, and every brain injured child actually has the capability of learning at the rate of the child he most closely resembles in terms of function – provided always that we know enough to be able to adequately stimulate him. So, if a child is six years old, but has the functional ability of a two-year-old, his learning capability is that of the two-year-old, not the six year old.

Very often, the biggest danger in teaching our children about their world is to assume they are not taking in the information, when in fact they are. This is the road to boredom, and should be avoided at all costs.

The I.Q. Test

Although the I.Q. test is no longer accorded the same level of importance as it once was, many of our children have undergone such a test before they come to us. It is not unusual for a child to be said to have an I.Q. of 70 or less, and often one wonders how such a test could have been given, with any hope of accuracy, in view of the other, more obvious problems which the child may have.

Several years ago, it was decided by the powers-that-be that one of our children should be given an I.Q. test. Ian, who was eight at the time, was a severely involved, midbrain injured child, who, whilst being unable to control his arms and legs, was nevertheless as bright as a button.

The psychologist came to Ian's home to test him, and his first instruction was, 'Ian, open the door!'

Ian had no way of manoeuvring himself across the floor on which he was lying, since he could not creep on his tummy. Nor could he stand up to reach the door handle. So, of course, the door stayed shut.

He was marked down by the psychologist for NOT UNDERSTANDING THE INSTRUCTION!

The I.Q. score is as much a label, and a stigma, as any of the others which I outlined at the beginning of Part 2, and had I not raised a protest on Ian's behalf, his ability to understand simple commands would have been denied, as a result of this episode.

The measurement of I.Qs as they relate to our children is in many ways a nonsense. At least, it is in the case of those authorities who still rely heavily on the results of such testing, since they expect that the I.Q., once measured, will not change by more than 10 points either way during the rest of the child's life.

In our present educational system, normal children are no longer faced with I.Q. tests. The eleven-plus exam is discontinued, and it is now the norm that a child will enter primary school at five, and complete his secondary education at sixteen, without being required at any stage to take such a test. UNLESS HE IS BRAIN INJURED.

For a brain injured child, the rules are often different, and designed in such a way that he has to virtually PROVE that he is worthy of being allowed to mix with normal children before he is allowed to do so!

Our programme, by its very nature, must be, and is capable of radically improving an I.Q. score.

So there is a way round the system!

CHAPTER 33
Dominance

The brain of a human being consists of two separate halves, or hemispheres. There is also a cross-over network which links each hemisphere to the opposite side of the person. Therefore, the right hemisphere of the brain runs the left side of a human being, and the left hemisphere, the right side.

The majority of people tend to prefer to use their right side, whenever there is a need to choose. They sight a camera with the right eye, write with the right hand, listen with the right ear, or kick a ball with the right foot. However, a not insignificant number of people are precisely the opposite – *they* always choose the left, and generally speaking have found the world unsympathetic to their needs. Left handed scissors or potato peelers are often difficult to locate, and as the majority of people are, and always have been, right sided, the 'lefties' have been regarded as being somehow odd or strange. The Latin word for 'left' is SINISTRA. From this derived our English word SINISTER – an obvious example.

We do not mind which side people prefer, so long as they are all 'right' or all 'left'. In either case, one hemisphere is dominant, and the other then looks after sub-dominant activities and interests, like music, rhythm, and artistic abilities. We are, however, very concerned when there is evidence of 'mixed dominance'.

Of course, a great many people are ambidextrous, or prefer the right eye, but the left hand; the right ear but the left foot. If they have no problems in learning, or in functioning, then this mixed dominance does not matter. However, when a child has reading and learning difficulties, and is found to have a mixture in dominance, then something has to be done.

Let us take as an example a child who is right handed, but who prefers to use his left eye. Whenever he attempts to write something, one half of his brain is controlling his vision, whilst the other is looking after his hand movements. The discord thus created is counter-productive, and he finds it very hard to write legibly or sensibly.

Some years ago, we saw a nine-year-old boy who had major learning and reading problems. On testing his dominance, we found that he was right handed, right eared, right footed, but left eyed. We designed a programme for him which included a number of activities aimed at encouraging him to use his right eye, and one technique involved was to put a patch over his left eye for periods of time each day.

The family went home with the intention of carrying out our programme with their son, on a repetitive basis, for several hours each day. The next day, however, whilst they were getting ready to begin, fate intervened.

Their son was playing out of doors, and happened to be on the edge of a quarry where, unknown to him, blasting was taking place. A small piece of stone flew up, and struck him in the left eye, causing serious damage. He was taken to hospital, and following an operation on the left eye, it was bandaged up for several months.

When the bandages were finally removed, it was found that his sight in that eye had been saved. However, and very importantly from our point of view, in the six months that his left eye had been totally closed off, or occluded, his reading age had increased by eighteen months. What we had to a limited degree recommended as a part of our programme – occlusion – had been wholly necessary as part of the healing process, and he had had no choice but to use his sole remaining eye – the right one – in order to see. In practice, he had become totally right sided, and the previous confusion in his brain created by the mixed dominance had been eliminated.

Whenever we see a child who has reading or learning problems, or whose fine motor skills are below par for his age, we automatically test him for hemispheric dominance. We note which eye he uses to look through a telescope; to sight a camera; to look at an object through a small hole in a sheet of paper. We ask him to point to a small torch held by the tester, so as to tell which eye he lines up with which hand. He is given a telebinocular test, to tell us a great deal more about his visual ability, and to establish what degree of sight he has in either eye, and when using both eyes together. He is also presented simultaneously with two texts, which differ in eight respects. His choices are recorded, to provide further evidence of his 'right' or 'left' visual preferences.

He is invited to pick up and listen to a sea-shell, to listen at a key-hole(!), and to listen to a single earphone.

He is asked to pick up a pen and to write his name, or to draw a picture; to pick up and to throw a ball; to take an object out of a bag.

He is asked to kick a ball; to hop from one side of the room to the other; to climb the stairs; to step up on to a box, and to step down again.

In each of these tests, no instruction is given to the child as to which eye, ear, hand or foot he should use, and careful note is made of the choice he makes. If a child lacks the physical or intellectual skill to perform the tests, then his problems are sufficiently severe to take precedence over any dominance problems he might have, and we concentrate instead on overcoming these.

Once the child's dominance has been established, we then recommend to the family a number of different activities, which they can carry out each day with their son or daughter in their own home. If, as is usually the case, only one of the four functions is out of line, then it is relatively easy to decide that a child should be right sided or left sided. Encouragement is therefore given to promote the use of the correct eye, ear, hand or foot. If, on the other hand, a child is totally 'mixed', then we have to make a decision as to whether to create 'right' or 'left' dominance.

In the old days, children who were naturally left-handed were strongly discouraged by teachers in school from writing with their left hand, and were made to write with the right hand. Doubtless many learning problems resulted. Nowadays, we know that there is no such thing as 'correct' dominance, only consistent dominance, and when this has been achieved, many of the academic problems faced by so-called slow learners often disappear.

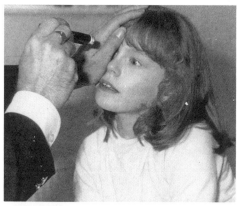

17 'Basic Vision'. (Photo by Jennie Painter).

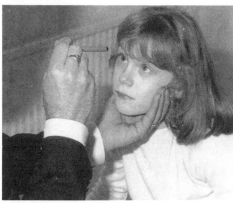

18 Encouraging visual convergence. (Photo by Jennie Painter).

19 'Cortical Opposition' – The Pincer Grip. (Photo by Jennie Painter).

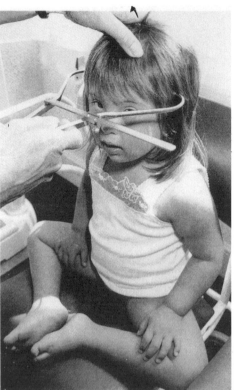

20 Left. Measuring lateral head growth with a pair of calipers. (Photo by Jennie Painter).

21 Below. '. . . with a little help from my friends!' (Courtesy of *Daily Mirror*).

22 Opposite. Sarah, Duchess of York meeting one of our children after opening our new pool – November 14th, 1989. (Photo by Jennie Painter).

23 Opposite left. 'Ladders all round the house . . .'

24 Opposite right. . . . No longer needed!

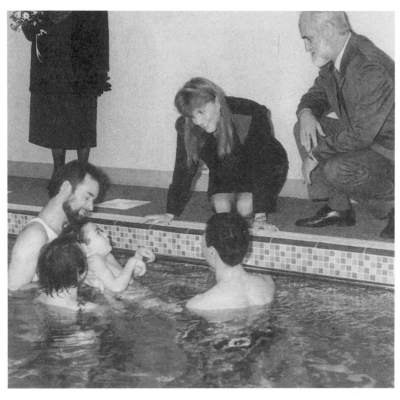

25 The Alison Centre's first patient – Brigid Nunan with the team.

26 Our first initial assessment & teaching week at the Alison Centre. April 1997.

PART FIVE

More About How

CHAPTER 34

The Brain's Own Environment

All the procedures which I have so far described have included techniques which either stimulate the brain or give opportunity for better function. In every case, use has been made of one or more of the five pathways into the brain: vision, hearing, feeling, tasting or smelling.

There is, however, another approach to the improvement of brain function. If we can enhance the physical environment of the brain itself, then we can often encourage better neurological organisation, and in the process correct various behavioural problems.

Masking

Of all the factors crucial to human life, breathing is one of the most vital. We can go without food for days, without water for hours, but if our supply of oxygen is interrupted for more than a few minutes, death becomes inevitable.

If we were to look at the case histories of all our children, and were to ask the question: 'Why did the brain cells die?', in the vast majority of cases, the answer would be: 'Because of a lack of oxygen.' Although the brain in an adult male represents only 2% of his total body weight, it uses more than 30% of the total oxygen available. The brain of a five-year-old child requires even more – about 50%. Thus, oxygen availability is a most important item for any human being.

Some of our children breathe very poorly. They take in less oxygen than a well child, their breathing varies in both depth and rhythm, and they are prone to colds and respiratory infections. Because of posture problems and lack of function, their chests are small and underdeveloped, and it is often a major effort for them to breathe at all.

In many of our children, their lack of function is the result of an obvious difficulty in obtaining enough oxygen.

We know that function determines structure, and that were it possible for the children to breathe more deeply, and more often, the dimensions of their chests would increase, thus producing a bigger reservoir of available oxygen.

Many people can remember times, during their schooldays, when the teacher ordered their class to carry out deep breathing exercises. This activity was not done just to use up excess energy. The physical action of raising the arms above the head allows the diaphragm to expand, and the lungs can then receive a greater than normal volume of oxygen. This extra supply stimulates the brain, and 'wakes you up'.

In the current *Highway Code* there is a recommendation that drowsy drivers should stop, get out of the car and breathe deeply, to restore alertness. Signs on Motorways warn that 'tiredness can kill' and advise motorists to 'take a break'.

Deep breathing exercises, if carried out regularly, are known to increase the breathing capacity, as well as improving individual alertness and efficiency.

Unfortunately, many of our children are precluded by their physical condition from carrying out such exercises, or their level of understanding is too low to follow instructions. So we have to find another way.

The brain has incorporated in it a safety mechanism called the carotid bodies. These nerve cells act as monitors, and their role is to keep a constant check on blood acidity and alkalinity, and the amounts of oxygen and carbon dioxide present in the blood. There is a direct relationship between the oxygen and CO_2 levels; when one is high the other is low, and vice versa. This is how we are able to regulate our breathing, in response to the amount of oxygen needed at any given time.

An increase in the amount of CO_2 present in the bloodstream triggers off a requirement for more oxygen, and the brain's response is to require an increase in breathing rate.

How, in practice, can a safe, temporary increase in the CO_2 level be arranged, regularly, in our brain injured children?

Each of us breathes out CO_2, which normally dissipates into the atmosphere. By encouraging a child to wear, for a strictly controlled period of time, a specially designed mask which prevents this dissipation, yet allows the breathing of some oxygen at all times, we are able to provide a source of CO_2 for the child to re-breathe.

Blood circulation within the brain is separately controlled from that of the rest of the body. Therefore, drugs which have a positive effect on the body's circulation do not improve the movement of blood within the brain. Some years ago, it was discovered that CO_2 was an excellent promoter of brain/blood circulation. In fact, it is probably the most powerful of all blood vessel dilators. Within 30 seconds of the introduction of extra CO_2 into the system, there is a marked increase in blood circulation, and thus improved oxygen availability.

Put in its most simple terms, masking has both a long term, and a short-term effect. In the long term, it helps to produce a bigger 'tank' of available oxygen. In the short term, it helps to increase the size of the 'plumbing'!

Naturally, as with every technique we use with our children, there are strict rules for masking. Before any child is masked, he has a very thorough medical examination, and if our doctor finds any contra-indications, the technique is not used.

We teach parents how to mask properly, and procedures for keeping the mask clean and hygienic. We also give them the following set of rules:

1. They should mask their child for a very precise period of time, which should never be exceeded.
2. A sufficient period of time should always be allowed between maskings to allow the whole system time to settle down again.
3. Masking is not normally a job for volunteers, and is the responsibility of the parents themselves.
4. No child should EVER be left alone when wearing a mask.
5. Masks should always be kept safely out of the reach of ALL children.
6. Masking should not be carried out if a child has a heavy cold, or is otherwise congested.
7. If a child ever shows signs of acute distress, the mask should be removed immediately.
8. If the mask should at any time split, it should be cut up into small pieces and disposed of. No attempt should be made to extend its life by sealing the sides with sticky tape, a most unhygienic practice.
9. Immediately after use, the mask should be cleaned, using a mild disinfectant, and dried out thoroughly.

In the last twenty-five years, I have been responsible for carrying out masking procedures with over 1,000 children, and the technique must have been used by our parents several million times. I have never had one instance where a child was hurt by this procedure.

On the contrary, regular use of the mask by many, many children has provided us with very clear evidence of increased chest development, improved breathing capacity, and better long-term oxygenation of the whole system.

Respiratory Patterning

Although Masking can temporarily alter a child's breathing rate, and can in the longer term, encourage deeper breathing, it cannot reinforce the *rhythm* of breathing, and it is the latter which we must also improve if some children are to have the chance of functioning more normally.

The rhythm and regularity of breathing are controlled by the brain, and change in relation to our need for more or less oxygen. Therefore, when sleeping, we require less oxygen and breathe slowly, whereas in the daytime we breathe faster, especially when we are exercising.

Twenty-three years ago, I.A.H.P. in Philadelphia first became aware of the inadequate breathing rhythms present in many brain injured children. Their inhalation and exhalation was so poor, and the consequent lack of oxygen was so chronic, that they did not move or speak. All they could do was to breathe – badly. Given the 'choice' of breathing or functioning, they invariably 'chose' breathing, and the tremendous efforts which some of them made simply to obtain enough oxygen to survive, raised the question whether anything could be done to make it easier for them to breathe. A number of existing techniques were tried, including the use of artificial respiration, but in every case, the methods used could not be sustained over a long enough period of time to be of any lasting benefit, as they tended to exhaust the therapist.

Some children breathed so shallowly and irregularly that it was impossible to obtain an accurate measurement of their breathing rates. Others were 'breath-holders', who could literally hold their breath for over a minute at a time – thus totally defeating the object of the exercise! Still others hyperventilated, producing an unbelievable result when measurements were attempted.

We knew that it was possible to override the chaos of poor mobility through physical 'patterning'. The new question became: 'Can we eliminate the chaos of poor breathing rhythms by 'patterning in' more appropriate information?'

The answer to this question, which took several years to find, became known as 'Respiratory Patterning'.

The first method used involved an air pump, sufficiently sophisticated to allow air to be sucked out of an enclosed space for a measured period of time, and then to be shut down for another measured period of time. This cycle had to be repeated regularly.

A child was placed inside a plastic cape, with only his head and hands left uncovered. A metal frame was placed over the upper abdomen, to prevent any undue pressure being placed on the chest. When the pump was switched on, air was evacuated from the cape, creating a partial vacuum, and the child's chest expanded to meet this vacuum. Thus the child breathed in whenever the pump became activated, and breathed out whenever the pump stopped. Because the effect of the pump was to use negative pressure to encourage inhalation, this technique became known as Negative Pressure Respiratory Patterning.

With several children whose breathing rhythms were particularly poor, we used this method for a number of months. They were given respiratory reinforcement for periods of six hours each day, five days at a time, and the technique was repeated every four or five weeks. The results were interesting. Some children improved their breath control to the point where they began to function better. We saw improvements in mobility, vision, and manual dexterity. We also recorded positive changes in digestion, appetite, circulation, constipation, sleep patterns and awareness.

However, with some children, negative pressure did not appear to produce any beneficial response. Their problems appeared to be more involved with *breathing out*, rather than breathing in. As they could not rid their lungs of carbon dioxide, they were unable to obtain sufficient oxygen for their needs, and because of poor breath control many of them could not speak.

A double-walled plastic waistcoat was therefore designed, which could be coupled up to the same air pump. The action of the pump was reversed and, instead of sucking air, it now blew air under pressure into the waistcoat. When worn by a child, the waistcoat tightened up sufficiently to encourage him to breathe out, without putting undue pressure on the rib cage. When the pump stopped, the pressure eased, and the child was able to breathe in without difficulty.

This Positive Pressure Respiratory Patterning was then used with children who had not responded to Negative Pressure, and we were pleased to find that several of them showed improvement, especially in speech.

For those of us who have no difficulty in breathing in and out, it is hard to imagine how it must feel to have a constant problem – in fact a survival problem of the most basic type. Breathing is one of the most vital functions of our body. The prevention of breathing can lead to a very swift death: in under 4 minutes without oxygen, brain cells begin to die and rapid, permanent deterioration of function quickly follows. Nevertheless, it is possible to temporarily simulate the problems of many of our brain injured children, and some years ago, we demonstrated this to a group of parents.

We lined up five volunteer fathers, whose physical condition had first been medically checked. The first one was given a sip of soup off a spoon. The second was asked to sing 'Happy Birthday to You'. The third had to walk a straight line. The fourth read aloud a passage from a book. The last had to sign his name, as if on a cheque.

Each volunteer was then asked to run up and down a very steep hill, and to repeat this activity until he was respiratorily exhausted.

Before each had had the chance to get his breath back, the same tests were repeated. The first was given a second spoonful of soup, which he promptly spat out, as he preferred to breathe! The second got as far as 'Happy..', then stopped, because he couldn't breathe. The third could not walk along the line, and staggered all over the place. The fourth read only the first three words, then stopped and threw down the book – he, too, preferred breathing. The last valiantly signed his name, but the signature looked nothing like his previous effort, and would never have passed the bank!

Happily, within a few minutes, each of the subjects fully recovered, and was then able to function quite normally. Yet, for as long as they were 'out of breath', their abilities were markedly below par.

Once Respiratory Patterning became a regular feature of our stimulation programme for 'poor breathers', regular weeks of in-patient breathing reinforcement began to be scheduled. However, although children often showed signs of improvement during their five days with us, the effects tended to wear off once they returned home and were able to slip back into the chaos of their own, uncontrolled breathing.

There was only one practical solution to this problem. A way had to be found to provide the children with continual reinforcement, at home.

There were two possibilities: either each family concerned would have to invest in an air pump, imported from the USA at considerable cost, and we would have to accept all the risks associated with the equipment when used away from our own rigorous supervision; or a new technique would have to be designed which parents could use themselves: one which carried no risks, and which could produce results just as good as those of the air pumps.

This technique became known as Manual Respiratory Patterning, and involved the use of a jacket, custom-made to fit each child, which could be tightened or slackened around the chest by two people placed on each side of the child. To ensure an appropriate rhythm, a metronome was set to the target breathing-rate of the patient.

When we first began to use these methods of improving breathing rates, it was essential to know some basic data. For instance, how many breaths per minute does a normal three-year, or four-month-old boy or girl take? Without these norms, it was impossible to set the air pumps correctly for each individual, so we made enquiries. It was hard to believe, but no-one appeared to know the answer. In the end, we purchased some expensive measuring equipment and set off to various local schools to discover the breathing rates across a full range of normal boys and girls. We then came across another problem – as soon as you ask someone to breathe normally, they don't! We had to ask the children to concentrate on something else, like drawing or reading to themselves, before we were able to record normal rates.

Now, after twenty-three years of investigation, we are in a position to provide substantial help for children whose breathing rhythms are so chaotic as to prevent or delay normal function. We can measure their abnormal inhalation and exhalation rates; we can initially use respirator pumps to override these abnormalities; we can teach their parents how to reinforce more normal rhythms at home; and we can regularly monitor and change the information which is being fed to each child so as to reach, in the end, the best of goals: good, regular breathing.

Nutrition

When we first see many of our children, they are still struggling for survival, and are weak because they lack nourishment. Although eating is their life-line, the very act of eating can tire them, so they do not eat enough. Their ability to absorb the nutritional components of the food which they eat is often poor, so despite an apparently adequate diet they do not put on weight, and remain lacking in energy.

In other children, hyperactivity is a major problem. They are constantly on the go, exhibit temper tantrums, and are completely unable to concentrate.

Profuse dribbling, general lethargy, continuous chestiness and an overproduction of nasal mucous are other symptoms which we believe are often directly associated with diet, and all these may be correctable.

The second half of the twentieth century has seen the widespread introduction of 'fast foods', convenience meals, and foodstuffs which contain artificial colourings, artificial flavourings, and other chemical additives. Many of these are recognised as being responsible for behaviour problems in children, and are capable of producing intolerances in both young and old.

Whilst it is easy to lay the blame for so many problems on the use of such chemicals, some of the difficulties which occur are triggered off by foods which we normally consider to be perfectly safe.

Cow's milk, for centuries in daily use by millions of people, is not necessarily the best drink to give a brain injured child. Many of our children have an intolerance to cow's milk, and respond far better to goat's milk, sheep's milk, or soya milk.

Sugar, whether refined or not, can play havoc with teeth. This is true for well children. It is even more true for our children, since their tongues are often less mobile, and the normal scouring effect of the tongue on the teeth is therefore reduced.

Sodium salicylate occurs naturally in many foods, and in particular in citrus fruits. Unfortunately, many hyperactive children have been found to have an intolerance to salicylates.

Sometimes, something as innocent-looking as a tiny piece of chocolate can turn a normally reasonable, although brain injured child, into an uncontrollable, gibbering idiot. His hands may flap wildly and aimlessly; he may chew his tee-shirt; he may pull out handfuls of his hair; he may produce meaningless non-stop movements which can continue for hours; he may kick out, and even dribble profusely.

The British Government recommendations, as they apply to daily vitamin and mineral requirements in both children and adults, do not take into account the very poor metabolism apparent in brain injured children. In fact, in the case of Vitamin C, the recommended daily allowance is 25 mgs, enough to prevent scurvy, but not enough to give our youngsters any form of real protection against even the common cold!

In some areas of Britain, water is still supplied to households through lead pipes. Although the lead content of the water may be very small, it can be enough to upset the very delicate balance within our children. Cooking with aluminium pots and pans can again produce mineral traces in food capable of creating adverse effects.

In the last twenty-five years, I have consistently advised parents to avoid 'junk' foods, and to put their children on a wholefood diet. In addition, I have recommended vitamin and mineral supplements in sufficient quantities to help overcome poor metabolism and low absorbtion rate. Nutrition is an important part of our programme, and, as every child is different, nutritional requirements are carefully monitored whenever at each visit.

Children receiving additional vitamins A, B Complex, C, D & E, together with folic acid, B6 and other specific B vitamins, have been found to be healthier, less prone to respiratory infections, and are usually the last ones in their families to catch a cold! Whether this is because they are on a good diet, or whether the vitamin supplementation, in combination with the increased daily stimulation they receive from our programme, is solely responsible for their improved health, I do not know.

Nevertheless, there is overwhelming evidence that the children whose parents follow our nutritional recommendations do develop more energy, begin to put on weight, cease being constipated, and function better.

In attempting to reduce hyperactivity, we think it important to attempt to identify any particular foodstuff which may be responsible. Lists of salicylate-free foods are provided, and families are urged to avoid any fresh or tinned produce which contain artificial flavourings, colourings, or additives.

Sweets and chocolate, the natural stand-by of every granny, are strictly prohibited.

Where a child does not gain weight, or has an irregular bowel function, we need to look for the cause. It may be the lack of a particular foodstuff essential for that child's needs; it may be an intolerance to gluten, a constituent of wheat, rye, barley and oats, in which case a gluten-free diet may eliminate the problems. Sometimes, the withdrawal of wheat alone may be all that is necessary.

Since similar symptoms can be seen in children when they are bored with the foods they are given, and as a lack of physical exercise can also be a factor, it is very important to check all the possibilities before deliberately eliminating foods.

Good nutrition, perhaps because it involves an often radical change in the types of foods which are eaten and the way many foods are cooked, is an acquired habit. Most parents think that they feed their children well, and don't always take easily to the notion that fish and chips, cornflakes, milk, and toffees – on which they may have been brought up – may be part of the cause of their children's problems. Yet too many good results have been obtained from improving the diets of our brain injured children for this aspect of our programme to be taken lightly.

CHAPTER 35

Fits

Historically, the subject of fits has been open to a number of different interpretations, ever since the days of Neanderthal man. Even the language used to describe a fit ranges from the colourful to the totally professional. 'Turns', 'episodes', 'little do's', 'spasms', 'attacks', 'convulsions', 'epileptiform seizures' – all these words mask a deep fear, present since the dawn of mankind, of a life threatening occurrence.

Until very recently, it was a fear of the unknown. Various theories were offered to concerned relatives by those in authority, and most of these explanations had a religious bias. Ten thousand years ago, fits were thought to be visitations of the devil; if the skull was opened up, the evil spirits could be released. The condition of skulls dating back to that time, which contain small burr-holes, or square openings known as fenestrations, indicates that the patients survived this crude surgery, which would have had the effect of relieving cerebral spinal fluid pressure. This is a classic example of doing all the right things for all the wrong reasons!

In the time of Hippocrates, those who suffered from fits were thought to be communing with the Gods on Olympus. Again, surgery was often employed. Hippocrates wrote that the brains of those suffering from fits appeared excessively moist – and the patients often survived!

In the Middle Ages, many hundreds of people were burned at the stake for witchcraft. Sometimes, the only available evidence presented to tribunals was that the accused suffered from fits.

In the nineteenth century, it occurred to unscrupulous people that sufferers from fits were a ready source of income. They were herded together in centres such as Bethlehem Hospital in London (a name later shortened to Bedlam), and the general public was invited to pay sixpence for the pleasure of laughing at the antics of these unfortunates.

The twentieth century brought a more enlightened approach, and advances in scientific knowledge led to the development of medications useful in the prevention of fits. On the principle that fits caused brain damage, they had to be avoided at all costs, and drugs were introduced to control seizure activity. As more and more anti-convulsant medications became available, the use of one single drug was superseded by a broader approach, where several drugs were prescribed in combination.

There are many different types of fits. Some are so mild that the only evidence is a flickering of the eyes, or a nod of the head. These 'petit mal' attacks may occur occasionally, or may appear as one of a series. A more severe form, called a 'grand mal', can involve the jerking of limbs, the upward turning of the eyes, foaming at the mouth, involuntary screams, unconsciousness, and other distressing symptoms. One specific type of seizure involves the nodding of the head and inward movement of the arms, suggestive of an eastern greeting – hence the title 'salaam spasm'. The most serious condition of all is 'status epilepticus'. When this occurs, a patient is in a constant state of fitting, and a tremendous strain is placed on the heart. It is almost always necessary to administer medication in order to interrupt the sequence and bring the child round.

What causes a fit? There are many different theories, and it is not surprising that we have one of our own.

Whatever the type of attack, there is one physiological factor which they all have in common. In every case, during the fit, the heart-rate speeds up considerably, and very often, the patient appears to be lacking oxygen.

We can find no evidence that fits cause brain damage. There is, however, considerable evidence to suggest that fits are a symptom of existing brain injury.

This symptom appears to us to relate very closely to the amounts of oxygen and CO_2 available at any time.

Let us suppose that a child has suffered brain injury at some stage, either before, during or since birth. The injury, being widespread in nature, has not only affected more noticeable functions like mobility and speech, but also less obvious mechanisms in the brain, including those which control breathing. In these circumstances, a child may simply 'forget' to breathe in, and run short of oxygen, or breathe out too often, leading to a shortage of CO_2. Either way, the brain is faced with a problem.

Shortage of Oxygen

In the first case, if nothing is done, further brain injury may result from the lack of oxygen. An attempt is therefore made by the brain to obtain more oxygen, and 'messages' are accordingly sent out.

These 'messages', resulting in the many different symptoms of fits, appear to be uncontrolled and random. However, one message which always gets through is the one requiring the heart to beat faster, pumping more oxygenated blood round the system.

I have seen hundreds of brain injured children who suffered from fits. Once the fit has commenced, I have noted this increased demand for oxygen, and the increase in heart rate. I have also noted that if such a child is assisted in his attempt to gain more oxygen, the fit can very often be controlled. Artificial respiration has been employed with many patients at the time a fit is occurring, with significantly good results. It would appear that as soon as the need for oxygen has been met, the fit subsides.

Shortage of Carbon Dioxide

Some children have a tendency to hyperventilate, which is to say they pant for no particular reason. This excessive exhalation, and the reduction in CO_2 in the bloodstream which occurs as a result, can also cause fits.

OUR ANTI-CONVULSANT STRATEGY

Although it is important in the short term to control a fit, the long-term elimination of the *need* for fits is even more essential. There are five factors which we believe to be crucial in eliminating seizure activity.

Improved Depth of Breathing

For those children whose supply of oxygen is insufficiently regulated, the use of the breathing mask encourages, over a period of time, a greater vital capacity, and a larger reservoir of oxygen for the brain. The short term effect, of temporarily enlarging the blood vessels leading to the brain, helps to provide oxygen in larger quantities immediately following the removal of the mask.

Improved Rhythm of Breathing

The objective of Respiratory Patterning is to instil in the patient's brain a better rhythm of breathing, improving the control and regularity of both inhalation and exhalation.

Replacement of CO_2

The use of the mask, and its ability to provide a ready source of CO_2, can rapidly help to eliminate any temporary shortage caused by hyperventilation. It can not only circumvent the onset of some types of fit, but can sometimes bring immediate relief when a child is actually experiencing a fit.

Diet

The elimination of stress factors, including 'junk' foods, artificial flavourings and colourings, and unnecessary chemical additives has proved very helpful in reducing seizure activity. Vitamin supplementation, and in particular the use of Vitamin E in improving the absorption of oxygen throughout the system, assists in providing an improved internal environment in which the brain can function.

Improved Neurological Function

The whole of our programme aims to create a better level of organisation and control within the brain and central nervous system. Once the brain's ability to function begins to improve, and better control of the breathing mechanisms develops, we would expect seizure activity to reduce.

Each of the above represents an important part of our overall anti-convulsant programme. One other resource is also open to us.

Anti-Convulsant Medication Elimination

The use of medication to control fits, whilst more logical and scientific than the historical approaches discussed earlier, has one immense drawback. Anti-convulsant medication tends to create a barrier between the patient and his environment. Awareness is dulled, the amount of information reaching the brain is reduced, and although the fits may become controlled, the price paid in terms of function is heavy.

Our programme of activities is designed to stimulate children. It is our experience that if a high level of appropriate stimulation can reach the brain, a greater level of function may result. Any procedure which *increases* the density of the barrier between the brain and the environment must therefore reduce the effectiveness of stimulation, and a better alternative must be sought.

In 1982, we carried out a survey of those of our children who were prone to fits. We found that a considerable number were receiving three or more anti-convulsant drugs each day. Some children were being given daily medication for fits, although they had not actually had a fit for two or more years. One child was receiving *nine* different drugs each day, and despite this was still having fits!

With the agreement of the children's parents and their own doctors, our medical officer began a new approach. A very slow elimination of all anti-convulsant drugs was commenced, with each child being weaned off medication over a period of several months.

The results were most encouraging. There was no dramatic increase in seizure activity. Some children exhibited the same number of fits with or without the drugs. A significant number showed an actual reduction in fits, once the drugs were eliminated. A number ceased having fits altogether!

This elimination programme has continued ever since, and as at 1st May 1995, 107 children for whom I was responsible had been successfully weaned off all anti-convulsant medication. As a result, they were more alert and responsive, and their progress was no longer impeded by a chemical barrier.

It is important to note that all these children have followed a full-time comprehensive programme of activities which we have recommended, a factor which I believe to be essential to the success of our drug elimination strategy.

UNDER NO CIRCUMSTANCES DO I ADVISE ANYONE TO ATTEMPT THE ELIMINATION OF ANY ANTI-CONVULSANT MEDICATION EXCEPT UNDER MEDICAL SUPERVISION.

CHAPTER 36

Coma

The children who come to us have a variety of different problems. Some have physical difficulties; some intellectual and quite a number have social problems, linked to hyperactivity, and frustration. Yet no child is more challenging than the one who is in coma.

There is no condition which is closer to death. To have no vision, no hearing, no awareness of physical sensation, no mobility, no speech, and no hand function; to breathe – badly; to be completely out of contact with the world, and yet to be still in the world, is surely one of the worst of all possible states. It is also the most un-predictable.

Were we to seek a medical prognosis of a patient after only one week in coma, the probable response would be 'guarded'. Following a severe physical injury to the brain, there is often a degree of bruis-ing, and an increase in the amount of fluid present within the tissues. This tissue swelling is known as 'cerebral oedema', and it can take up to 3 months to subside. After this point has been passed, any medical prognosis is likely to be pessimistic, since in the majority of cases, spontaneous recovery is rare.

What, therefore, can be done?

I believe from long experience working with brain injured children that if the right stimulus is applied to the brain, with the appropriate Frequency, Intensity and Duration, function can be encouraged and often re-generated.

In coma cases, the Frequency and Duration are important, since a regular repetition of the stimuli is necessary if any information is to be retained, and a consistent effort is called for, day after day and week after week, if their cumulative effect is to be successful in wak-ing the patient up.

However, for the comatose patient, the most important of the three, by far, is INTENSITY, since it is the *strength* of the stimuli which will determine if the barrier can be broken.

Once again, it is to the same five sensory pathways into the brain –

sight, hearing, touch, taste and smell – that we must turn, if we are to be effective.

If, as is often the case, the comatose patient has to begin to learn, all over again, the most basic of information, then it is up to the therapists to provide that information, in as INTENSE a form as is compatible with safety.

Examples of the levels of Intensity which we might use include:

A bright light being shone into both eyes, simultaneously, for a short period of time.

A loud noise being sounded, close to each ear, again for a short time.

Where the skin condition allows, the application of hot water bags, and the contrasting sensation of ice bags; the use of a vibratory massager; rubbing all over with a rough towel.

The presentation of a variety of strong smells – ammonia, disinfectant, smelling salts, French perfume etc.

The introduction of a variety of strong tastes – curry powder, mustard, lemon juice, etc.

Brain injury creates a barrier between the environment and the brain itself. By increasing the strength of the information coming from the environment, we have often succeeded in breaking down this barrier.

In March 1985, during a visit to Holland, I was approached by two families, whose children were in coma. One was a thirteen year old girl, who had fallen from climbing bars in a gymnasium, striking her head on the ground. The other was a young man of nineteen, who had asphyxiated, swallowing his tongue.

I taught each family an individual series of activities which we call our 'Coma Programme'. They were to carry these out many times each day. Within two months, Dik, the young man, regained consciousness. I heard no news of the girl for five anxious months. Then a message came from Holland: 'Astrid woke up!' She certainly did. The last time I saw Astrid she was walking up the main staircase at Knowle Hall!*

Of all the families faced with the problems created by brain injury, the family of a comatose patient is probably presented with the biggest shock. Coma is very often the immediate result of a traumatic injury, and it is very hard to adjust to the fact that this morning their loved one was fine, and talking to them, and now he or she is in intensive care, linked to life only by a series of tubes. The feeling of desperation is intense, and so is a desire to do something – anything – to try and restore normality.

*I have told Astrid's story in detail in Chapter 46.

The first important thing to do is to discover the depth of the coma. Is there any response at all from the patient to any sensory stimulation? After the first few days, there may be some indications that light, sounds, or voices do elicit some response, however minimal. The family should ask the hospital staff to keep them fully informed, and keep a diary, in which they should record every reaction, however small.

Every patient is different, and before any attempt is made to carry out techniques such as those described above, a decision must be made as to the most appropriate and practical Frequencies and Intensities of the stimulation. Because many of these techniques could, if incorrectly used, be harmful to the patient, I do not advise anyone to attempt a 'do it yourself' approach; rather, I will be pleased to advise any family facing this problem, if they contact me.

Our coma techniques, like any other techniques, carry with them no guarantee of success, but the results obtained using methods such as those described above have sometimes succeeded where more conventional, non-invasive and 'wait and see' attitudes have failed.

CHAPTER 37

Warm Water

Ever since 1934, when, as I have described, Dr Temple Fay first realised that brain injured children could develop new skills if given sufficient sensory stimulation, and enough opportunity for motor activity, a series of dedicated pioneers have sought new and better ways to improve the functional abilities of their young patients.

It is fair to say that in the majority of immobile children, or those whose mobility was below par, the use of 'Patterning' when coupled with 'The Floor', or other appropriate techniques produced improvements. Children who were totally immobile responded by becoming able to creep on the tummy, to crawl on hands and knees, and even to walk and, eventually, to run.

However, in the period between 1st January 1980 and 31st December 1989, 143 children, who had come to us totally immobile, did not improve in mobility despite receiving daily stimulation for periods ranging from 6 months to 5 years.

One factor which appeared to be common to over 60% of these children was their level of stiffness. In many, the muscles were so spastic as a result of their brain injury that even our own staff, despite their experience, could only obtain limb movement with great physical effort. The children appeared to have no way of overcoming such a level of rigidity themselves.

Other patients, when placed prone on the floor, tended to assume the foetal position, leading us to the conclusion that, as a result of their brain injuries, they were – at least as far as mobility was concerned – still below birth level in function, and were assuming the 'in utero' position of the unborn child.

It has always been a basic principle of our philosophy that where a child has missed out a particular stage of development, we should return him to this level, and encourage the establishment of the missing function. A child who never crept on his tummy, crawled poorly and walks with poor co-ordination would, following this principle, be given every chance to learn how it feels to creep, and would be encouraged to creep along the floor. Once he could creep well, and in a good cross-pattern, we would expect his crawling and walking to improve automatically.

The two questions therefore appeared to be: 'How could the very high levels of spasticity in these children be reduced?', and: 'How could a child be successfully returned to an *in utero* state, and be stimulated at that level?'

One of the guests at our first International Conference at Knowle Hall in 1986 was the Director of the Australian Institute, Tim Timmermans, who, with his wife Claire, has for the last twenty-six years specialised in teaching tiny babies to swim. I have maintained close contact with Tim since 1973, when I first met him, and his wife Claire, in Philadelphia, and on the subject of the use of water as a therapeutic medium, they both know what they are talking about.

Tim presented a paper to the Conference, in which he described the rapid improvements gained in a severely brain injured boy as a result of giving him regular immersion in warm water, and an increased amount of sensory stimulation.

Of course, hydrotherapists have known for many years of the beneficial effects of warm water on spastic muscles. Yet, to my knowledge, no-one had ever attempted to carry out our type of therapy with a child WHILST HE WAS IMMERSED IN WARM WATER.

Perhaps this approach would help to answer both our questions, since not only might we be able to reduce spasticity for long enough to enable us to stimulate the child's brain and obtain some degree of response; we might also be able to reproduce the 'in utero' environment we needed to trigger fresh development.

Further investigations were carried out by my wife, Valerie, during 1987. She was able to immerse children's hands, disabled by spasticity, in warm water, using normal bathroom facilities. When coupled with sensory/motor activities, this procedure worked. Valerie and I talked to hydrotherapists, who agreed that in principle, our proposition made sense. We learned a lot about hydrotherapy pools.

In May 1988, a National Appeal for £95,000 was launched, to build a Very Warm Water Pool with a number of special features.

We would need to be able to 'pattern' children and young people in the water; therefore an overhead hoist would be required to help take the weight of older children and young adults.

We would need to be able to give children the opportunity to creep on their tummies in warm water, at a depth of a few inches. We would also want to encourage other children to crawl on hands and knees in warm water, at a depth of twelve or more inches. Others would need to be able to walk in warm water. This problem of a variable depth facility was most easily solved by incorporating into the pool a false floor, which could be raised and lowered by pneumatic pressure.

The normal temperature of the human body is 98.6 degrees Fahrenheit. For 'in utero' conditions, we would need a system which could reliably, and automatically, heat the pool water to at least that level.

We would need control equipment sophisticated enough to cope with all the normal problems of pool hygiene, plus the extra difficulties associated with incontinent children.

We would need a jacuzzi area, with sufficient water pressure to produce good tactile stimulation.

Construction work on the new pool began in April 1989, and by the beginning of November it was ready for use. And for us, it heralded yet another new voyage of discovery. We learned how to 'pattern' in warm water. We learned that many of our physical techniques could be successfully used in the pool. We were not surprised, but very pleased to find that many children began to relax in the water, and that after regular immersions, their stiffness could be kept at bay for longer and longer periods. We found that we could reproduce intra-uterine movements in the children, an impossibility on land. And that when we did so these movements reinforced the effects of patterning.

The Pool could be used clinically in several different ways. Children could be exposed to warm water during their normal, two-day reassessment, and after observation, new routines could be suggested, involving this medium, which parents could carry out with their youngsters at home, in the bath.

Children and parents could be invited to stay for a one-week or two-week period, so that they could use the pool several times each day as part of their child's programme.

A session in the pool could also be incorporated into the evaluation procedures, so as to monitor the improvements produced by the new warm water techniques.

Almost all the children so far introduced to this new programme environment DID begin to respond. And, what is even nicer, they *enjoyed* the experience.

CHAPTER 38
Autism?

In the constant professional search to find acceptable words to describe our children's problems, autism seems to have become another 'catch-all', like 'mentally handicapped' or 'backward'. Yet what good is it if a child fits a checklist or a one-line description?

Does this produce an instant and successful solution, or is it just another 'box'; another label to make it easier to categorise a child's problems?

The word 'autistic' is not so much a diagnosis of a child's problems as a label used to describe his symptoms. Over the years, attempts have been made to codify autism by means of a 'check list' – the 'nine points' of autism – by attempting to define as autistic 'someone who carries out non-goal-directed activities'; and by introducing a grading system which very often attempts to minimise the problems, using phrases like 'mildly autistic', 'having autistic tendencies', 'showing signs of autistic behaviour', 'on the autistic continuum'; or descriptive words which 'accentuate the positive', like 'hyperlexia'. More recently, all variations of autistic, hyperactive, and attention deficit disorders have been codified. There are several syndromes including Asperger's and Tourette's. Then we have the confusing proliferation of acronyms, some of which are related to autism, like 'OCD', 'SPD' and 'MSD', and some of which are most definitely not, like 'ADD', ADHD' and the sad 'ODD'.

Over the last 30 years, use of the 'nine points' check list, and the more recent wide ranging criteria produced by the American Psychiatric Association have led people to give a diagnosis of variants of autism, since such children could be more easily identified. However, why has this procedure not led to a successful treatment regime? The nine points and the 'criteria', however detailed, are surface observations. They are, again, descriptions of symptoms. The real question is WHY? Is the behaviour totally illogical, or is it in fact absolutely logical, given certain sets of circumstances or a different reasoning on the part of the observer.

If a child is withdrawn, WHY is he withdrawn? If he cannot relate to other people, lacks eye contact, hates being hugged or is constantly waving his hands in front of his eyes – WHY? And what can be done about it?

Let us for a moment set aside the checklists and labels, and imagine a child who has sustained severe brain injuries which have affected his sensory pathways: his sight, hearing, touch, taste or smell. No, he is not blind, deaf or paralysed, but he certainly does not see the world the way we do; hear the world the way we do; or feel the world the way we do. He lives in chaos. And he cannot unscramble the chaos, however hard he may try.

Suppose, instead of having normal sight, and the ability most of us possess to see things in stereo, and in an ordered fashion, he cannot control the constant bombardment of fresh images which assault him. Because he cannot perceive dimension, everything he sees is 'out of true'. Worse, he may be hyper-visual, and may stare for hours at some tiny object, a small piece of lint, or a moving toy, which will give him especial pleasure. He may suddenly change position, altering the visual range of the object he is staring at. Conversely, he may be visually hypo-sensitive, and will rock to and fro for hours. He will be strongly attracted to light, and will stare at the sun, or at shadows. He will be afraid to climb or descend stairs, and cannot cope with any swift movement.

Suppose the sounds which he hears are undifferentiated; one sound follows another without meaning or pause: a constant pandemonium. Or perhaps he is hyper-sensitive to noise, so that to him a whisper is a loud shout, and a simple instruction is just an unbearable Babel of sound. His only method of survival is to block out noise, either externally, by blocking his ears with his hands or fingers, or by switching off *internally* and behaving as if he were totally deaf. Because his hearing is so acute, he may well listen avidly to noises we cannot hear, such as those produced by strip lighting, or a mains hum. Maybe he has the opposite problem, and has hearing so hypo-sensitive that he seeks constant noise. He will place his ear next to the hi-fi loudspeaker, the washing machine or the vacuum cleaner. He will make noise by repetitively banging doors, running water, or smashing one toy against another.

Suppose he is oversensitive to touch; he hates being hugged, feeling trapped by the arms which encircle him. Tickling is for him tantamount to a beating, and for his cheek to be stroked is worse than a slap across the face. Or perhaps his ability to feel is so dulled that he cannot feel pain, and self-mutilates as a poor attempt to give himself pleasure. He is almost wholly 'tuned out' to his own body sensation, and has a tendency to move all or part of his body in a rhythmic way.

Suppose his sense of smell is acute to the point that he cannot bear being near other people: he simply cannot stand the way they smell! His olfactory sense is quite possibly as acute as any dog, and he is nauseated by any strong smell. He will often avoid going to the toilet, as he cannot stand the smell of his own wastes. Or perhaps his sense of smell is so weak that he is constantly trying to reach for any smell and sniffs everything and everyone. He is likely to concentrate his attention on his own body smells, and may have constantly wet hands, through mixing his saliva with his own body odour to enhance his own smell.

Suppose he has an overabundant sense of taste, and rejects most of the food given to him, because he cannot adjust to its taste. Bland foods like milk or scrambled eggs are too strong for his taste buds, and a flavoured dish like mild curry or chilli can often produce vomiting. This child cannot tolerate variations in taste, and is consequently a problem to feed. Or, perhaps his ability to taste is underdeveloped, and he will put anything and everything in his mouth, including coal, wood, ink or disinfectant.

So far I have described the two ends of the sensory spectrum – the Type A ('hyper') child and the Type B ('hypo') child. There is a third category, harder to distinguish, but nevertheless very real.

This is the Type C child – the one whose problems Dr Carl Delacato, an expert in the sensory difficulties of children, describes in his book *The Ultimate Stranger* as being 'white noise in the system'. This child seems to be more interested in what he can see *inside his eyes* than in the world around him. He will rub, or press his eyes to make changes of light or colour in his *internal* visual perception. He is fascinated by the noise of his own heartbeat, or by his own internal plumbing. He may constantly hum to himself. He is so busy producing his own favourite tactile sensations by pinching, biting or scratching HIMSELF that he ignores outside tactile stimuli. He behaves as if he has a constant smell present in his nose, and is trying to dislodge it by blowing up into his nose, or by stuffing objects up it. He is always sucking his own tongue and cheeks, as if he has an ever-present taste in his mouth.

There is no question that these are difficult children. Yet the difficulty lies just as much in making the right diagnosis as in deciding on the most effective treatment, since every child is different, and may have behaviourisms in abundance which I have not described, but which nevertheless fit one of the fifteen possibilities which I have described. Yet it is often very hard to determine which of the senses is aberrant. A child may be rocking forwards and backwards because he is hypo in vision, or hyper, or he may be hypo-tactile. It is therefore necessary to look for other symptoms before a clear picture may begin to emerge. Very careful observation of the child is needed, on more than one occasion, and a deliberate avoidance of any readiness to jump too quickly to conclusions, if an accurate determination is to be made of which senses are affected, and in what way.

Before coming to us, one of our children had exhibited all the characteristics of deafness. He had even been supplied with a hearing aid, when only eight months old. When in desperation he himself finally threw the aid away, his parents sought our advice, and we found that he was actually hyper-sensitive to noise. The hearing aid was the very last thing he had needed!

A further complication must also be borne in mind. It is quite possible for a child to be a total mixture of Types when all five senses are taken together. Whether a child is Type A, B, or C, or a complicated mixture of all three, successful treatment requires a two-stage approach. First we must normalise the sensory channel; then we must feed it with carefully structured information.

Vision

For hyper-visual children, a reduction should be made in the amount of available light, whether sunlight or flashing lights. Instead of the child being allowed to vary the amount of light he sees, this should be done for him. If he likes to watch moving light, YOU move it for him. If he likes to wave objects in front of his eyes, YOU move them instead.

If he is hypo-visual, then he needs plenty of light, and brightly painted objects to look at and to play with. He needs to be given the opportunity to learn about depth, and where things begin and end. This can be done by letting him feel things, so that he can learn where the edges are. He must be encouraged to look directly at things, since they are most clear to him when in his direct line of vision, and 'blinkers' can be useful.

For the Type C child, you must gain his visual attention, however briefly, and repeat the exercise over and over again until his attention span increases. Do not let him look *inward*. Control what it is he looks at, so that YOU are in charge of what he sees. Draw the curtains so that the room is dimly lit, and, using a pencil torch, move the light YOURSELF. It should be possible to develop his attention quite quickly, and coloured lights can then be used.

Auditory

The hyper-auditory child needs protection from noise. Try to cut down loud sounds as much as possible, and avoid any environment where there is likely to be a lot of noise. If this is difficult to achieve, use ear plugs. Do not talk to him – WHISPER. Gradually he will begin to respond, once the level of sound has been controlled for him, and it ceases to be a threat.

The hypo-auditory child needs sound, but it should be controlled sound. A tape recording of specific sounds can be used, but each must be specific, and not a mix of many sounds as in a piece of music. He should be encouraged to make sounds of his own, especially in the bath, where the acoustics are usually good.

The 'white noise' child needs to be introduced to *external* sounds, and his habit of listening to himself should be interrupted as often as possible. Talk to him. Give him things to do. Let him watch and listen to external stimuli like video tapes and TV. Games and toys involving sounds are helpful in teaching him that sound is external as well as internal.

Tactile

The hyper-tactile child has to be able to control the amount of sensation he receives, or he becomes terrified. Even a slight pain can make him hysterical, and any body contact, like hugging, should be very gentle. He cannot handle large variations in temperature, and his environment needs to be temperature controlled, and preferably cool. Observe what he likes to do to himself, and then do it to him, but very, very gently. Be prepared to stop whenever your stimulation distresses him.

The hypo-tactile child needs sensation. He craves it. Rough towelling, warm and cold water, strong hugging, tickling, and the use of a vibratory massager will be sources of great pleasure to him. Be particularly aware of the areas of his body which he tends to mutilate, as these need particular tactile stimulation from YOU. And remember, he does not feel pain very easily, so be careful not to cause inadvertent harm to him.

The Type C child needs to learn how to experience EXTERNAL stimulation. Make it obvious to him that you are going to hug, tickle or stroke him. Tell him what you are going to do, and what you are doing whilst you are doing it. Once he begins to learn about the tactility reaching him from outside himself, he can be exposed to more and more tactile experiences.

Olfactory

The hyper-sensitive child should be protected from as many strong odours as possible. Keep his environment as free of smells as possible, and well ventilated. Once the threat presented by smells has diminished, you can begin to introduced mild, gentle smells, although not close to his nose. People, and their particular smells, should only be introduced when he is able to tolerate a range of other odours. Remember, people are one of the strongest sources of smells he can experience.

The hypo-sensitive child should be exposed to as many smells as possible, naming each one as he smells it, and putting each right under his nose. Play 'smell' games with him, having him choose between two different smells, and gradually reduce the strength of the smells, as his skill improves.

The Type C child needs to learn about EXTERNAL smells. First create for him a smell-free environment, and make him, himself as smell-free as possible. Then, make a collection of little bottles containing strong smells: bleach, disinfectant, manure, Chanel perfume. Choose one, and use it for the entire day, naming it each time he smells it. Put a drop of it on his clothes, and on his body. Once he can recognise strong smells, you should introduce other, milder smells, until he has mastered a full range.

Gustatory

Of the four tastes – sweet, salt, sour and bitter – the hyper-gustatory child should only be given the first two to experience until he can cope with sweet and salt. Fizzy drinks should be avoided. Give him only small quantities of bland foods to eat. With any new, mildly tasting food, put a drop on the tip of his tongue, and another immediately behind his upper teeth. Starting with very bland tastes, sweet and salty foods should precede sour and bitter ones, and the latter should only be introduced when he can cope with sweetness and salt.

The hypo-gustatory child needs to be protected from all harmful tastes, since he is totally unable to discriminate. He should be introduced to bitter tastes, applying these to the back of the tongue. Then, sour tastes on the sides of the tongue, followed by salt tastes on the tip of the tongue. Sweet tastes should come last, also to the end of the tongue. Each sensation should be continued for two weeks before moving to the next. At the end of eight weeks, begin again with bitter tastes. Once the child can distinguish between the four, move on to choosing a 'daily taste'. In time, different tastes can be used during the course of each day.

The Type C child needs taste to be introduced from *outside himself*. First, however, the sensation in his mouth and tongue need to be enhanced, and a regular brushing of the mouth and tongue, as well as the teeth, will help. Try each main taste to see which he will most readily accept, then start with that one. When he has become accustomed to all four, begin teaching him how to tell the difference between them, starting with sweet and salty tastes on the tip of the tongue.

The above techniques are essentially aimed at normalising the particular sensory aberration which a child may have. Once this has been achieved, then he can be introduced as appropriate to the many other techniques which we use with brain injured children. His behaviourisms are, after all, just another group of symptoms of his real problem – brain injury.

CHAPTER 39
The Family

So far I have described some, but by no means all, of the techniques we can use to overcome the effects of brain injury. One of our most important 'techniques', however, can easily be forgotten – so basic is it to our entire philosophy. This technique is the use of the FAMILY.

A brain injured child responds to extra stimulation. He responds even more to extra stimulation provided, on a one to one basis, by a caring adult. He responds best to extra stimulation provided by those he loves the most, and by those who love him the most.

Our job is not, in the first instance, to treat the children. It is to TEACH their parents. Using parents as therapists is one of our major weapons in the war to combat brain-blindness, brain-deafness and brain-paralysis.

Our parents are fantastic. They care more about their children than anyone else could, and they do more for their children than anyone else would. They don't start at 9 o'clock in the morning, and stop at 5 o'clock in the afternoon 'when the bell rings'. The job of any parent is a 24 hour-a-day job, 7 days-a-week, and this is even more true when their child is brain injured.

When people talk about brain injured children, they tend to localise the concept to the child himself. Yet, in fact, any family which contains a brain injured child is a 'brain injured' family. And the only way to treat a 'brain injured' family successfully is to treat the brain injured child successfully. So why should such a family not have the joy of seeing the results of their OWN efforts, and feeling the particular pleasure of achieving something which is supposed to be impossible?

Our families are so often underestimated. The idea of a family doing something, themselves, about one of their members who is hurt, still seems foreign to many people.

Yet, in the days before the specialisation and sophistication of our present civilisation, it would have been considered barbaric and unnatural if the family did NOT take care of its own. During the five years I spent in Zambia, I often observed African families camped out in the grounds of the local hospital, cooking for their mother, father, brother, sister or child who had been admitted for treatment. They wanted to be nearby. They wanted the one who was ill to feel that the strength of the family was being brought to bear on the problem. Is this attitude 'uncivilised', or is it perhaps a demonstration of the solidarity that exists within a family, provided that officialdom is not allowed to intervene?

Our parents are told that they should not exhaust themselves working with their child; that they – the mother and father – deserve a life of their own; and that carrying out an exhausting daily programme could eventually lead to a breakdown of their marriage.

Those who give such advice cannot possibly have any idea what it is like to see a child whom you love fail to develop, whilst all the other children living in your street achieve their milestones, and progress in leaps and bounds. How can any mother or father be expected to 'live with' that situation? Or to proceed gaily to have a happy life of their own?

Do these counsellors have any idea how much time has to be spent just looking after such a child? Do they not realise that it can take most of a parent's energy and strength just to feed, clean and calm a brain injured youngster, not to mention the constant need to guard against his injuring himself, or to anticipate the next fit? However much time is spent stimulating him is POSITIVE activity; it is aimed at trying to solve the problem, so that *then*, once this has been achieved, Mum and Dad *can* enjoy life.

Of course some marriages of parents following our programme do break up. A considerably larger number of marriages of parents NOT following our programme have broken up, just as a considerably larger number of marriages of childless couples have broken up. To imply that it was the programme that broke up the marriage is not just unfair, but is untrue.

(It is worth mentioning that we have never had a case of suicide amongst our parents. The suicide of the parent of a 'mentally handicapped' child is not an unknown occurrence in society generally.)

On the other hand, it is by no means unusual for our programme to have the effect of bringing the marriage partners closer together, in a mutual effort to try and solve a shared problem.

The myth that parents don't have enough energy or commitment to tackle a programme like ours with their children is easily disposed of. On the first day of each Initial Week that we hold, a group of parents arrives at the Alison Centre. Each set of parents is unknown to every other parent, and no doubt many feel uncomfortable in the presence of other families and their hurt children. Five days later, each mother and father will not only have had the energy to learn, and to practise each technique needed for their own child; they will also have had enough energy left over to have helped other families to pattern *their* children. And when families return for their first, fourth or even tenth reassessment, they often ask about the progress of 'that tiny little paralysed girl' whom they helped to pattern on their first visit. They have had enough strength to complete their own programme, and enough left over to be interested in the condition of another child who doesn't even belong to them!

What about the siblings, the brothers and sisters? As I have said, having a brain injured child in the family is a problem, not just for the mother and father, but for everyone in that family. A 'normal' life for ANY of the members is virtually impossible, and the stresses and strains brought about by extra worry, and the extra attention which the hurt child in any event demands, are shared by all.

Brothers and sisters can be a tremendous asset. Very young ones are often experts at creeping and crawling, and delight in joining in, if given the chance. Older ones feel important and useful if asked to help with some of the techniques.

One day, when our youngest daughter, Heather, was six years old, she climbed on to a stool when her sister Alison was lying on the table, ready to be patterned, took hold of Alison's head in exactly the right way, and announced that she was 'ready'! Our natural reaction was to tell her that she wasn't old enough, and to get down off the stool. Then we thought, 'Why not? It cannot harm, just for a minute, and Heather will have felt part of it all.' I therefore took a leg, Valerie the other leg, Susie and Judy an arm each, and we began.

We were amazed at how good a rhythm Heather kept up! We all went on for a full five minutes, and thoroughly enjoyed the session. And the nicest thing was that the whole family was helping Alison, from the littlest to the biggest. That seemed a healthy thing to me then, and it still does now.

There are other bonuses. All three of our well children learned to read long before they went to school. They picked it up, whilst listening to us teaching Alison to read!

It is always easy to fall into the trap of concentrating on the hurt child to the exclusion of the well brothers and sisters. We advise our families to guard against this, and recommend that each day's plans should always include ALL the children in the house. Whenever Mum and Dad are both available, or enough helpers are present, one adult should spend as much time as possible with the rest of the children.

I have heard it said that we offer false hope to desperate parents. Families come to us with hope – or else why would they come at all? They hope that we will tell them what is wrong with their child. They hope we will teach them what to do to try and solve all the problems. They hope they will be treated with courtesy, and not patronised.

Above all, they hope our programme will produce the results they seek. To begin any undertaking without hope of success would seem to be a rather futile exercise. They know, because we tell them, that we cannot give them any guarantees, other than the assurance that they face a lot of hard work; that we believe our objectives for their child may be more positive than those they have previously been offered; and that we promise them our support and help for as long as they want it.

If, after all their efforts, our programme is not successful, and their child does not significantly improve, the parents know that, at the very least, they and we have tried hard.

If all our efforts lead to a successful conclusion, then their hope was justified. If not, then they will look elsewhere, in the hope that someone else will be able to help them. That is what we did, for three long years, when we were desperate for help. We saw sincere people. They tried, and we tried. We all failed. But we did not become consumed with the agony of false hope. We didn't have time for that luxury. We simply kept on looking, and we kept on hoping!

And in the end, we found some answers.

The opposite of 'false hope' in most people's minds is probably 'fulfilled hope'. There is an alternative: 'false despair'. This condition is far worse, for in reaching it, all hope has been given up, too early and without justification. As Samuel Taylor Coleridge wrote, 'He who can inspire hope is the best physician.'

It is not a crime to hope. Far from it. Hope is the well-spring of action, and of endurance, and to give up hope for a child is to give up on a child, something we will never do.

Of course, working all day and every day is not every parent's choice. Nor should it be. But for those mothers and fathers who want to 'Do It Themselves', there should be somewhere that they can go to learn all they need to know, and someone to provide the essential and regular monitoring of their efforts, without which they can soon 'run out of steam'.

That is our function.

CHAPTER 40
Helpers

Contrary to the belief of many people, we do not run an in-patient unit. Our children are treated in their own homes.

Our programme is therefore designed to be carried out in the home, whether that home is in England, Scotland, or Wales; in Amsterdam, Athens, Valletta, Cairo, Berlin or Warsaw.

Each item of equipment which we use must be capable of being reproduced at home. Each activity we recommend must be both practical and possible, since every house is different, and space is sometimes at a premium.

As should by now have become apparent, many of the techniques which have proved to be so effective in accelerating the development of our children are simple, and can easily be carried out by one person. But some, which involve lifting, or the simultaneous movement of arms, legs and head, call for a number of people to be involved. The movements are not complicated, nor do they require professional training; in fact, all that is needed are extra pairs of willing hands, and a desire to learn a new approach.

In the case of a small child, three people can easily carry out between them all the activities which may be prescribed. A sixteen-year-old, on the other hand, may well need a team of five to meet the needs of the programme.

I estimate that over 8,000 volunteers give, on average, one hour of their valuable time, each week, to brain injured children, in the UK alone!

When parents come to see us for their first interview, we discuss with them their need to find helpers. Reactions vary considerably. Some parents, who have relatives living close by, can find all the support they need from within the family. Others have already received offers of help from their community. The rest are given advice about where help may be found, and how to obtain it.

One family from Essex was very worried about finding people willing to help their little girl. They were farmers, living out in the country with few neighbours, and were sure it would be impossible to find enough assistance. I suggested that they contact the editor of their local paper, who might be persuaded to publish a very real 'human interest' story about their daughter, and her chance for a better future. To their amazement, and the editor's, over two hundred readers responded to this appeal for help, and they were able to set up a two-weekly rota, with *reserves*!

Helpers come in all shapes and sizes. Some are as young as ten years old, others are in their seventies! Many do not know each other the first time they arrive at the house, but all are motivated by the same desire – they want to help, and are glad to be needed.

It is not all one-way traffic, either. Initial timidity disappears as they discover that our children are not all as fragile as they first thought. Pity turns into enthusiasm once they see a child beginning to respond to their efforts, and a real bond of achievement develops.

Some years ago, their local vicar accompanied one of the families when they came for their child's reassessment. The little girl had done very well, and had not only learned to creep and crawl, but could now walk and run as well. We decided that she no longer needed to be 'patterned', and both we and the family were very pleased with this decision, as it indicated just how much progress had been made. The vicar, however, looked worried.

When I asked him why he was so worried, thinking that perhaps he had not realised the significance of the decision we had made, he explained that on his patterning team was a member of his congregation who was an alcoholic. This man had not had one drink since becoming a patterner, and now I had taken patterning out of the child's programme!

Of course, there was an answer. The word 'patterner' implies someone who gives their time purely to pattern a child. The word 'helper' is much broader in concept, and we know of many cases where people have offered their time, not just to help carry out the programme, but to give a hand with the many chores which tire out even the most energetic Mum.

Not everyone in the world is well co-ordinated; not everyone can happily work with a brain injured child. Yet they can still help: with the shopping; by looking after the other children for a while; even by making the tea!

One of our daughter's helpers went through a complete nervous breakdown, unknown to us. She never missed her turn, was always smiling and cheerful, and we never knew that the only time she ever left her house, week after week, was to keep her promise to help Alison.

Many volunteers never realise just how important they become to the children. One of the ways parents have of telling us how much their child's sight has improved is to say, '. . . and now he can recognise each of his helpers.'

Some teams design and make their own individual 'uniform', often a tabard in brightly coloured material. At least one of our mothers has so organised her volunteers that each team wears a different colour, to help teach her child all the colours of the spectrum.

Older children can become very bored when being patterned, or when they receive a half-hour or more of respiratory reinforcement. To combat this, we often suggest that the helpers each choose a topic they have 'swotted up' during the week, and talk about it to the child for a predetermined amount of time. It is amazing how much *everyone* learns!

A common fear, voiced by both parents and professionals, is that the daily demands of the programme may prevent our children from enjoying social contact and interaction with other children. Yet many helpers bring *their* children with them when it is their turn to lend a hand, and there is no better reinforcement for a child who has to spend time on the floor, than to enjoy the company of other youngsters for whom the floor is their natural playground.

At first, older people are often very concerned that they might hurt the child. Our children are much tougher than they think: they have had to be, just to survive. One mother, faced with the problem of an older helper whose hands became wet with perspiration caused by the fear of making a mistake, equipped all her volunteers with white gloves!

Where do all these wonderful people come from? Some respond to adverts placed in the local press, or in the local newsagent's window. Some come from the congregations of local churches. Others are members of service organisations, like Rotary, Rotaract, Inner Wheel, Round Table, Ladies' Circle, the Lions, the Buffs, and the Moose. Youth Clubs, sixth form and college community projects, Duke of Edinburgh Award schemes, Scout and Guide groups – all these provide volunteers. Of course, if one of our mothers has two neighbours who will drop everything and come whenever she needs them, she only needs two helpers. Yet most of our families rely on between thirty and forty people each week, thirty or forty 'pretend' Aunties and Uncles, for this is often what they become.

Helping a hurt child can become so much a part of one's life that it becomes difficult to stop. I have had several calls from people who have moved from one part of the country to another, and who would like to help one of our children in their new neighbourhood.

But perhaps one of the nicest stories is of the brain injured child who, having overcome his own problems and become able to survive, in due course became a helper for another.

At this point I would like to pay tribute not only to our own helpers, who did so much to give Alison a future, but also to the many volunteers around the world upon whom our work, and our children's achievements, has depended, and still depends.

CHAPTER 41

Discipline

I am sure that many of you will think it strange that I should want to include this subject in a book about brain injured children.

The parents of a mid-brain injured youngster, who is bright as a button, but cannot move, would probably feel that this subject simply doesn't apply to them, since a lack of discipline is the least of the problems they have to face every day. The parents of a hyperactive child probably wish that they *could* introduce a measure of discipline into a totally chaotic situation.

Other people might say, 'Shouldn't we all concentrate on making the children's lives as happy as possible, to make up for their having so many problems to cope with?'

If there was no way of creating any improvement in brain injured children, then there might be some validity in this argument. But, since, as we know, our children do not remain static, and generally speaking respond well to our programme, it is just as necessary for us to consider ways of helping them to learn how to live in *our* socially-orientated world, rather than creating a 'special' world just for them.

Our world is full of rules. And all of us are constantly presented with options. We can learn the rules, and obey them, in which case we can live our lives relatively free from interference by 'authority'. Or, we can opt to break the rules, in which case we have to take into account what will happen when we are caught. Our society is organised on the basis of deterrence. If we break a rule, we pay a penalty. The penalty is judged to be enough to deter us from breaking the rule, and if it doesn't, then either the penalty is insufficient, or we have to experience the penalty in order to be deterred from breaking the rule again.

If our social behaviour is unacceptable, other people avoid us, and in extreme cases we can be made social outcasts. Our society tries to make rules for the good of all, and if we break them, we have no real cause to complain.

We learn very quickly what is, and what is not acceptable, and, initially by trial and error, we also learn to conform.

The first new phrase which each of my well three children learned, when they began to go to school at the age of four, was 'You are not allowed . . .!'

Why should this be any different for brain injured children?

If a two-year-old screams and shouts because he cannot get his own way, we adults take appropriate action, whilst accepting that such behaviour is part of childhood. But, if a twenty-two year old throws a similar tantrum, we are faced with a very different situation. What is the appropriate action? And how do we even begin to explain to on-lookers that he is brain injured, and that his brain actually functions at a two-year-old level.

All children have to learn the rules, and also have to learn what happens if they are broken. The built-in deterrent must be experienced enough times for them to decide that being 'good' is more rewarding than being 'naughty', and that their own happiness is linked to other people's happiness.

It is part of growing up to 'test the edges'. All children are constantly involved in growing up, but whilst well ones learn where the 'edges' are quite quickly, hurt ones often learn very, very slowly.

Consistency

One of the reasons that we are able to function successfully in society is because the rules do not change, minute by minute, and they apply to everyone.

Since the 'family' can be viewed as a microcosm of society as a whole, this same consistency should, and must apply not only to the brain injured child, but also to everyone else in the family.

Johnny asks his mother if he can go out to play, and she says 'No'. If he then asks his father, who promptly says 'Yes', Johnny has learned an important lesson. The next time he wants to go out, he won't bother asking his mother, and will head straight for his father.

This has created one sort of problem for the two parents. But, what if the next time Johnny asks his father, he is refused permission? Now he is confused, and bewildered, since the rule he thought he had learned has suddenly changed.

If he asks to be allowed to go out to play, and is refused without explanation, and he then hears his brother or sister given permission to do so, he is once again bewildered and confused. The rules appear to be different for him, and he becomes resentful.

Suppose only Johnny's mother is available. He asks her nine times if he can go out to play and is refused nine times. But, on the tenth occasion, she is so tired of his persistent nagging that she agrees. Johnny has now learned a different rule. He now knows that he needs to ask ten times before he can get his own way.

All these examples demonstrate a lack of consistency in Johnny's family. We have the beginnings of chaos, where no-one knows where they are.

All good parents try to avoid the situations I have described. At least, they do as far as their well children are concerned. But when it comes to bringing up a brain injured child, it is all too easy to fall into the trap of making different rules, or avoiding having rules, BECAUSE HE IS BRAIN INJURED.

This is the most effective way I know of creating a spoiled brat; a little 'monster' who will in time grow up into a big, and totally unmanageable 'monster'.

It is even more important for brain injured children to grow up within a framework of rules than it is for ordinary children. Since the learning process is often more difficult for the hurt child, and since he finds it much more of a problem to adapt to change, he needs to know that there are as many unchanging factors in his life as possible.

Many of us who are used to getting up at the same time every day to go to work, view the occasional day off, or lie-in with pleasure. Not so the hurt child, who is accustomed to a routine, and becomes quickly unhappy if this is in any way altered.

In the days when young brain injured students used to fly to England from the USA to spend some time at Knowle Hall, they took up to two weeks to overcome the effects of jet lag! Their ordered lives were suddenly disrupted, both by a time change, and by a whole new set of rules. In addition, they found it very hard indeed to cope with the 'culture shock' of coming to England.

The children on our programme are surrounded by 'coat-hangers', upon which they 'hang' their day. They get up at the same time every morning; they carry out the same regular sequence of activities every day; they stop for lunch and tea at the same times every day; they go to bed at the same time every day. They are cushioned by routine.

The same principle applies to discipline. A basic set of rules should be agreed by everyone in the family. These may be particular to only that family, but they cover such things as behaviour at table, tidiness, obedience, helpfulness, and consideration. They should also apply to EVERYONE in the family.

They should be adhered to. They should become a part of daily living. Only in this way, with this level of consistency, can the hurt child ever learn that the same rules apply just as much to him as to everyone else, that there is a difference between right and wrong, and that 'No!' means no.

What is the deterrent? The answer depends entirely on the level of understanding of the brain injured child, but is basically the temporary removal of something he likes.

If he is able to understand and interpret the look of pleasure or disappointment on his mother's face, and if the former is accompanied by hugs and cuddles, he can begin to learn that it is nicer to be smiled at and hugged than not to be, and if he breaks the rules, he doesn't get smiled at and hugged.

If he is able to react to a tone of voice, or to spoken words, he will gradually learn that when he behaves appropriately, he will be praised, and when he doesn't, he will trigger a less pleasant response.

If he can understand two-step commands, and deals, then he will be able to recognise the feeling of being ignored, or of not being allowed to do what he wants, in much the same way as his well brothers and sisters.

Millions of words have been written on the subject of bringing up children. Very few thoughts have been published about how to bring up brain injured children, and almost all of these have assumed that the problems of these children cannot be alleviated, and that therefore the problems themselves are punishment enough.

The best possible way to reward a brain injured child, however hurt, is to tell him, in every way you can, that you are pleased with him. The only practical way to punish him, if this is called for, is not to reward him.

When families return to us for reassessment, parents are often anxious that we see their children at their best. Their 'best' may only be a new ability to move six inches on their tummies without help, but the amount of cheering and clapping that accompanies such an achievement can leave the child in no doubt that he has done something wonderful.

Some years ago, two of our parents were at a loss as to what to do about their son's behaviour. He regularly threw a tantrum whenever he had to carry out a particular activity in his programme which he didn't like, and was disrupting his schedule and upsetting his helpers. Unfortunately, it was also a technique which he badly needed, and could not therefore be simply left out.

We suggested that they should try to overcome their typical English conservatism, and give him a great deal of positive reinforcement every time he did anything praiseworthy. Whenever he threw a tantrum, however, he was to be removed from the room, left on his own and totally ignored for fifteen minutes, without toys or other distractions. In other words, he was to be temporarily 'sent to Coventry'. When the time was up, he was then to be brought back into the room, and the programme was to be resumed without comment.

Although his mother and father were doubtful about this suggestion, they agreed to give it a try. It took three weeks of consistent application before the tantrums stopped!

Before they begin our programme, brain injured children live in a world of their own. However chaotic, or unreal, they do at least know *that* world, and they do not know *our* world. It is therefore hardly surprising that some of them should initially protest, when we begin to introduce them to reality, as they prefer the relative security of their chaotic world to the insecurity of ours.

Nevertheless, none of our parents would dream of giving their children the vote as to whether or not they should stay in their own world, if there was any way they could become part of ours. If it were left to the children, they would stay the way they are, because they have no way of knowing what 'well' is. Parents *do* know what 'well' is. They know it is worth striving for, and this is one occasion when they cannot afford to let the child win. If he wins . . . in fact he loses.

It is one of the responsibilities of being a parent to have to decide what is best for one's children, and this is even more true and difficult if the child happens to be brain injured. It is therefore very important to determine whether tantrums or unacceptable behaviour stem from fear, discomfort, or an attempt to 'test the edges'.

If fear is the cause, we need to build confidence by taking things very steadily, and giving a great deal of praise.

If discomfort is the problem, then we need to investigate carefully the circumstances surrounding the specific activity. One child I know used to scream all the time he was in a particular room. It transpired that he had hypersensitive hearing, and was greatly disturbed by the noise emitted by the fluorescent ceiling lights, a sound outside the audible range of well people.

Only if it is clear that the unacceptable behaviour is truly linked with the need for discipline, should firmness and consistency be applied, as in the example of temporary 'banishment' which I have described.

It is worth remembering that all human beings respond to the way in which they are treated. If a child is treated like an idiot, he will become an idiot. If he is treated like a two-year-old, he will behave like a two-year-old, whatever his chronological age.

Children rise to our expectations. We should continually set those expectations at the highest possible level to which the children can respond. Therefore, if we want a ten-year-old brain injured child to behave more like a well ten-year-old, and less like a two-year-old, we must encourage him by treating him as much as possible like a ten-year-old. Consistently.

PART SIX

The Final Programme
. . . and its Effects

CHAPTER 42

Working out a Programme

When we refer to 'the Programme', as I have done many times in this book, we tend to forget that most readers will not have the foggiest idea of the practical meaning of these words. I have talked about our stimulating brain injured children; about increasing the Frequency, Intensity and Duration of the stimuli they are given; about providing them with lots of opportunity for practising the new skills we want them to learn. But I am sure the reader may still have no idea what a child's programme might look like. Since every child is different, each programme is also necessarily different, because the routines we recommend for each child must vary in order to meet his individual needs. But the discussion which takes place between us before a final decision is agreed is always very similar. Every activity or technique which could be included is always carefully considered under the three headings of:

Would it be nice for him to have it?

Would it be good for him to have it?

Must he have it?

Once we have established within which of these three categories a technique falls, we then eliminate the first two, and are left with the MUSTS – those stimuli which are of the greatest priority.

Each is then given its own time requirement. Homolateral Patterning will probably require 5 minutes. Basic Vision will take 1 minute. Masking will vary in time, depending on the age and breathing ability of a child.

We used to present each family with a list of techniques, showing the length of time that each one should last, and the number of times they should carry out the technique, each day. However, as this required a family to work out for themselves what was, in effect, a *sequence* of activities, we found it was easier for them if we simply presented them with a ready-made sequence. Certain additional recommendations, covering procedures which cannot be incorporated within the sequence e.g. diet, could then be listed separately.

Since, as I have said, every child's needs are different, and as we have over five hundred available techniques, there cannot, by definition, be such a thing as a typical sequence of activities. The following will, however, give a clearer picture of the principle:–

Activity	Length Of Time
Mask	1 minute
Basic Vision	1 minute
Roll Pattern	2 minutes
Trunkal Pattern	3 minutes
Mask	1 minute
Basic Vision	1 minute
Tactiles	3 minutes
Frequency Tape	1 minute
Mask	1 minute
Basic Vision	1 minute
Homolateral Patterning	5 minutes
Mask	1 minute
Assisted Creeping on Tummy	5 minutes
Mask	1 minute
Basic Vision	1 minute
Tactiles	3 minutes
Hang from Hands	1 minute
Mask	1 minute
Basic Vision	1 minute
Suspended Inverted Rotation	3 minutes
Rolls	1 minute
Orals	1 minute
Mask	1 minute
Basic Vision	1 minute
Arm & Leg Swings (side to side)	1 minute
Arm & Leg Swings (front to back)	1 minute
Suspended Rotation	3 minutes
	46 minutes

In Addition:	Nutrition Programme
	Intelligence Programme

The above sequence would, in practice, take a family approximately one hour to carry out, and, depending on the age of the child would be carried out in total between 4 and 6 times per day. (The daily FREQUENCY)

The INTENSITY of each technique would be individually taught to each family, depending on their child's needs. The DURATION would be a period of approximately four months, after which time we would want to see the child again for reassessment.

Under normal circumstances, our families return to see us at regular four-monthly intervals. The reassessment is carried out over a two-day period, and involves the same thorough series of investigations, which characterises the first day of an Initial Assessment week.

Now, however, we are able to measure a child against his own initial status, both medically, functionally and physically, and can clearly see if he has changed in any respect, whether positively or negatively. Once again, the parents are an invaluable source of information for us, and although we will only record on the child's Development Profile those positive changes in function which we ourselves observe, we nevertheless make careful note of any small changes in ability which Mum and Dad feel to be significant.

A Word of Caution

If you are the parent of a brain injured child, or a professional therapist interested in trying a different approach, please remember that designing an effective programme for a brain injured child is not easy. Whilst it is possible, as I have done in this book, to give an example of a sequence of activities, the particular sequence described would only be applicable to a very specific child, whom I have imagined for the purposes of the exercise. It isn't difficult to work out a sequence, or a full programme, but it can be very, very difficult indeed to write the RIGHT sequence or programme for a child. For this reason, I advise you to contact me directly before *doing* anything.

CHAPTER 43

Physical Measurements

There is a constant yardstick against which each of our children is measured: the ability of normal children. This comparison is in itself one of the biggest problems we have to overcome. Our children remain 'different' until such time as their progress makes it virtually impossible to distinguish them from the rest of their chronological peer group.

'Physical Growth' can be regarded in two different ways. It can mean 'an improvement in the physical abilities of a child', which would include walking and running, hopping, jumping, and manual dexterity. It can, however, also mean the physical *status* of a child; whether his body is developing correctly; whether his size compares favourably for his age with other children; whether his bones, muscles and organs are growing properly.

Earlier in this book, I explained that the brain 'runs' everything. This is just as true for physiological development as it is for physical and intellectual control, and when brain injury takes place, whether before, during or after birth, physiological growth can very often be affected adversely as a result.

Brain injured children tend to be smaller in stature than their well counterparts. Their chests can be less well developed; their heads are often smaller; their height and weight can be below normal. Since 'function determines structure', a lack of function can result in poor structure. Muscles can remain undeveloped; tendons can be too tight or too slack; inappropriate pressures can cause bones to bend and distort; poor nutrition, malabsorption and poor respiration can further retard proper physiological growth. Unless action is taken to correct such conditions, permanent deformities can result.

I mentioned earlier that when a family first embarks on our programme, they attend an Initial Week's course at the Alison Centre. The first day is entirely devoted to finding out as much information as possible about the child, and in addition to a long clinical history, and both medical and functional examinations, the child is very carefully physically measured.

These measurements, which form the basis for all future comparisons, must be as accurate as possible. For this reason we use equipment originally designed by anthropologists to measure bone, skull and rib cage dimensions.

Length of Body

If a child can stand up really straight, this data can be obtained vertically. However, as many children cannot stand, and those who can often exhibit a poor posture, we prefer to obtain this information with the child lying on his back. Where one leg is longer than the other, the reading is taken from the heel of the longer leg to the crown of the head.

A child's sitting height – the distance from the base of the pelvic girdle to the crown of the head – is separately recorded, as vertical growth in the trunk can occur without corresponding growth in the legs.

The Hips

The distance is measured between the hips, excluding as much as possible the effect of any fatty tissue.

The Chest

We measure the breadth of the chest, the depth and the circumference. As this latter can vary considerably when a child is lying supine as opposed to sitting up, the circumference is recorded in both positions.

A badly twisted spine can dramatically affect the surface contours of the chest. Some children have a narrow breadth, and broader depth (pigeon-chested). Others are flat chested, or exhibit a frontal cavity. For this reason, all three dimensions must be recorded, since later growth in any one field may not be apparent in terms of overall change.

The Head

Again, we measure in three different dimensions. A reading is taken from front to rear, another from side to side, and the circumference is also recorded.

Weight

Modern electronics have improved considerably the accuracy of this investigation, and as conversions between British stones and pounds and European kilos are now available at the push of a button, we can provide this information to parents in whichever scale they prefer!

Heart and Respiration Rate

When practical to do so, both these are recorded twice; first when the child is relaxed and inactive, then immediately after exercise.

All these statistics would be meaningless were there no standard norms against which we could make a comparison. Fortunately, norms do exist, both for males and females, from birth up to 18 years of age, and we are therefore able to ascertain how the physical dimensions of any of our children compare with accepted averages.

Of course, these norms are not the only criteria which must be applied. Parents themselves vary considerably in *their* measurements, and if both parents are small or light in weight, these factors must also be taken into consideration.

PHYSICAL GROWTH

The many different activities which make up our programme can, in themselves, create physical growth in children.

When we hang a child upside down to increase his spatial awareness, the traction which this produces can encourage an increase in height; it can also help to reduce a spinal deformity such as scoliosis, which can change or distort the dimensions of the chest.

The improvement in the rhythm and depth of breathing, by means of masking, respiratory patterning, and running, can, over a period of time, greatly increase the size of the chest.

An appropriate diet and the introduction of vitamin and mineral supplements can dramatically affect a child's weight.

NEUROLOGICAL GROWTH

Whenever a new item of data is stored in the brain, a process takes place which is called myelination. A protective fatty sheath, called myelin, forms around the newly active neuron, and consequently, the space it takes up in the brain becomes microscopically greater. In the case of only one brain cell, the extra space requirement is so small as to be insignificant. But, if ten million become myelinised, there is sufficient demand for more room to require expansion of the skull, and it is this growth which we are able to measure.

Amongst the many labels which are 'attached' to our children before they reach us, is the term 'microcephalic'. This description relates to the size of the head, compared to normal. On a scale of 1 to 100, where 100 represents the largest known size of human head, and 1 the smallest, and where 50 is the exact mean average of all known sizes, if a child's head circumference places him in the bottom 2%, he is said to be microcephalic, or 'very small brained', on the assumption that the size of the head indicates the size of the brain.

Our findings over the last 25 years indicate that when a child receives a great deal of extra stimulation and begins to respond with improvements in function, his head grows at a rate faster than would normally be expected. The process of increased myelination would explain this accelerated growth. We also know that the brain grows by use, and we believe therefore that our programme for brain injured children can actually eliminate 'microcephaly'.

There are, of course, other possible causes of accelerated head growth. One of the more well-known of these is hydrocephalus, or 'water on the brain', when an excessive amount of cerebral spinal fluid becomes present inside the skull. This leads to an increase in fluid pressure, which forces the skull to expand. The brain is simultaneously placed under intense pressure, which can result in a loss of function, and even further brain injury.

Any noticeable increase in a child's head dimensions must always be regarded in the context of function. If he is gaining in ability, and head growth is accelerating, then all is well. If his abilities are deteriorating, and the head is expanding, then corrective action must be taken immediately, and the advice of a competent authority sought.

Many of our children have a fear of white coats, which they associate with discomfort and restraint. White coats are banned at the Alison Centre!

Nevertheless, children do not always enjoy being measured! Sometimes they cry; sometimes they struggle; sometimes they refuse to co-operate. This is understandable. In most cases, they have been examined, poked and prodded many times, by many people, before they arrive at our Centre, and are ready to sound a note of protest as soon as they are held down, or encouraged to keep still.

We always record the demeanour of a child during a measurement session, as this can be useful information when interpreting the figures.

Each time a child returns for re-assessment, we carry out a complete re-measurement. In view of the physical effects of the programme in encouraging growth, we are never surprised to find that a child's height, weight, chest or head has grown 300%, 400% or even 500% of the normal expectation, for a given period of time.

If our children have to compete with well children, then they must have a chance to catch up physically. Through regular measuring, we can determine not only how much they are below par, but also monitor their progress towards this goal.

Figure 11   Development Profile (Results)

BRAIN - NET
DEVELOPMENT PROFILE

NAME OF CHILD _____

AGE AT INITIAL EVALUATION _____ AGE TODAY _____

RE-ASSESSMENT NUMBER _____ EVALUATED BY _____

INDEX NUMBER _____

PRESENT DATE _____

DATE OF INITIAL EVALUATION _____

MONTHS SINCE LAST ASSESSMENT _____

SENSORY			TIME FRAME	LEVEL	MOTOR		
VISUAL DEVELOPMENT	AUDITORY DEVELOPMENT	TACTILE DEVELOPMENT L R			MOBILITY	LANGUAGE	MANUAL COMPETENCE L R
Able to read fluently with appropriate visual dominance	Understanding of complete vocabulary consistent with age level using appropriate dominant ear	Able to identify by touch using appropriate dominant hand	PEER LEVEL IF OVER 6 YEARS	8	Able to move with coordination of age level consistent with appropriate dominant foot	Able to converse appropriately at age level	Able to write at age level using appropriate dominant hand
Able to read single words [Proficient]	Able to understand complex sentences	Able to identify tiny objects by touch	6 YEARS	7	Able to hop, skip, jump and kick a ball	Able to speak in complete sentences	Able to write single words [Imperfect]
Able to recognise symbols and letters within experience	Able to understand two-step commands and simple time concepts	Able to differentiate between similar objects	3 YEARS	6	Able to run in cross pattern [Imperfect]	Able to speak in short sentences	Able to use both hands together purposefully
Able to recognise pictures within experience	Able to understand simple commands	Able to differentiate between dissimilar objects	18 MONTHS	5	Able to walk with arms no longer required for balance	Able to say two words together	Able to simultaneously oppose index finger and thumb of both hands
Able to focus both eyes simultaneously, and to perceive depth	Able to understand single words [Imperfect]	Awareness of the third dimension	12 MONTHS	4	Able to walk with arms used for balance	Able to say single words [Imperfect]	Able to oppose index finger and thumb of either hand
Able to see details within an outline [Imperfect]	Able to recognise meaningful sounds [Imperfect]	Able to react to light touch	6 MONTHS	3	Able to crawl in cross pattern on hands and knees [Imperfect]	Able to make sounds culminating in communicative sounds	Able to grasp objects purposefully
Able to see outline	Vital response to threatening sounds	Awareness of vital sensation	3 MONTHS	2	Able to creep in cross pattern on tummy [Imperfect]	Able to respond by crying to vital threats	Able to release in response to a vital stimulus
Reflexive response to light	Reflexive response to loud noise	Babinski reflex	BIRTH	1	Free voluntary movement of limbs	Able to cry	Reflexive grasping with hands

Profile Copyright Brain-Net 1996

CHAPTER 44
'Results' and 'Achievements'

As all our parents know, we use our own Developmental Profile to assess the abilities of each child we see. As we have already seen, this Profile takes account of the six major functional abilities present in human beings – namely Vision, Hearing, the Sense of Touch, Mobility, Speech and Manual Dexterity – and records the eight most significant skills which all normal children acquire in each of these areas during their early lives.

If we find that one of our children has no ability in respect of a specific function, then the Profile is marked as 'absent' in that 'box'. If the ability is present, but is not fully established, then the marking is shown as 'imperfect'. Only when a child is able to demonstrate a full level of function is he given credit for this, and the Profile 'box' is marked as 'proficient'.

The Profile is first marked, in blue ink, after a child's Initial Assessment. It is marked again, this time in red ink, after each subsequent reassessment. Where new abilities have been gained, these improvements can be readily identified, and by comparing the red and blue entries, it is easy to see the overall changes which may have taken place.

There are ten levels of function on the Profile which we regard as being particularly significant. These are:

VISION	Level 3	(Imperfect)	– Beginning to see.
	Level 7	(Proficient)	– Beginning to read.
AUDITORY	Level 3	(Imperfect)	– Beginning to hear.
	Level 4	(Imperfect)	– Beginning to under stand.
MOBILITY	Level 2	(Imperfect)	– Beginning to creep.
	Level 3	(Imperfect)	– Beginning to crawl.
	Level 4	(Imperfect)	– Beginning to walk.
	Level 6	(Imperfect)	– Beginning to run.
LANGUAGE	Level 4	(Imperfect)	– Beginning to talk.
MANUAL COMPETENCE	Level 7	(Imperfect)	– Beginning to write.

Our computer has been programmed to store and retrieve Profile information. Therefore, whenever a child reaches one of the above Levels for the first time, the computer registers a new 'Result'.

There are thousands of improvements which can occur in children. Whilst the ten that I have listed have special significance, it would be a great pity if we were to ignore all the others, especially when some of them mean a great deal to a family. The day a child became fully toilet trained; the day he swam his first width of a pool; the day he was finally and successfully withdrawn from all anti-convulsant drugs; the day he won his Scout Collector's badge; all these 'red-letter' days deserve recognition, so whenever one of our children gains an important new skill, or overcomes a particularly difficult problem, we award him an 'Achievement'.

A Certificate, describing his new victory, is given to the family, and a copy is entered in our 'Book of Achievements' which is kept on public view at the Alison Centre.

RESULTS

BIBIC

If we look at all the children who were helped by BIBIC between January 1st, 1980 and March 1st, 1995, there were 721 who had been seen on more than one occasion. We are therefore able to compare the profile markings of these children at their latest reassessment with the original markings obtained during their initial assessment.

Of these 721 children, 500 (69.3%) achieved significant improvements. The average number of gains per child was 2.0.

Specifically, the following achievements had occurred:

52 children, blind as the result of brain injury, gained their sight.

221 children who could not read any words, learned to read. Forty-two of them did so at an age younger than might have normally been expected.

7 children who became able to read had had no effective sight at their first assessment.

34 children, who were deaf as the result of brain injury, became able to hear. Nineteen of these also became able to understand spoken language.

114 children who could only hear sounds learned to understand spoken language.

155 children, 44 of whom were previously immobile, learned to creep forwards independently on their tummies.

73 children learned to crawl on their hands and knees.

62 children learned to walk.

68 children achieved the ability to run.

19 children who had been immobile learned to creep on their tummies, crawl on their hands and knees, and to walk. Five of these also learned to run.

111 children gained the ability to talk.

85 children learned to write, 5 of them ahead of their chronological peers.

Additionally,

35 children were accepted for full-time mainstream education.

32 children were currently receiving, or had benefited from, part-time education in normal school, as a part of their programme.

107 children had, since 1st January 1983, been successfully withdrawn from all anti-convulsant medication, with no ill-effects in terms of increased seizure activity or deterioration in behaviour.

The above list does not take into account the number of children who were more aware, more healthy, who were no longer hyperactive, or who had been awarded any of the 1,281 Achievement Certificates which had been presented in the previous fifteen years.

MALTA

If we then look at the 52 children treated by the Institute for Brain Injured Children (Malta) between June 1st, 1996, when Brain-Net began to help create and develop a Centre in Malta, and May 8th, 1998, 41 had been seen on more than one occasion.

Of these 41 children, 32 (78.0%) had achieved significant improvements. The average number of gains per child was 1.8.

Specifically, the following changes occurred:

3   children, blind as the result of brain injury, had gained their sight. One of these had also learned to read.

20   children, who could not read any words, had learned to read. Three of them had done so at an age younger than might normally be expected.

2   children, who came to us neurologically deaf, had begun to hear sounds. Both of these children had also learned to understand spoken language.

5   children, who could only hear sounds, had learned to understand spoken language.

11   children, 5 of whom were previously immobile, had learned to creep forwards independently on their tummies.

2   children had learned to crawl on their hands and knees.

1   child had learned to walk.

2   children had learned to run.

1   child, who had begun the programme immobile, had learned to creep on her tummy and to crawl on her hands and knees.

6   children had learned to talk.

4   children had learned to write.

Sixty Achievement Certificates had been awarded.

It is worth remembering that in Malta, unlike Britain, the summer temperatures rise on occasion to 40 degrees centigrade, and environmental conditions do not favour the types of programme which our children need. Yet, in relative terms, both the percentage of children succeeding and the average gains per child are very similar, in both countries.

CHAPTER 45
Perspective

We are very proud of our results. To the best of my knowledge, ONLY Brain-Net and BIBIC publish results of any treatment applied to brain injured children in Britain, and this is a great pity. If the results achieved with brain injured children by the use of alternative methods of treatment were available, we would have some means of comparison, and so would you, the reader.

There is another factor to be taken into account when assessing the progress of our children. I call it the 'lack of perspective' syndrome.

Most people in this world are not used to brain injury, or to brain injured children. The majority of human beings, when confronted with a child who cannot walk, talk, see or hear, tend to feel uncomfortable or embarrassed, and the obvious differences between themselves, as 'well' people, and the hurt child, immediately stand out.

People rarely notice the similarities: that they share with our children the same human characteristics – both groups have hands, both have heads, both bleed when they cut themselves. So obvious are the differences; so often are they immediately apparent that the positive images are ignored, and only the negative ones are noticed.

It is rather disheartening when you have worked every day with a child for several years; when you have helped him to learn to creep, to crawl, and to take his first hesitant steps; when you have watched him gradually become aware of light and darkness, outlines and then details, and have 'jumped for joy' the first time you gained eye contact with him; if, after all that, you hear a visitor say, quietly, 'But hasn't he got such a long way to go!'

'A LONG WAY TO GO!!!!!'

'Have you any idea just how far he has already come?'

If only people could appreciate the incredible distance which you and he have already travelled, together, from the darkness, the stiffness, and the emptiness.

These difficulties of perspective do not belong to the brain injured child. They are OUR problems. It is for us to realise them, just as it is for us to realise that the only difference, in fact, between the hurt child who cannot move and we so-called well people who can move, is the relative number of brain cells which have been lost along the way. Remember, we are ALL brain injured to some extent.

Not one of us still has, intact, the brain we had when we were born. The question is not, 'Who is brain injured and who isn't?' The real question is, 'Does it stand out?'

In our children, it stands out. Gradually, as our programme takes effect, it stands out less and less, but as it is in the nature of human beings to notice the differences between us all, and not the similarities, it still stands out.

Next time you meet one of our children, notice the similarities, not the differences. That way, you will be able to enthuse, as we do, about that wonderful, dynamic thing called PROGRESS!

CHAPTER 46
Eight of Our Children

The children who come to us range in age from five months to sixteen years. We could help younger children, but it often takes several months before parents are able to fully grasp the size of the problem, and have had enough time to assess and evaluate the amount of help available to them.

We do help older patients if their injuries are the result of trauma such as road traffic accidents or other mishaps, when there may be some retention of function, or if they are comatose. Generally speaking, however, once a child is over sixteen, he is no longer a 'child', and whilst our methods may still be capable of producing good results, the amount of help required to carry out our programme with an adult can often be a barrier to its successful implementation.

Some of the children who are brought to us have been hurt at conception. Others have suffered brain injury whilst still in the womb. Many have become hurt during the birth process – 'the most dangerous journey any of us ever makes'. For others, who have survived all the risks up to and including birth, the tragedy has occurred days, weeks, months or even years later.

ZOË

Zoë has Down's Syndrome. At the time of her conception, a genetic error occurred, and the normal blueprint determining the characteristics of each cell of her body became flawed.

Let her mother begin the story:

'When we were told the news, twenty-three hours after her birth, we were advised that a good special school was available, but that, once she reached sixteen, there was not much on offer. When I left the hospital, I was told we could always bring her back if we couldn't cope.

'During her first and only visit to us, our health visitor asked me how my family and neighbours had reacted to the news. I was so upset by her insensitivity that I didn't see another health visitor for about two years. We then met a very good one, who helped and encouraged us a great deal.

'We took Zoë to Great Ormond Street Hospital for a second opinion. We learned that her heart was sound, [heart problems are often associated with Down's Syndrome], and the specialist told us that our daughter's future was 'up to us'. He inspired us with confidence that we ourselves could help Zoë.

'When she was a year old, Zoë began to go twice each week to a hospital assessment play group. That year, she had two separate assessments.

'Twelve months later, we heard about the local Down's Syndrome Association. As Zoë had not yet begun to talk, and was becoming more and more frustrated at her inability to communicate properly, we became interested in both this local association, and the national Down's Syndrome Association in London. However, we were told by our assessment unit paediatrician not to waste our time with either of these organisations, as her unit was quite capable of catering for all Zoë's needs.

'It was fortunate that we ignored this advice, as the local Down's Syndrome Association introduced me to a sign language, which had a dramatic effect on Zoë. She quickly became less frustrated as she learned how to ask for things, and in no time at all began to talk. We were soon able to discontinue sign language altogether.

'Zoë had been recommended 'Pedro' boots when she was one year old. I kept on and on asking for help to get her walking. The medical profession kept avoiding the issue, and I was told that she would walk in the fullness of time, when she was ready. She finally started walking at three-and-a-half, and because she was so late, she was delayed in going to nursery school.

'Just before her third birthday, Zoë's assessment unit paediatrician announced that she was ready to be 'statemented' for her future educational needs. We felt this was far too early, and after my husband protested, and stood his ground, this process was postponed until she was four-and-a-half.

'We had been advised not to begin potty training until Zoë was three years old. In fact, I did start a little earlier than this, but success was a very long time in coming. I now know I should have started much earlier.

'We were told that Zoë could join a normal play-group, but were advised not to put her in a nursery school, as it would be too advanced for a Down's child. One specific private one was mentioned as an example. At a later stage, Zoë did join this one, and was able to proceed to mainstream primary school.'

Zoe came to us in September, 1986, when she was four-and-a-half years old. Our initial evaluation of her functional skills showed that in vision, her ability to focus both eyes together was impaired by the presence of a left divergent strabismus, which is to say that her left eye tended to turn outwards; although she could read most of the words she was shown, knew the letters of the alphabet and a number of different shapes, Zoë could only recognise one or two numbers, and had no idea of counting.

In auditory ability, she did not respond by blinking to any sudden sounds; she became unduly distressed by loud noises; could not follow any two-step commands, and was only just beginning to understand simple time concepts.

In tactility, her Babinski reflex was imperfect in both feet; she was hypersensitive to light touch all over her body; and although she could appreciate the third dimension with either hand, she could not differentiate between even the most dissimilar of objects.

She could walk, and was beginning to develop running skills, but her ability to creep on her tummy was marred by disorganisation and poor limb control, and, at a higher level, she could not hop, skip, jump, and could only kick a ball with her right foot.

She found it difficult to make the 'F' sound, and her sentences were limited to three word combinations.

Zoe's manual dexterity was surprisingly good, considering her poor tactile awareness. She could manipulate a zip fastener, and was starting to develop the ability to unscrew the lid of a jar, and to button and unbutton. She was beginning to use a pen, and could make circles and crosses on a piece of paper.

Zoe's initial programme was based upon a specific sequence of activities, and we asked her parents to carry out this sequence with her eight times each day, seven days per week. The sequence included masking; homolateral patterning; creeping on her tummy; brachiation; crawling on hands and knees; a variety of techniques to challenge and improve her balance and co-ordination; upside down; regular brushing with soft fabrics to reduce her hypersensitivity to touch; and several different manual activities. We also advised the discontinuation of the Pedro boots, a decision which overjoyed Zoe when she learned that she could at last choose and wear pretty shoes.

Zoe's intelligence programme included reading words and sentences; our language development programme; writing; further toilet training; and a continuation of her three-hour-per-week attendance at nursery school. (On this day, her sequences were reduced to five).

Our nutritional investigations had revealed that she was very sensitive to cow's milk, and we therefore proposed that all dairy products should be eliminated from her diet. Wholefoods, and mineral and vitamin supplementation were also recommended.

At her first re-assessment, six months later, her parents reported that Zoe's time concepts were improving; the catarrh from which she had regularly suffered in the past had cleared up completely, and her appetite was greater and more universal; she was now more curious about her world; she would now allow her hair to be cut without complaint; she was beginning to invent games for herself; her writing was more spontaneous; her vocabulary had increased, and she was more willing to use it.

Our own functional evaluation revealed that she now had a much broader understanding of numbers, and not only knew all the words she was shown, but could indicate the parts of her body to which some of the words referred. She also demonstrated that she could read several sentences with understanding. Although still hypersensitive to external light touch, especially on her feet, she was beginning to control her own ability to feel things, and could now differentiate between some unlike objects.

We did not make any major changes in Zoe's programme for the next four months, feeling that essentially she needed 'more of the same'. We did, however, add some sprinting to her other physical activities, and C.V.S. cards were now included in her intelligence programme.

As there was a history of sensitivity to apples in the family, we also suggested that apples and apple juice should be eliminated from her diet, as she was suffering from a skin rash.

At Zoe's next visit, after a total of ten months of intensive stimulation, her parents reported that she was now able to concentrate more, and for longer periods; her running was more controlled, and in a better pattern; her articulation was clearer, and her sentences more structured; her memory was better; she could now write short letters; she was using both hands together to perform tasks, and with more control; and she was becoming more emotionally mature.

By now, Zoë was 5 years 4 months old. Under test conditions, we were able to confirm that she could now understand more complicated sentences and some abstract concepts; her hypersensitivity to light touch had disappeared; she could select dissimilar objects without difficulty by touch, using her right hand; she could carry out a whole range of bi-manual activities without difficulty; and she was indeed able to write her own name, and several other words spontaneously, just as her parents had said.

Following this reassessment, Zoë began to attend mainstream primary school one day each week, whilst keeping up with her programme on the other six days.

We continued to see her at regular four monthly intervals, and on each occasion, noted both highly significant (or 'profile') changes and functional improvements. She gradually integrated more and more into her school activities, progressing from 1 day, to 2 days, to 3 days and finally, in March, 1989, to full-time school. At weekends, and after school, her parents were able to offer her some extra stimulation through a 'back-up' programme which we designed especially for her.

A 'red-letter' occasion took place in November, 1989, when Zoë took part in a two and-a-half hour musical show staged by the dancing school which she had been attending since the summer. As a result of this experience, the following month she behaved like an 'old hand' in her school nativity play, knew her cues, and performed with confidence in front of an audience.

At the end of January, 1991, four-and-a-half years after her first visit, Zoë's mother summarised the positive changes which had taken place.

'Since Zoë began her home programme, we have seen major improvements in concentration; confidence; walking, and walking up and down stairs; running; social and sociability skills; speech; reading, writing and spelling; and reaction to noise.

Zoë is now in full-time school; she is learning French; she is a member of the local Brownie Pack, and attends ballet and tap dance classes. She has begun piano lessons and goes horse riding.'

Her mother adds, 'We can now look forward to a much more independent future for Zoë. I am sure that, in time, she will hold down a regular job, which she will be able to enjoy. And, no doubt, she will drive a car.'

Update
After a seven year interlude, Zoë's mother was pleased to fill in the gap, and bring her story forward to the present.

'During the last seven years Zoë has attended a school for children with moderate learning difficulties. She now reads well, and her 'joined-up' writing is excellent. Her speech is much clearer, and her conversational skills are much improved. She has an extensive vocabulary.

'Her swimming has improved, and she has gained two swimming certificates.

'She is still learning ballet and tap dancing, and up to 1996 she continued to sit exams, competing with her peer group. She has gained two more grade certificates, and in 1996 she won a Special Certificate for Merit.

'She continues to ride, and has taken part in several gymkhanas. This year she was placed 3rd in two events.'

JOOST

Joost also has Down's Syndrome. For him, too, a genetic error occurred, and the normal pathway through childhood became strewn with problems.

His mother writes:

'Joost is our elder son, and was born on May 17th, 1987, in Haarlem, Holland. Within the first five minutes of his life, it was clear to us that he had Down's Syndrome.

When he was five years old, we heard that Keith Pennock was to give a lecture in Nagele. We had heard about the therapy which he recommended, through friends of friends, and our curiosity was aroused. We decided to get in touch with his Institute, and we asked to be put in contact with other parents whose children were Down's Syndrome, who were following the programme, and who we could visit to see the therapy in practice.

At the end of 1987, we visited two families in England, and all the information which we were able to gather only made us feel more and more enthusiastic.

We asked our family doctor for his opinion. He summarised his feelings as follows:

Would Joost be prepared to carry out the daily routine, with volunteer helpers?

Would we, his parents, be able to cope with having volunteers in the house every day, at the cost of our privacy?

Could we afford the costs involved?

He did not see any disadvantages to Keith Pennock's approach, and very much wanted to be kept informed. He was happy to leave the decision to us, and was willing to co-operate fully.

Our major concern was the thought that if we put off starting the programme until later, we would lose precious time. If, on the other hand, we started as soon as possible, but did not have success, we would at least know that we had tried. So, in June 1988, we went to England for the Initial Week.'

When we saw Joost for the first time, on June 20th, 1988, he was thirteen months old. Our initial evaluation of his functional skills showed that in vision, he had a good, fast pupil response. His ability to focus both eyes together at near point was excellent, but he had problems focusing at far point, and consequently had difficulties with depth perception. He was interested in pictures, but was unable to differentiate between two of them (hardly surprising, considering his age).

In auditory ability, his startle reflex was mature; he was not unduly distressed by loud noises; he could understand meaningful sounds, and a variety of single words, and could follow one or two simple commands, but not yet consistently.

In tactility, his Babinski reflex was immature in his left foot; his sensitivity to both pain and light touch was appropriate on both sides of his body; but although he could appreciate the third dimension with either hand, he was not yet able to differentiate between even the most dissimilar of objects.

He had a full range of movement in his limbs, and could creep on his tummy, but in no recognisable pattern. His parents told us that whilst he could not yet sit himself up, he could pull himself up to standing from a sitting position, by holding on to their hands.

He could produce a loud cry when appropriate, but had a limited range of other sounds, and his parents confirmed that he had only three words which he could use appropriately, but only occasionally – Mama, Papa, and No.

He could grasp objects purposefully at will, and was beginning to develop a pincer grip in either hand.

Joost's initial programme was based upon a specific sequence of activities, and we asked his parents to carry out this sequence with him six times each day, seven days per week. The sequence included masking; trunkal patterning; homolateral patterning; creeping on his tummy; rolling; swinging; hanging from hands and feet; and tactile stimulation to his face and particularly to his mouth. We advised his parents to take him swimming as often as possible, and, to encourage

Joost to begin to develop independent creeping on his tummy, we introduced an 'anti-roll' device to be used when he was on the floor.

Joost's intelligence programme included C.V.S. cards, our language development programme; simple commands; and activities to help him develop cortical opposition and bi-manual function.

Our nutritional investigations had revealed that Down's Syndrome children are particularly sensitive to cow's milk, and we therefore proposed that cow's (and goat's) milk should be eliminated from his diet. Whole-foods, and mineral and vitamin supplementation were also recommended.

At his first re-assessment, eight months later when he was 20 months old, his parents reported that Joost could now sit upright on his own. He had also learned how to pull himself into a standing position with support from furniture, and had begun to cruise. His breathing had improved in quality and depth.

Our own functional evaluation revealed that he had now developed adequate depth perception; he could now recognise a good range of pictures; he could follow many simple commands and several two-step instructions, and was beginning to grasp simple time concepts; he could differentiate between dissimilar objects with his right hand; he had started to crawl on hands and knees; he could make a variety of understandable sounds, and had begun to use several single words appropriately and spontaneously; and he was beginning to develop a pincer grip in both hands.

We also found that Joost's chest circumference had increased by 4.5 centimetres, which was nearly four times more growth than would be expected for a normal child of his age and sex over the same period.

We felt that this was an excellent initial response to the programme.

In response to all the improvements which had taken place in Joost's abilities, we made several changes in his programme. Several new spatial techniques were introduced; more time was allowed for him to consolidate his crawling on hands and knees; he was encouraged to stand up and to take a few independent steps; and a tricycle was recommended. Tactile stimulation to his face was suggested immediately before meals. More C.V.S. cards were included in his intelligence programme, and reading words were introduced.

His nutrition programme and vitamin supplements remained unchanged.

At Joost's next visit, after a total of ten months of intensive stimulation, his parents reported that he had taken three steps independently; was cruising around furniture more; was developing more imaginative play; was more inquisitive; and had begun to develop a better idea of how to swim. His breathing and circulation were continuing to improve.

In Joost's new programme, few changes were made, as most of its elements were still needed. However, we did decide to introduce Cross Patterning, to reinforce his crawling, and to encourage more independent walking. Bi-manual activities were now to be emphasised, and he was to be exposed to two-step commands and simple time concepts. Toilet training was to be given a higher priority.

We continued to see him at regular four monthly intervals, and on each occasion noted both highly significant (or 'profile') changes and functional improvements. He began to attend a mainstream play-group. He learned to read; to understand complex sentences; to identify tiny objects by touch with either hand; to walk, run, hop, skip, jump, kick a ball, roller skate, swim and ride a bicycle independently; to speak in complete, spontaneous sentences; and to write.

Joost went on from play-group to mainstream school, and gradually integrated more and more into his school activities, progressing from half-days to full-time school in April, 1992. At weekends, and after school, his parents were able to offer him some extra stimulation through a 'back-up' programme which we designed especially for him.

In August, 1994, five-and-a-half years after first beginning our programme, Joost's parents proudly told us of the diplomas he had gained in both swimming and gymnastics.

In June, 1996, Joost's mother summarised the positive changes which had taken place.

'Joost is lucky not to have heart problems. His physical condition is good, and he has developed beyond everyone's expectations.

'Our church provided us with volunteers, so we never had problems finding enough helpers. The fact that a local doctor, having retired, made public the fact that he wished to become a volunteer, and has been a regular member of the team for the last six years, has given us very good PR.

'Joost has enjoyed his programme almost all the time, and we have seen constant improvement in concentration, self-confidence, walking, running, talking, reading, writing, spelling, cycling, swimming, to name only some of his gains. At 2 years old, Joost went to regular nursery school, and at four, went on to regular primary school. Next year he will be in group 5. In practically every subject, he is integrated with his peers. The only exception is Maths, where he gets a special programme. Every week he gets speech therapy.

'He has already obtained the A and B swimming certificates, and has now begun keyboard lessons.

'In December, 1989, Joost got a baby brother – Daan. They get along very well. Joost can read, something that Daan cannot yet do. Daan does not like this, but he knows he will learn to read at school next year. Although Daan is developing normally, Joost is still ahead of him in many areas. Daan is gaining on him, and may well overtake him, but we don't expect problems with this.'

She adds, 'Looking back, we consider ourselves to have been very lucky. Our family doctor and our paediatrician have always been very supportive, and have always provided us with the help we asked for. As a result of the programme, and the extra time and energy we have put into his education, we hope Joost will be able to get a good job in the future, and be able to live independently.'

There is no reason why he shouldn't. Joost has already achieved **50** positive changes on the Profile, and is still improving.

Down's Syndrome is a more well-known condition which can occur at conception. There are many others, and some can be frightening, as well as challenging.

GEERT-ELIAS

His mother writes, 'Directly after birth, Geert-Elias had severe breathing problems. Apart from being a very floppy baby, he had club feet, the fingers of his right hand were webbed, and the end section of his left index finger was missing.

'A medical team from the Wilhelmina Children's Hospital, which had come to our home in Ermelo to treat Geert-Elias' breathing problems by intubation, decided to take him by ambulance to Utrecht.

'This was the beginning of a search for a true diagnosis. After many medical examinations, and for us some very tense weeks, as our son sometimes stopped breathing, a diagnosis was finally reached. In view of his abnormal eye movements, lack of functioning vocal chords (which was causing the breathing difficulties) and an inability to produce or imitate sounds, and no ability to swallow, it was concluded that Geert-Elias had Moebius Syndrome. All these problems were caused by three non-congenital and 3 partly congenital brain nucleae.

'By the time this diagnosis had been reached, Geert-Elias was three months old, but unfortunately, no solutions were proposed. He was a child in need of 24 hours-a-day intensive care, and was therefore kept in the intensive care unit, but we kept on saying, *'Please, find a way for us to have him at home!'*

'This proposal required a major switch in the thinking of the medical staff, since in the first 4–5 weeks of Geert-Elias' life, they had seriously considered euthanasia – a proposition which we did not want at all!!

'When his condition improved, we were told that our son still needed 24 hours-a-day hospital nursing care, but as far as we were concerned, this too was no solution. Then the decision was made to give him a tracheostomy and a gastrostomy, and at the same time to correct both his feet. The artificial channels to his trachea and stomach, and the correction to his feet, were all done in one surgical session when he was six months old.

'Eight weeks later, he was ready to come home. At last!

'Then, everything really began for us. We had virtually our own hospital at home, with 24 hours-a-day intensive nursing, to care for the two artificial tubes, plus the two plaster-casted legs, and a severely disturbed sleep-wake rhythm.

'The hospital's advice? 'Give him a cosy corner in the room, and give him a lot of LOVE' (with capitals). According to the staff, no physiotherapy was needed. 'If he is capable of movement, he will move on his own.'

'After a long search high and low, and with the full support of our family doctor, we finally found a physiotherapist living nearby, who was willing to begin exercises with Geert-Elias. They both told us afterwards that at first they offered their help because WE wanted it, but after a while they became convinced that the exercises were beneficial to Geert-Elias. Unfortunately, this co-operation had to end, three years later, when our boy went to a rehabilitation centre.

'After three long years, during which we took turns to sleep four hours a night; during which we fought several ear infections and bronchitis; during which we gave him intensive physical treatment – all in the face of general opinion (other than our own, that of our family doctor and the physiotherapist) that Geert-Elias had no potential – we were forced for the sake of our own health to allow him to be admitted to a clinic as an in-patient.

'He went to a rehabilitation centre. After some time, it was decided that he was too mentally handicapped to benefit, and it was recommended that he should instead attend a centre for mentally handicapped children. Despite many discussions, and our protests, Geert-Elias was duly transferred to a centre for mentally handicapped children in 1985.

'At both these centres, we experienced a lot of frustrations in dealing with both physical and educational therapies; time and time again, we ran into the brick wall of bureaucratic red tape.

'At the end of 1985, one of our neighbours gave us a book about sensory-motor stimulation, which he knew about through his work. Some time later, this same neighbour gave us an article from the magazine *De Libelle*, about a Dutch family who were actually carrying out this type of therapy. After reading it, and reflecting on all the information which we had, we decided that this was what we wanted for Geert-Elias. This therapy was what he desperately needed.

'After the first approach to BIBIC, we had a personal meeting with its Director, Keith Pennock, in Nagele. This resulted in an appointment for us to attend an Initial Week with Geert-Elias in Bridgwater in September, 1986. To our relief, from the moment we arrived at Knowle Hall, we realised we were talking to people who did NOT look at the things Geert-Elias could NOT do, but rather who focused on all the things he COULD do.'

By this time, Geert-Elias was 5 years 8 months old, and should have been functioning at least at Level 7 on our Profile. But, when we did focus on Geert-Elias' abilities, this is what we found.

In Vision, he had no trouble seeing both outlines and detail. He could not converge both eyes together very well, and had a nystagmus in both eyes, but could nevertheless recognise a few pictures.

He could understand a good range of meaningful sounds, and single words, and was beginning to comprehend simple commands. However, he did not blink at all in response to a repeated sharp sound, and became very upset when he heard threatening sounds.

He could react appropriately to pain and to light touch, and could tell the length, breadth and depth of objects by feel. However, he was only just beginning to tell the difference between unlike objects, and his Babinski reflex, in both feet, was immature.

He had full use of his limbs, and could crawl on hands and knees, although he tended to use his head as a '5th limb', to help maintain balance. He could walk, and didn't need to use his arms to help him balance, but he had a curious gait, and preferred to tumble around the room. To get from one place to another, he chose to roll, or to somersault. During the early stages of his development, he had missed out creeping, and had no idea how to move forwards on his tummy.

His language skills were severely limited by his tracheostomy, but whilst he had no words of speech, he had evolved a series of blowing sounds which his parents could understand.

He could grasp and release objects with either hand, despite the abnormal shape of his right hand and having webbed fingers. The use of first finger and thumb to pick up small objects was still a very new skill, and he did not do this consistently.

Whilst his three sensory functions and his mobility were those of an 18 month old, his language skills were, as expected, only at a six months old level, and his manual dexterity were at the level of a 12 month old.

Because of the presence of the tracheostomy, and to avoid the very real possibility of infection, we decided first to concentrate on his crawling abilities. Unusually, therefore, we taught Geert-Elias' mother and father Cross Patterning, initially for 1 minute at a time, but gradually building this up to three minutes. Following each Cross Pattern session, Geert-Elias was to spend 5 minutes crawling on hands and knees with assistance. To give him a lot of spatial stimulation, we included suspended rotation, garden swing, balance beam, and stepping stones. To encourage more controlled walking, we suggested that he should climb up and down a ladder 5 times each day. To strengthen his grasp, we included one minute in each sequence of hanging from a D-ring. To develop his facial muscles, so long inactive because of the tracheostomy, he was to be given tactile stimulation to his face and mouth.

For obvious reasons, he could not be masked, or hung upside down, at this stage.

His Intelligence programme included C.V.S. pictures, Words, Simple Commands, Visual Tracking, and a lot of Manual and Bi-manual activities.

He was put on a wholefood diet, and Vitamin supplements were recommended.

One would have thought that this little boy had enough to contend with. Yet, within three months of his starting the programme, we heard that Geert-Elias had broken a leg! This injury, whilst not permanent, necessitated several changes in his programme, to avoid any weight-bearing on the fractured limb.

Five months after his initial visit, we saw him again, and despite the expected set-back of the fracture, Geert-Elias had begun to respond to all the extra stimulation we had recommended. He could now recognise a considerable number of pictures. He could understand and follow a good range of simple commands, and could now pick up objects simultaneously with both hands (though still using the second finger and thumb in his right hand). His parents told us that his awareness had improved, his sense of humour was beginning to develop, he was chewing and swallowing better, and that before the fracture, he had begun to crawl properly.

We made very few changes to his physical programme at this point, as he had not yet fully benefited from it. However, in his Intelligence programme, we introduced C.V.S. cards, with both pictures and words; increased the number of word cards he was to be shown; began his exposure to simple time concepts; and suggested that he be given a chance to hold a pencil, and learn how to draw lines, circles and crosses. Because he was having difficulty in swallowing tablets, his parents had found an excellent Dutch liquid multi-vitamin preparation.

Five months later, in July 1987, Geert-Elias showed us that for the first time, he could READ! He was beginning to follow two-step commands and more complex language; he could now zip, thread, and pour; and he had started to creep on his tummy. He was taking more interest in the world around him, his balance was better, his social behaviour was improving, and he was playing more with his brother.

It was time to do something about the tracheostomy, and in his next programme, we asked that his mother deliberately stop-up the tracheostomy tube for 1 minute, 40 times each day. Since he was beginning to creep of his own accord, 5 minutes of creeping was added to his sequence of activities, and this sequence, which would take in all over 1 hour to accomplish, was to be repeated 5 times each day. We also suggested that he be encouraged to walk up stairs, to horse-ride, to swim, and to ride a tricycle as often as possible.

As reassessment followed reassessment Geert-Elias continued to improve in all areas.

In 1988, he became able to recognise symbols and letters; to read sentences; to differentiate by touch both dissimilar and similar objects; to understand two-step commands and simple time concepts; and to run, jump, and kick a ball. The same year, his tracheostomy was finally removed.

In 1989, he began to say single words; to understand complex sentences; and became fully toilet trained.

In 1990, he finally mastered the skills of creeping in cross pattern on his tummy; crawling on his hands and knees; and identifying tiny objects by touch with either hand.

In 1991,Geert-Elias' mother and father reported that, amongst many significant changes, his concentration was much better; he could count to ten; his social behaviour was much improved; he was becoming far more independent; and that he was communicating better.

By the end of 1992, he was able to say a variety of single words consistently and appropriately, and was beginning to use couplets; he could now oppose the first finger and thumb of both hands simultaneously; and his tactility was almost at the level of his peers. He had also achieved full left hemispheric dominance, was beginning to understand musical rhythm, had started to develop road sense, and had begun to experiment with different facial expressions.

1993 was the year Geert-Elias became more extrovert. He was now less frightened of new situations; was becoming more skilled in self-care; was more confident in water, and his swimming skills were more evident. His understanding of time and other abstract concepts was becoming more mature.

A summary of our observations in 1994 reads: loves walking on rough terrain; better fine manual and bi-manual skills; better concentration; more independent; more adventurous; showing more logical thought; more willing to help in the house; pen and paper skills improving.

His parents summarised his progress like this. 'We had seven years of hard and intensive work. We coped very well, because we were very motivated by the results, and we knew this was our job, and no-one else's. By doing everything we were taught at BIBIC, we found we could so manage our lives as to have some time for ourselves as well (without feeling guilty!).

'Now, ten years later, Geert-Elias has become a boy who breathes normally, swallows normally, and eats normally (due to a wonderful speech therapist at the rehabilitation centre). So, no more tubes! He can run, rides his bike, likes to help with domestic chores like washing the dishes, doing the shopping, making tea or coffee, pouring drinks . . . there is so much to list!

'Although his speech is still not very clear, he is very capable of showing his emotions. He can cry, laugh, be angry, stubborn or self-willed, but of course that's how you are when you are 15 years old. He feels very happy in society, and in the world around him.

'In short, he now has a personality, and that personality is still developing. At the moment, he is very interested in computers. With the help of specially developed software for multi-handicapped people, Geert-Elias is already quite capable of using a mouse.

'Ten years later, we don't doubt for one second our decision to start the therapy. We are convinced that without it, Geert-Elias would not have become the person he now is – a very nice boy with a lot of humour, knowledge of the world around him, and the opportunity to develop even further.'

And let us not forget that 'in the first 4–5 weeks of Geert-Elias' life, euthanasia had been seriously considered'!

DANIELLE

Danielle was a first baby. Sometime during her pregnancy, her mother caught a viral infection, and Danielle sustained severe injuries to her brain. Her mother writes:

'Danielle's was a full-term, normal delivery, although in retrospect the second stage was long. We were ecstatic with our baby girl, and loved her instantly even though she looked very bruised and swollen, as she had passed through the birth canal with her hand up by her shoulder. She passed all her initial tests, and her microcephaly was not detected as her head size could have been normal for a smaller baby.

'I breast-fed her without too many problems initially, but after two weeks she started crying and screaming a lot, especially during and after feeds. I would spend hours feeding her and cuddling her until she settled down and fell asleep. We didn't go to the doctor at first, as we thought she was suffering from colic, plus a cold which in any case made feeding difficult. But, as the weeks multiplied, and all she did was feed, scream and sleep, we became more and more worried.

'At the seven week reunion with the other mothers I had met at the ante-natal classes, I was shocked at their responsive babies. *Their* babies were smiling, alert, stronger somehow and aware. By far the most noticeable difference between them and Danielle was that *they* looked you in the eye. I spent hours trying to get Danielle to look at me, but she never did. I had been disappointed that she never looked at me before going to the clinic, but after seeing all those other babies, I *knew* she should have done.

'I went to see my G.P. He assured me that nothing was wrong, that all babies get wind to some degree, and that all babies develop at different rates. He made me feel like a very young, neurotic, inexperienced, first-time mum and I was in no way reassured.

'We now had a baby nephew, and at six days old he was stronger, and more alert and responsive than Danielle, who was two months older. Although the rest of my family didn't entirely agree, I felt that something was dreadfully wrong, and that it wasn't just her eyesight that was at fault. I went to our Health Visitor, and she agreed that she wasn't happy either. I asked our G.P. for a hospital referral, and as he didn't share my anxiety, we were given a non-urgent referral, and had to wait six weeks before we could see a paediatrician.

'Once at the hospital, Danielle was immediately admitted for extensive tests. There was now a suspicion that she might have physical, and even metabolic problems, but no-one mentioned 'intelligence' or 'brain damage', and we didn't ask, although I am sure that is what we were all really thinking. The tests became a nightmare, and I could hear Danielle screaming from the next ward when she had her lumbar puncture.

'Two weeks later, we returned to the hospital to hear the results of the tests. We saw a lady locum consultant, who was obviously sympathetic, and who really didn't know how to tell us, straight out. She said that the brain scan and most of the tests were normal, and that the only test which had proved positive was the CMV, where a high level of Cytomegalovirus antibodies were present in Danielle's bloodstream. The diagnosis was strengthened by her microcephaly, and delayed development.

'We asked what this meant, and were told that Danielle would have 'problems'. My brain just wasn't functioning properly, and I could only sit, frozen, while my husband asked the questions.

'Will she go to normal school?'

'No.'

'Will she walk and talk?'

Very quietly, *'Probably not.'*

'Although I had suspected that we were not going to hear good news, and although we had spent four months thinking and talking about it, we still weren't prepared for the shock of definite confirmation. I remember looking at our beloved baby, sound asleep as we spoke, and it was as if she had suddenly been exchanged for another baby; all the future events that we had anticipated for her had evaporated.

'The next few weeks were awful. We were grieving for the baby that we thought we had had, and coming to terms with the handicapped child we actually had.

'We had to return to the hospital for another appointment four weeks later, and were sent home with no support or back-up at all. It would definitely have helped to have been able to speak to a family who had been through a similar experience themselves. I had no contact with or from my G.P. until several months later, when I attended the surgery for Danielle's final DTP injections. He said nothing until I was leaving, hand on door.

'Coping all right?'

'Very soon after we had heard the diagnosis, we had realised that Danielle was still our baby, and we knew we loved her very, very much. So, although we never doubted the diagnosis, it was not long before we were thinking 'What shall we do? How can we best help her?

'We had read about intensive stimulation programmes for parents to carry out, but when we went for our out-patients appointment at the hospital, our consultant was immediately dismissive of this idea.

'Too much strain on the family causes divorce, job losses and stress,' he told us. *'Although stimulation helps, just because you do something that produces a result, doing it a hundred times isn't going to give you a hundred times the result.'*

'We felt that he didn't understand the issue at all, and I have often wondered what he would have said, or done, if he himself had had a handicapped child. To have a child who doesn't progress and can't do anything for itself is in any case a strain on the family, and we just had to try and help Danielle in whatever way we could. What do you do to stimulate a child who can't *do* anything, and who doesn't even look at you?'

Danielle's parents heard about us from another family, and in December, 1985, they brought her to see us for the first time, when she was 10 months old.

We found that visually, Danielle had a very slow pupil reflex; whilst she had good outline perception, her appreciation of detail was poor, and whilst she could focus her eyes at near point, we doubted that she had any ability to see in three dimensions at any distance. She could not recognise any pictures.

She did not blink at all in response to a sudden sharp sound, and only reacted to a very limited range of meaningful sounds.

She was aware of being stroked on the face, the soles of her feet and her right arm, but showed no response to being lightly touched on her body or legs. She was aware of the third dimension, and could curl her fingers in hair, around her toes or a rattle if first prompted.

Danielle had a full range of movements in her individual limbs, good head control, could 'kick' with her legs, and could roll over from her back on to her front. She had no ability to move forwards on the floor.

She could produce a limited range of sounds, and some communicative cries which her mother could interpret.

She had begun to develop a prehensile grasp, and would occasionally take hold of some toys with either hand if the hand was first tapped. She could hold her toes quite tightly.

Taking account of her age, we taught her parents a sequence involving 31 minutes of activities which we asked them to carry out five times each day, seven days per week. We included basic vision; masking; visual pursuits; tactile stimulation; trunkal and homolateral patterning; creeping down a ramp; hanging from hands; swinging side-to-side and head-to-toe; and hanging from feet.

We recommended that Danielle should spend all her free time on her tummy on the floor. She was to be shown picture cards consisting of large, bright fluorescent pictures in two colours, on black card. Danielle was to be talked to as much as possible, and told exactly what was happening all the time. She was to hear regularly one or two simple commands – 'Touch your nose', 'Look at Dad', or 'Clap your hands' – which were to be within her physical capabilities to perform, and were always to be given using a consistent phraseology. Basic vision, each time lasting one minute, was to be carried out 55 times each day.

She was to be put on a wholefood diet with the introduction of extra protein in the form of fish, chicken and cheese. Her mother was advised to watch Danielle's weight carefully, and to have her weighed every month, to avoid her becoming overweight.

We saw Danielle for her first re-assessment in April, 1986. Her mother and father told us that she was more aware of her surroundings, and of people; she was beginning to follow simple commands; she could say 'mum', 'dad', 'dada' and 'daddy'; she was moving more on her tummy; her arms were stronger; she was beginning to weight-bear, and her legs were more solid. She was very good at tracking with her eyes, and seemed to be able to see things at a greater distance. She had begun to pass objects from hand to hand, was now reaching out for toys, and was starting to manipulate them.

Our own functional assessment confirmed that Danielle no longer had a fixed squint, was now able to see details within an outline, and could recognise a few pictures; she could understand some single words, and could follow a few simple commands; and she could grasp objects purposefully with either hand. Her dribbling was less pronounced, and she was beginning to develop a sense of humour.

At this first re-assessment, we made very few alterations to her programme, feeling that she was responding very well to the amount of extra stimulation she was receiving.

We saw Danielle and her parents one further time in that year, and were delighted at the improvements which were continuing to occur.

She could now recognise a much greater number of pictures, as well as some shapes; her understanding of meaningful sounds and single words was now at the level of her peer group, and she could respond to a variety of simple commands; she could distinguish between dissimilar objects purely by touch; she had learned how to creep along the floor on her tummy; she could produce a normal range of communicative sounds, and had a greater vocabulary of single words, which she used spontaneously and appropriately.

When drinking from a beaker, she could now hold it for herself, and was beginning to respond to toilet training.

In the months and years that followed, we continued to see Danielle regularly, and she went on from strength to strength.

In 1987, she learned to understand and follow two-step commands; her balance and co-ordination improved and she began to crawl on her hands and knees; she began to develop visual depth perception; she learned to chew and to finger-feed herself.

By the end of 1988, Danielle could walk unaided, even without shoes. She could negotiate steps and could walk without problems on uneven ground. She had developed a pincer grip in both hands and was starting to use both hands together to manipulate objects. She could now read several single words.

During 1989, she learned how to put pen to paper; she began to develop jumping and somersault skills; she began to use couplets, rather than just single words; and she was able to understand conversations not directed purely at herself.

At the end of 1990, Danielle's mother summarised the progress which her daughter had made:

'When we first decided to take Danielle to BIBIC, we knew we were in for a lot of hard work, but we both felt we could cope with it, and that following the programme would be the best thing we could do for Danielle. Even if we only did it for a few years just to start her off, so to speak, the work, however hard, had to be infinitely better than the terrible feelings of helplessness, despair and frustration which we had found impossible to live with.

'Now, after five years, we feel that Danielle is a real tribute to the BIBIC programme. Nearly everything she does has had to be taught to her, and even now she rarely learns anything new for herself. Before we started her programme, we would have to wait weeks for the smallest improvement to happen; once she began to follow her daily routine, there was a dramatic increase in her development. We now have a happy, healthy, friendly, well-behaved little girl whom we can take out with us, and can enjoy. She, in turn, benefits from a more able life-style. Language is still a problem, but her overall understanding is quite good, and in the last year she has gradually become a lot more vocal, which seems promising. We also feel that there is still more that can be achieved from the programme.

'My husband and I are very happy with the achievements she has gained, and very proud of what she can do.'

So are we! Danielle's Developmental Profile shows **twenty-eight** positive and significant changes which took place in that same five year period. They are a testimony to a family's love, care and hard work.

Update

In a recent note, Danielle's mother summarised her most recent achievements, now that she is twelve and-a-half.

'Danielle now has a 70 word vocabulary which she uses spontaneously and appropriately. Most of this comprises single words, but she does use some couplets on occasion.

'She can feed herself.

'She now walks better, faster, and with more co-ordination and confidence. She manages steps with more skill.

'She is happy and sociable, is more eager to communicate, and can make many of her needs known to us.

'She can swim independently, and has so far achieved 10 metres on her back.

'She has learned to pedal an exercise bike.'

JELLE

Jelle was born by Caesarian section. He was examined immediately after birth by a paediatrician, but no problems were discovered, and he developed normally, though rather slowly, until he was one year old. The only remarkable thing about his first year of life was that he was often ill, and feverish.

His mother writes: 'Suddenly, he couldn't sit any longer – a skill he had already developed. Our family doctor could not find an explanation, so he referred us to a paediatrician, who concluded that Jelle was suffering from *a delay in development*. He then underwent all kinds of tests and examinations so that a diagnosis could be determined, but to this day, none has been reached.

'The only factor which has been discovered is that the left hemisphere of Jelle's brain contains less 'windings', and has larger vacuoles than normal. However, according to the doctors, this could not be the cause of his psycho-motor lag in development. We were just over-anxious parents.

'By the age of two, Jelle still couldn't speak. At this stage it was acknowledged that he would probably not be able to make up for his delay in development. At two and-a-half, he went to a nursery school for two mornings each week; he was also receiving half-an-hour of physiotherapy, and half-an-hour of speech therapy a week.

'When he reached three-and-a-half, Jelle went to a school for children with speech and language problems. He left after nine months, because the standard was too high.

'The next year, he went to a special school, but, because we were sure that Jelle had more potential than was obvious at that time, we kept looking for better alternatives.

'Then we read an article in a Dutch women's magazine about a girl who had made a lot of progress through the BIBIC therapy. To get more information, we then went to a special meeting which was held to explain more about the therapy, and what was involved.

'We decided to try it with Jelle, and travelled to England in October, 1993, for an Initial Assessment week, when he was four years, seven months old.'

On the first day, a very careful assessment was made of Jelle's functional abilities.

We found that visually, Jelle had a good, strong and immediate pupil reflex in both eyes. He had good outline perception, his appreciation of detail was also good, but he could not fully converge his eyes. He could recognise and name a good range of pictures but had little comprehension of shapes, probably because he had never been shown them. He could not read any words.

He did not blink at all in response to a repeated sharp sound, but coped well with a threatening sound. His parents told us that he knew a large number of household sounds, and could understand not only single words, but also a number of single-step commands. Although he had begun to develop a sense of humour, and some reasoning ability, his understanding of two-step commands and simple time was very inconsistent.

He demonstrated a mature Babinski reflex in both feet; he reacted normally to pain and light touch; was aware of the third dimension; but could not consistently differentiate between dissimilar objects with either hand.

Jelle had a full range of movements in his individual limbs, and good head control. He could creep on his tummy, but not in consistent cross pattern, and his feet were up in the air. He could crawl on hands and knees in cross pattern, but again his feet were up in the air. He could walk, but with an unsteady gait, and rather stiffly. The nearest he could get to running was a fast, uncoordinated walk, with his arms flapping.

He had a wide range of communicative sounds and single words, but had problems in pronouncing certain sounds. The longest sentence he could manage would consist of no more than three words.

He had an adequate prehensile grasp, but had not yet fully developed the ability to oppose the first finger and thumb of either hand, individually or together. He could unzip and zip, unscrew the lid of a jar, but not button or unbutton. He could not hold a pencil, or write any words.

As Jelle's school had agreed to allow his family to combine schooling with therapy, he attended school two mornings each week, and did his programme at home the rest of the time, with the help of 40 volunteers. We taught his parents a sequence involving 31 minutes of activities. These were to be carried out four times a day on school days, and six times a day on non-school days. We recommended masking; tactile stimulation; homolateral patterning; creeping; brachiation; S.I.R.; crawling; stepping stones; balance beam; simple varied jumps and somersaults. Simple ball games and sprinting were also to be included, once or twice each day, outside the sequences.

Jelle was to be shown C.V.S. cards, reading word cards, and to carry out number work and learn simple time concepts. He was also to be given the opportunity to develop a pincer grip in either hand, and to develop more bi-manual skills.

He was to be put on a whole-food diet, with the introduction of extra protein in the form of fish, chicken and cheese.

We saw Jelle for his first re-assessment in March, 1994. His mother and father told us that his general level of understanding had improved; he had a better idea of time, and was beginning to talk in longer sentences. His balance was better. His hand/eye co-ordination had improved, and he could now put pen to paper, and draw circles and crosses. He was more self confident, could now ride a pony independently, and was almost independent in riding a bicycle.

Our own functional assessment confirmed that Jelle could now converge his eyes at both near- and far-point, and was beginning to recognise shapes. His reflexive response to loud noises had matured. He could now reliably detect dissimilar objects with either hand purely by touch, and was beginning to extend this skill to similar objects. He could now creep on his tummy, and crawl on his hands and knees proficiently. His walking was now in a good cross-pattern; he had started to run, and to jump and kick a ball. He was now regularly putting two words together. In line with all these improvements, we noted that Jelle's head circumference had increased by a half a centimetre – 357% of the normal head growth expected in a boy of his age over a five month period.

We felt that this was an excellent beginning!

At this first re-assessment, we made very few alterations to his pro-gramme, feeling that he was responding very well to the amount of extra stimuli he was receiving. We did, however, change Homolateral Patterning to Cross Patterning, introduce hopping, and target games, and increase the levels of challenge in several of the other activities. His Intelligence programme was extended to include Language De-velopment, multiplication tables, and letters of the alphabet, and we suggested to his parents that they read books to him regularly.

We saw Jelle and his parents one further time in that year, and were delighted at the improvements which were continuing to occur.

He had begun to read; he was now using four-word sentences; he could now differentiate between similar objects purely by touch; his understanding of time was better; his running was more co-ordinated; he could now ride his bicycle independently, and his horse riding had improved.

In the months that followed, we continued to see Jelle regularly, and he went on from strength to strength. He began to attend school for half of each day, to gain more experience of mixing with his peer group.

During 1995, he learned to understand and follow two-step com-mands; his speech and mobility improved further; he learned to interact better with other children; and his concentration and confidence in-creased. This same year, he was accepted for full-time school, and we adjusted his programme to accommodate this.

At the end of 1995, Jelle's mother summarised the progress which her son had made:

'When we started the therapy, Jelle could hardly speak, creep, crawl, run, jump, or cycle. He had no balance, depth perception, or concen-tration. After four months of therapy, he had made incredible progress. There were 11 improvements on his Profile. He learned how to crawl, his balance and speech improved, he learned how to run, and in that short period almost mastered the skill of riding a bike.

'Jelle coped very well with the programme, and even put up with patterning, which he did not enjoy. He enjoyed the work, partly because of the variety of the activities, and partly because he liked the many volunteers. The four monthly re-assessments were really essential, as each time they provided new techniques.

'Looking at Jelle now, we can see we are still far from the finishing line, but we have already accomplished a lot.'

KEITH

It is hard enough not being able do to what you want to do, and not knowing why. It must be far worse to watch someone else, who happens to be your twin brother, doing so many things that you would give your 'eye teeth' to do. A reversal of the old saying 'There, but for the grace of God, go I!'

Keith was such a twin. His mother says:

'My pregnancy was as normal as any twin pregnancy is – I had trouble with a threatened miscarriage and high blood pressure. Later scans showed Keith in the breech position, and his brother Andrew lying transverse just below my ribs.

'During my labour, Keith's heartbeat dropped to 54. The midwife was instructed to give me oxygen, and the emergency Caesarean section, which the obstetrical team had anticipated, was not carried out as the birth of my babies was too imminent.

'When I was told to push, it was discovered by the midwife that Keith was in fact in the breech position, and not lying head-first, as she had thought. A doctor was called to perform a forceps delivery, and Keith was born immediately, but did not cry. The paediatrician took him away for 15 minutes, saying that she would give him oxygen.

'Keith was returned to me just as a protesting Andrew was born, and both the paediatrician and the midwife told me that Keith was fine. I was suspicious, as no-one had bothered to tell me that *Andrew* was fine.

'Keith's eyes were continuously darting from side to side, and we commented that he appeared to be looking everywhere. No-one else said anything – did they know it was a nystagmus?

'We were sent home without comment from the medical staff. Keith was quiet – he cried quietly, startled easily and sucked poorly. We wondered, but there was nothing obvious until Andrew smiled at nine weeks – and Keith didn't.

'At three months, Andrew had blossomed into an alert, interested, interesting baby. We suddenly realised that Keith didn't appear to see or hear anything. His darting eyes certainly weren't taking in anything. We took him to the baby clinic, where our Health Visitor carried out a developmental test. He failed almost everything. She referred us to our GP, who conducted more tests and expressed his concern.

'Within two days, we had an appointment to see the paediatrician at our local hospital. He suspected (although we only found this out later) that as Keith's development was so poor, and as he had not been discovered to have problems at birth, he might have a degenerative brain disease. More tests followed in hospital, and fortunately, it was found that he did not have a degenerative brain disease. It was felt that Andrew's obvious lack of brain injury showed that Keith's injuries must have occurred during his birth, and not whilst in the womb.

'We saw the same consultant two weeks later, when all the test results were through. When I told him that Keith, now aged four and-a-half months, had smiled, he looked absolutely delighted, and said *'There's hope!'* I was left feeling that he must previously have decided that there was 'no hope'.

'The consultant was very helpful. He referred Keith to eye and ear specialists, and when I asked how we could best help his development, we were referred to an excellent paediatric physiotherapist, who saw him weekly until he was a year old.

'At eight months, Keith never bothered to swallow his food unless it ran to the back of his throat. I then met a speech therapist, who sorted out his feeding problems almost overnight.

'At ten months, my wonderful Health Visitor arranged for a community worker to come to our house five mornings each week to help me with Keith. At this stage, he was still sitting blankly, whenever he was not being worked with on a one-to-one basis.

'In September, 1986, when he was a year old, Keith's physiotherapist was changed, and the new one could only see him at home once every three weeks. This was called 're-organisation'.

'Keith was progressing, but had a dullness about him, and showed little interest in anything. We were always saying, 'Well, he **CAN** do that, but . . .' It was the frequency, and the definiteness that was lacking – we still had to initiate everything ourselves.

'We heard of the work of the Institute from my community helper's supervisor, who told me of two other families in the area whose children were responding well to the programme. I wrote to Knowle Hall, and following a preliminary interview, we attended an Initial Week in August, 1987.

'Until this point had been reached, I hadn't told any of the professionals of our plans. Generally speaking, they were all dedicated, but 'reorganisation' and maternity leave resulted in a lack of continuity. Everyone was very guarded about a prognosis – *'See how he goes'*.

'Once we started the programme, the physiotherapists dropped us like a stone. Other therapists continued to support us, especially when I explained to them that I wasn't criticising their individual abilities and skills, but was merely looking for MORE for Keith.'

And more was quite definitely what Keith's parents found. Much, much more.

At his Initial Evaluation, when he was twenty-three months old, we found that he had overcome his previous nystagmus, or eye-flicker, but had developed a convergent strabismus, or squint, where his eyes were turned in towards his nose. As a result, it was difficult for him to focus his eyes together at both near and far point, but this did not prevent him from being able to recognise an adequate number of pictures.

Whilst his startle reflex was normal, his response to loud, threatening sounds was delayed. He could understand single words, but was inconsistent in following simple commands, and often needed prompting or reminding.

His tactile awareness was that of a twelve-month-old child, and he had not yet learned to differentiate between even the most dissimilar of objects.

Keith could walk, but he was still using his arms to help him balance, had a poor gait and lacked good co-ordination. Not surprisingly, his ability to creep on his tummy was very poor and also lacked co-ordination.

He could use a number of single words, but his articulation was poor, and he was only at the earliest stage of putting two words together.

He had some trouble in opposing the index finger and thumb of his left hand, and showed little evidence of any bi-manual skills.

We designed for him a 40-minute sequence of activities. This sequence was to be accomplished five times each day, and seven days per week. It included masking; homolateral patterning; creeping on his tummy inside a 'creeping tunnel'; visual pursuits; hanging by his hands from a suspended D-ring; upside down; oral stimulation; suspended rotation; garden swing; crawling on hands and knees, including crawling downstairs; rolls; ball games; and bouncing on a trampette.

In addition, but outside the sequence, we recommended that he should spend a total of 10 minutes a day learning to ride a tricycle; should begin learning to swim; should experience a full Intelligence programme including learning to read; bi-manual activities; our language development programme; and toilet training. We also suggested a wholefood diet, together with vitamin supplementation.

We saw Keith and his parents again four months later.

We recorded **eight** specific improvements on his Developmental Profile. He was now able to respond normally to threatening sounds, and could understand and follow an adequate number of simple commands. He was beginning to differentiate between unlike objects with his left hand; he could now creep on his tummy in a good cross pattern of movement, and walked with his arms no longer required for balance. He was now speaking in short sentences. He had developed a proficient pincer grip in his left hand, could zip, unzip and unscrew the lid of a jar, and was using both hands together much more in play.

We also noted that his squint had reduced; he had better side-to-side control of his eyes; he had learned sufficient breath control to be able to blow; he was beginning to run and jump; and his awareness of his surroundings and of other people was much greater.

His parents thought that he had made a very good start, and we agreed with them!

We made several alterations to his programme. Homolateral patterning was discontinued, and Cross Patterning took its place. The creep tunnel was no longer required. Further spatial and co-ordination activities were introduced, including a balance beam and stepping stones, and sprinting was added.

C.V.S. cards were incorporated into Keith's Intelligence programme, as were 'commands and choices'. We also suggested that he begin to attend a mainstream playgroup at the beginning of the next school year.

Four months later, we counted another 5 Profile changes.

Keith was now beginning to recognise numbers, and to read words; he could understand two-step commands; his right hand had caught up with the left, and he could now differentiate between unlike objects with either hand; he had a larger vocabulary of spoken words, and readily used couplets.

His concentration was noticeably better. His running was becoming more co-ordinated. His manual and bi-manual control had improved, and his parents reported that he was becoming more sociable, especially with adults.

Two and-a-half years later, Keith, at the age of 5 years 3 months, had achieved full-time mainstream school.

Although his squint had still not fully cleared, he could read at his class level (he could read a variety of single words when he was four and-a-half!)

He still had some problems with concentration and memory, especially in relation to long-range time, but he could understand vocabulary and abstract concepts at his peer level.

He could differentiate between a number of tiny objects purely by touch, and could tell the difference in feel between a 5p, 10p, and £1 coin. Tactilely, he was ahead of his peers.

He tended to run with his arms flexed, and he was rather heavy footed. He could hop, skip, jump, and kick a ball, but was still a little ungainly.

He could speak in complete sentences, with the vocabulary of a six-year-old. His diction and articulation were at times inconsistent, and he had some problems with the 'r' and 'th' sounds.

He had no problems at all with any bi-manual activities. He could write his own name spontaneously, was beginning to copy letters, and could hold a pencil with confidence.

After school each day, and also at weekends, he spent two hours completing a mini-programme of activities designed to eliminate his residual problems, and to reinforce and further improve his hard-won skills.

Keith has come a long way. The final goal is in sight. But, best of all, he can now look his twin in the eye.

Update
In May, 1997, Keith's mother responded to my request to bring Keith's story up-to-date.

'Keith's routine of full time schooling, reinforced by some programming, continued for the first two years that he was in mainstream primary school. In August, 1992, however, we all decided that it was time for Keith to stop any formal program, and to completely integrate with his peers. It was recommended that he should be encouraged to continue with daily running, bike riding, trampolining, swimming, gym classes, and bat and ball games, none of which might set him apart from his friends.

'Five years have passed, and Keith is now 12 years old. The trampoline is still in the garden and is used regularly. Keith swims twice a week at the swimming club, and although not as fast as his twin, Andrew, he is an excellent breast-stroker, and was a finalist in the district schools' swimming gala this year. He also swam a continuous 5000 metres in March in the BT Swimathon, an achievement for any child! He takes part in fun runs and duathlons to give him an incentive to keep up with his running. He has outgrown the gym classes, but now goes to a diving class (gymnastics in the water). He plays both the violin and the keyboard, and has reached Grade 1 standard in both.

'After seven years in a very supportive primary school, Keith transferred in September, 1997 to a mainstream secondary school, and he loves it! His reading age is at his peer level, and his general knowledge is excellent. However, he still has problems with his eyesight, and is starting to need text books and reading books enlarged. He also finds writing a labour, so only records a little of the knowledge he has.

'The future can never be guaranteed, but with support, he is coping and is happy, and is still in a strong position to achieve our ultimate aim – independence as an adult.'

So far, we have looked at six children. Three became brain injured at conception; two before birth; and one during birth. The number of possible causes of brain injury which can occur post-natally are almost infinite, so let just two examples speak for them all.

MICHELLE

This little girl was born three weeks prematurely, and by Caesarean section, on Boxing Day, 1985. Happily, there were no complications, and mother and baby were allowed home from the hospital a week later. Michelle thrived, had a good appetite, and enjoyed the extra attention given to her by her four-year-old brother and three-year-old sister.

By her fifth month, she was sitting up, and very active in her baby walker; at nine months, she could walk if someone held one of her hands. She could respond to facial expressions, could understand several words, and was beginning to follow simple commands. She was interested in toys, could pick up tiny things with thumb and finger, and was using both hands to play with things. She had a considerable range of sounds, and words were just beginning.

Then, at ten months, she caught an ear infection. Three weeks later, she contracted meningitis.

Her mother continues, 'Michelle was not expected to pull through, but she is a fighter, and after twenty-four days in hospital, she was allowed home. At this stage she no longer reacted to light, was having petit mal attacks, and was spastic down her right side. We were told that it would take her a long time to recover.

'We knew another family whose baby had left hospital without sight after meningitis, but had regained vision after about six weeks, so we were hopeful that Michelle would do the same. Then, she began to have more fits, and was sent to a neurologist, who diagnosed fluid on the brain. In January, 1987, a shunt was inserted to control the fluid pressure.

'At regular intervals, she was seen at the hospital, but no-one told us why she was not making any recovery, or what was really the matter. She was seen by an eye specialist, who said he couldn't help.

'Then, after six months, Michelle began to sit up on her own once again, and the spasticity down her right side eased. But from then on, her progress was very slow. I felt I could do more for her, but was at a loss as to *what* to do.

'By this time, I had reached the conclusion that Michelle was brain injured. I asked her physiotherapist about it, and she said, *'Michelle's 'computer' (meaning her brain) was damaged.'*

'We heard about BIBIC from my sister, who had a friend who was helping another child. We wrote to ask if Michelle could be helped.

'We saw our paediatrician, and asked him if Michelle was brain injured. After some hesitation, he finally admitted that she was. He also pointed out that only time would tell to what extent she was hurt, as she was still only eighteen months old.'

In February, 1988, Michelle and her parents came to us for their Initial Week.

We found that Michelle's vision was very poor. Her pupil reflex was delayed; her response to light, and her ability to track were not consistent; and she could not be relied on to respond to facial expressions.

She had a continuous startle reflex; she overreacted to sudden loud noise; and was only aware of a limited number of simple, meaningful sounds. She did not always respond to her name, and showed understanding of only two or three simple commands.

Her tactile sensation was that of a normal twelve-month-old, but she had no ability to select objects by touch.

She had a full range of movement in her limbs, and could roll from front to back and back to front, but had no forward movement.

She could make a few non-communicative sounds.

She could pick up objects with a whole-hand grasp, but the pincer grip was not fully developed. She was still susceptible to fits.

Michelle's initial programme was heavily weighted with techniques to encourage better vision, spatial awareness, mobility, breathing and hand function. Her sequence involved 33 minutes of intensive stimulation which would probably take 45 minutes to complete, and was to be carried out seven times each day, and seven days per week. In each sequence, we asked for five one-minute sessions of basic vision, and, outside the sequences, a further twenty-five, making a total of sixty each day.

Her Intelligence programme included additional visual stimulation, single step commands, a lot of being talked to, and opportunities to use both hands together. We also recommended a wholefood diet, and vitamin supplementation.

At her first re-assessment, six months later, Michelle's Profile had improved in six levels of function. Her vision had markedly improved. Her reflexive response to light was now normal; she instantly reached out for any object offered to her; she responded without hesitation to facial expressions, followed moving objects unerringly with her eyes, and looked with interest at fluorescent pictures.

She could recognise and respond to a wide range of meaningful sounds, single words and simple commands.

She was now able to creep along the floor on her tummy, with some assistance; could say the names of her brother and sister; and was beginning to help in dressing herself. Physically, she was stronger and healthier.

In the next twelve months, Michelle achieved another eight significant improvements on her Profile; the following year, a further nine.

By the time she was five years old she could focus her eyes together to some degree, although her left eye tended to turn outwards. This did not stop her from being able to recognise some shapes, and she could read a few single words.

She could follow many two-step commands, and could understand conversation even when she was not included in it.

She could select different objects with either hand purely by touch, although she was better with her left than her right.

She could creep along the floor on her tummy, although she did not use her right leg. She could balance on all fours, and had learned to crawl on her hands and knees, both on the floor and up stairs. She now liked to climb on to furniture, and would walk, rather stiff-legged, if someone held her hands.

She could say lots of single words.

Her pincer grip in either hand was proficient. She could use both hands to unscrew the lid of a jar and to pull beads apart. She was now beginning to learn how to manipulate a zip fastener.

Socially, she was happier, more co-operative, more alert, more assertive, and was more aware of danger. She had a sense of humour, was inquisitive, and liked to join in.

She had had no fits at all in the previous four months.

Her mother concluded, 'Michelle has responded well to the programme. Initially, we decided to do it for two years, although we hoped Michelle might not need it for that long. We were very optimistic.

'We are now beginning our third year, and Michelle is five. We will continue until she can walk independently, and can talk in sentences.

'Our Local Education Authority are anxious for us to send Michelle to school, but we feel that she is benefiting more from her programme than she would in school. How could she possibly get the same amount of stimulation and one-to-one attention in a class of children, especially handicapped children?'

Update
Michelle is now 11 years 8 months old. She is big for her age, and is already beginning to physically mature. Her mother recently wrote:

'Without our time on the programme, I dread to think what Michelle's life, and ours, would have been. Now, we tend to take everything for granted, and it is only when we look back that we can see how far she has come.

'She can now walk, jump, stand on tiptoes, and can run after a fashion, although she is very heavy footed. She can bounce and catch a ball.

'She has developed an excellent memory for songs and poems; has a sense of humour; knows right from wrong; and is for ever asking questions.

'She can pick out details in pictures, and can now spell simple words like cat, bed and dad. She will correct herself when she knows she has made a mistake, learns new things at a faster rate and in fewer attempts, and loves music.

'She can feed herself...... and she loves food!

'She is now toilet-trained during the day

'She can go unaided in a familiar environment, and will tell you, when asked, her name, address, telephone number and postcode

'Michelle has been attending school for four years. She became obstinate with her programme, and grew very heavy. This, coupled with the fact that we lost a lot of helpers, led us to think that school, and the company of other children (she loves company) would be beneficial to her.

'At her school, which is very up-to-date, she has horse-riding, rebound therapy, swimming, and the use of the light room.

'In September, she will be moving on to Abbey Hill, which has been featured in the press.

'Michelle is turning into a very happy young lady.'

ASTRID

It is always a shock to discover that you have a brain injured child. This is particularly true when a much-loved and beautiful daughter has developed into her teens, and then tragedy strikes. For Astrid and her family, just such a catastrophe called on reserves of the human spirit which most of us never have to tap.

Let her mother begin the story.

'Astrid was, and is, a daughter to be very proud of. For 14 years, we enjoyed our vivacious and healthy daughter. As a little girl, she was always happy, and as a teenager, she was someone who wanted to accomplish a lot. She was a bright student, and a good athlete, particularly in gymnastics, until a day in January, 1985, when she fell whilst performing on the rings. The safety mats had not been positioned correctly, and she struck her head on the floor.

'At first, it was thought that she had received a severe concussion to the brain, but unfortunately there were complications, and she needed emergency neurosurgery. Without that operation, she would not have survived.

'The operation lasted six hours, and her condition was critical. For the next three days, she was heavily sedated, but when the sedation was discontinued, Astrid did not wake up, and we were told that she was in a coma.

'Coma! Whatever were we to do?

' 'Just wait,', the doctors told us. 'Wait until she comes out of it.'

'After Astrid had been in coma for four weeks, one of her aunts showed us an article from the magazine *Libelle*, about a child from Nagele whose parents had been carrying out with him a daily stimulation programme. The article gave details of the therapy, which had also been used to wake people up from coma. We telephoned a contact number in Nagele, and were told that it was certainly possible for us to start this therapy with Astrid.

'Fortunately, Mr Keith Pennock, the founder of the British Institute for Brain Injured Children, whose therapy it was, came to Nagele shortly afterwards, and we were invited to meet him. He explained what was involved, gave us an initial programme to carry out, and told us it was most important to start stimulating Astrid as soon as possible.

'After Astrid had been in coma for 7 weeks, she was transferred to a nursing home. This gave us the chance to begin carrying out the therapy with her, and we recruited 25 volunteers to help us. We were with Astrid almost every day and night.

'Four months passed before she finally began to respond. She began reacting to her favourite band – BZN – and to the people around her. The response became stronger and stronger. We had succeeded!

The arousal therapy had worked! Astrid was no longer in coma!

'Now the time had come to call BIBIC in England. They too were overjoyed to hear the wonderful news.

'Keith Pennock came over to Holland with his staff to see children, and he visited Astrid in the nursing home. He examined her, and designed a special programme for us, so that we could continue to stimulate her. She stayed in the nursing home for two more months, and all that time we stimulated her, every day.

'In October, 1985, Astrid came home! What a celebration that was!

'More volunteers had offered to help us with her therapy, and Astrid made a lot of progress.

'One year after the accident, we took her to BIBIC for the first time. The staff at the Institute were very happy to see how much progress Astrid had made.'

We certainly were! At her Initial Assessment, and considering the injuries she had received, it was not surprising that she had a lot of problems. What was surprising was how many of her previous skills Astrid had regained! She had made remarkable progress in the five months since I had seen her in the nursing home.

Apart from being unable to focus at near point closer than 6', her vision had almost fully recovered. She could read, slowly but accurately in Dutch. She could also read several sentences in English, and insert missing words in the text.

With the exception of a now immature startle reflex, her hearing and understanding was almost back to normal. Her comprehension of time was good. We felt that she was below her peer group in general knowledge, but her family were convinced that she understood everything that was going on around her.

In Tactility, we could begin to see the effects of the accident. Her Babinski reflex was now immature in both feet. Whilst with her left hand she could tell the difference between dissimilar objects, she was much less skilful with her right hand, and had no ability beyond this level. She was, in reality, at the tactile level of an eighteen-month-old child.

It was in her Motor function that Astrid showed the greatest difficulty. In Mobility, she did not have a full range of movement in her limbs; her right arm and hand, and her left leg were stiff, and difficult for her to move. She could not creep, crawl, or even roll over.

Her Language was restricted to making a sound when she was in pain, and even this was muted.

Her Manual Competence was poor. She had very little ability to grasp with her right hand, and could only with great effort pick up an object with finger and thumb with her left hand. Surprisingly, she could hold a pen, and could laboriously write one or two recognisable words, but was now left-handed, whereas before the accident, she was strongly right-handed.

Astrid's new programme included Masking; Trunkal Patterning, Homolateral Patterning, Assisted Creeping, Sitting with D-ring, Suspended Rotation, Garden Swing, Rolls, and a lot of Tactile, Facial and Oral stimulation. She was to spend all day and all night prone on the floor when not carrying out her programme, eating, or being bathed or toileted. We recommended swimming once a week, and a considerable amount of bi-lateral foot manipulation, to avoid any risk of contractures.

Her Intelligence programme included reading words in Dutch, English, French and German; C.V.S. cards in all four languages to strengthen her general knowledge; writing; bi-manual activities; language development; and social outings with one friend at a time, to avoid tiring her.

Vitamin C was added to her already good nutrition programme, and we cautioned the family not to allow any weight gain which might further restrict her mobility. A gradual anti-convulsant reduction programme was also recommended.

Five months later, when we next saw her, Astrid had continued her astonishing progress.

She had gained five profile changes, in Tactility, Language, and Manual Competence. With her right hand, she could now differentiate between dissimilar objects without difficulty. With her left hand, she was almost as good as before the trauma. Similar and tiny objects, and complex tactile tasks were no longer a problem for her. She was beginning to make recognisable communicative sounds, and she had started to use both hands together, to zip and to screw up jar lids. Interestingly, she had switched back to her right hand when writing.

Her mother and father told us that she was more aware and alert; she could now stand and walk with support; she could roll over with little help; her focus had improved; no facial paralysis was now evident; her balance, co-ordination and circulation were all better. She had gained 3.8 centimetres in chest circumference – a 1900% increase compared to normal growth expectancy for her age

In view of all these splendid improvements, we made several changes to her programme, and added Cross Patterning – which may at first have confused her helpers, but certainly did not confuse Astrid's brain! Assisted crawling, using a supportive pommel, standing in a corner, and walking along an overhead ladder, were also added. Her intelligence and nutrition programmes, however, remained largely unchanged.

Her regular reassessments began to follow a pattern.

15.10.86	3 Profile Changes	7 Functional Changes	Verdict – Excellent Progress
04.03.87	4Profile Changes	6 Functional Changes	Verdict– Excellent Progress
13.07.87	3 Profile Changes	5 Functional Changes	Verdict– Good Progress
08.06.88	3 Profile Changes	4 Functional Changes	Verdict– Excellent Progress

By June of 1988, twenty-nine months after her first visit to the Institute, and forty-one months since the day of her accident, Astrid was able to read newspapers, and books of a fourteen-year-old level, and her convergence was down to 3 inches. Whilst her reaction time was still slowed, and her mathematical ability was not yet fully restored, she had regained a full understanding of everything said to her. Her Tactile ability was consistent with her age level. She had regained full independent movement in her limbs; had relearned to creep, crawl, and walk, and could navigate stairs with help. She had a vocabulary of eight words, used spontaneously and meaningfully, and was beginning to use couplets. Using both hands together, she could zip, button and lace; using her original hand (right), she could write sentences spontaneously, although not yet at her age level.

Her mother takes up the story again.

'After four-and-a-half years of daily therapy, we decided to send Astrid to a rehabilitation school in Arnhem. She went there until she was 20 years old, and then came home to live with us. Three days a week she now attends an activity centre for disabled people; the rest of the time she spends with us. We often visit a fitness centre, and we walk and cycle a lot. We keep stimulating her so that she will develop further. Through BIBIC, we have learned how to deal with Astrid's disabilities, knowing that stimulation is essential.

For us, as parents, this therapy has been very important. The doctors had told us that there was nothing we could do but wait, whereas BIBIC provided us with the opportunity to actively help our daughter. Generally, in such situations, parents just visit their children in day-care centres, and worry all the time about what to do to help. We were fortunate in being able to fully participate in, and carry out, a daily treatment programme. That was so important to us. Instead of waiting passively, we knew what we had to do. And, by doing it, we found a way to help overcome the grief. Thank you for everything you taught us.'

This was supposed to be the end of Astrid's story; the story of a brave girl, and a brave family, who performed wonders in giving her back a lot, if not all, of her former life.

On October 27th, 1996, Astrid died. She spent that night in a special care unit, one which she often went to, just to spend the night. She normally sensed when a fit was coming, but this time she didn't ring the nurse for help. Since she always slept on her tummy, it is thought that she must have suffered a major fit, fallen with her face in her pillow, and asphyxiated.

For such a thing to happen, after all her own efforts, and those of her family, and the many friends and neighbours who came to help, is inexplicable. But one thing is clear. Astrid came 'back from the dead' to spend eleven extra, happy years with those she loved, who loved her and who showed yet again the power which love can summon when facing even the most impossible situation.

Thank you for all the lessons you taught **me**, Astrid. We will miss you, and never forget you. Rest in Peace.

CHAPTER 47
On Being Professionals

There is a feeling of pride in being a 'professional'. It involves doing a worthwhile job; doing it well; and knowing that other people respect you for what you do.

The word 'professional' also implies efficiency, precision and competence, and it is all too easy to fall into the trap of feeling 'superior', and even beginning to patronise those who know less than you do.

Many of the families who find their way to us have already met other professionals. Some will have been sympathetic; some will have been anxious to impress with their own knowledge. All will, in one way or another, have thought of themselves as trying to help.

Each one will have expected their advice to be trusted, and followed.

Yet what happens if that advice does not produce results? No professional, however experienced, is *infallible*.

It is the mark of a true professional that the finding of a solution to a problem is more important than the name of the person who found it. No-one has all the answers, and this is just as true of brain injury as of any other problem.

At Brain-Net, we are presented with fresh problems every day. Some we have met, and overcome before. Others are outside our previous experience. Yet others are outside *everyone's experience*.

There are three important considerations which we constantly try to remember.

1. However difficult the problem, we are always prepared to try and solve it.
2. If we cannot solve it, we must be honest enough to admit it.
3. If *anyone else* may be able to succeed, even though *we* have failed, we must have enough humility to accept this, and to learn from *them*.

These principles are hard to live up to, and sometimes also hard to live with. Yet if we ignore them, we run the risk of convincing ourselves that only we are right and everyone else is wrong – a 'black and white' philosophy in a world which is made up of many shades of grey.

APPENDIX 1
Advice to Families

ESPECIALLY FOR FAMILIES

If you are the mother, father, brother, sister, granny, granddad, auntie or uncle of a brain injured child, and you have read this far, you may want the answers to several other, very specific questions. Let me try and answer them, if I have guessed right.

How Do Families First Hear About The Alison Centre?

I suppose one easy answer is – by reading this book! Another good source of information is from other families who are already following our programme. Helpers also tend to pass on the message, in their enthusiasm about the child whom they go to help every week, and the progress he is making.

Our work is occasionally featured on TV, and is often described in local and national newspaper and magazine articles, and advertisements.

A growing number of G.Ps, Health Visitors, Social Workers and other professionals tell families about us, and several of our children have been referred to us by their family doctors.

Must Our Child Be Referred To You by Our G.P.?

No, you do not need an initial medical referral. Our own Medical Officer will in any event contact your family doctor once you have decided to embark on our programme with your child.

What Is The Best Way For Us To Get In Touch With the Alison Centre?

Write to us. Tell us as much as you can about your child's difficulties, and if you think you know what may have caused the problem in the first place, tell us that too.

What Will Happen after We Write To You?

We will reply, inviting both parents and the child to visit us for an initial discussion.

At this early stage, there will be no examinations or tests. But, we will be able to discuss with you all the factors involved in carrying out our Programme. We can also arrange for you to visit other parents who are already following our recommendations with their child. You will have the opportunity to observe what they are doing, and talk to them, without any commitment.

Once you have decided whether or not to embark on our Programme, we would be pleased if you will let us know, so that we can react appropriately. If your decision is positive, we will offer you the first available date to come, with your child, for an Initial Assessment week.

What Happens During the Initial Assessment Week?

We will have five days to turn you into professional therapists for your child.

Our staff will be looking forward to meeting you, and want your time at our Centre to be both instructive and enjoyable. We know that to talk of 'enjoyment' when we are dealing with problems as large as brain injury sounds strange, but we think you will find it enjoyable, once you have settled down. It's that sort of week.

MONDAY – THE FIRST DAY

Today, you will be with your child all the time. You will see no-one wearing white coats, in case these might make your child uneasy. Nothing painful or unpleasant will happen, and you can relax.

This first day is all about 'finding out'. You will meet all our staff, and each will want to ask you a great many questions. Your child will be physically measured, and will have a full-scale medical examination. He will also be given a series of functional tests, to establish his levels of ability in Vision, Hearing, Sense of Touch, Mobility, Speech, and Manual Competence. You will meet other families who are, like you, at the Centre for their initial visit. Make friends with them. They will be feeling strange and new, just as you will, and the sooner you all settle down and make yourselves at home, the sooner you will begin to learn.

TUESDAY – THE SECOND DAY

Today, all the parents attend a series of lectures designed to explain our philosophy, and the reasons behind many of the techniques we use. For families who are not fluent in English, translation facilities are available.

The information contained in the lectures is very important for you to understand, and we are anxious that you should have every opportunity to concentrate. While you are listening to the lecturers therefore, your child will be looked after by our staff. They will not only play with him, or nurse him; they will also be able to find out what he is like when you are not there

– sometimes a very important factor we must consider in designing your individual home programme.

WEDNESDAY – THE THIRD DAY

The morning will be taken up with further lectures and explanations, and our staff will again care for your child. By now, they and he should be old friends, and his morning will pass quite quickly.

When the lectures end, you and your child will be reunited, and from then on, not only for the rest of this week, but also on all future visits to the Alison Centre, you will always be together.

During the afternoon, you will be taught some of the techniques which will form part of your programme, and will have an opportunity to begin to practise them yourselves.

THURSDAY – THE FOURTH DAY

During the day, you will be taught more parts of your programme, and will have further time for practice. We all want you to develop confidence, and would rather you made your mistakes whilst with us, than after you have returned home!

FRIDAY – THE FIFTH AND FINAL DAY

This will be the final day of your Initial Week, when all the remaining parts of your programme will be taught to you.

During the day, you will also have an opportunity to discuss with us any financial matters; to obtain any small items of equipment which you may need; to seek our advice about how to find voluntary helpers, and to resolve any queries you may have in constructing larger pieces of equipment.

We will also talk to you about the various government allowances available to you if you live in the U.K.

We hope that you will not leave until all your questions have been answered, and you have thoroughly understood everything. If you are not sure of anything, please ask. You have had a great deal to learn, and no-one minds any family asking questions. There is no such thing as a silly question at the Alison Centre.

How Soon Are We Expected To Begin Our Programme?

Once you return home, you will need to spend some time organising your helpers, and getting together any equipment you may need. Some activities which do not require help or equipment can, of course, be commenced as soon as you have recovered from your journey, but any attempt to try and carry out a full programme immediately would be foolish, and might well 'blow fuses'.

Build up the number of sequences you carry out over several days, and once you are achieving everything we have recommended, please let us know.

What Happens Then?

Once we know that your child is regularly receiving the extra stimulation we have advised, we will make arrangements for you to be visited at home, if you live in England, Scotland or Wales, by one of our staff whom you will already have met during your Initial week. She will call to help sort out any problems which may have arisen, and to make sure that both you and your helpers are not experiencing any difficulties with any of the techniques we have taught you. We will also arrange your first reassessment appointment at the Centre, which will be timed to allow your child to experience at least three months of full programme before we assess its effects.

What Happens At Our Reassessment?

Unlike your five-day initial visit, your reassessment appointment will be for two days. On the first day, we will repeat all the measurements and tests which were carried out on the first occasion you came to the Alison Centre, and will ask you a great many questions concerned with your child's initial programme, and your observations in regard to its effect.

On the second day, we will discuss with you the results of our examinations, and where we feel any progress may have been achieved, we will tell you. It may be necessary for us to make alterations to your daily programme, to take advantage of any changes which may have occurred in your child, and we will spend the rest of the day teaching you any new techniques which we may feel to be appropriate.

Regular reassessments of your child will thereafter be arranged at 4 monthly intervals, so that your programme can be regularly updated, and so that you can keep a frequent check on your child's progress.

Do We Have Any Other Contact with the Centre?

You can telephone or write to us whenever you need advice. We hope you will also contact us if, and when, something nice happens, and your child develops a new skill!

Extracts from the BIBIC/Surrey University Control Study

Extracts from 'Development of Brain Injured Children' by J.W.T Dickerson, Paula A. Tingle, Penny Barrington and J.K.Pennock, published in The Journal of the Royal Society of Health. August, 1987.

'. . . In the ten years since 1972, a considerable degree of improvement in many of its patients was recorded by the (British) Institute. However, although these results were easily verifiable by individual examination, no in-depth study had been attempted, and the Institute's philosophy and treatment methods were viewed with caution or suspicion by those holding more conventional attitudes. In 1981, it was decided to carry out an independent and objective assessment of the Institute's methods and results . . . This paper contains a description of the protocols followed and the changes which occurred in the 36 children studied in the period between January 1982 and January 1983.'

'. . . The 36 children included in this study had differing developmental needs. However, the changes in their developmental profiles during the study period showed that they achieved an average of 23% of the total score needed to bring their performance up to that of their normal peers. Because of the different conditions of the children the components of this achievement differed. A true assessment of the changes can only be appreciated against the background of their presenting disabilities. Thus, three children who could not see were able to see detail. Of those children who could not read, seven were able to read at the end of the study and by May 1986 the number able to read had risen to 13. Two children who were deaf were hearing sounds and understanding words. Two children who could not walk due to spasticity of their limbs were able to run. By May 1986 the number of children who were talking or writing had risen to four for each change. The significance of changes such as these to the children and to their parents should not be underestimated. The close involvement of the parents with their children's treatment and the results obtained probably leads to strengthening of the parent-child bond and an increase in the child's independence. The total of the changes can only be interpreted as an increase in the quality of the life of the children.'

Centres Associated with Brain-Net

Australia
The Australian Institute for the
Achievement of Human Potential,
P. O. Box 248, Mount Eliza,
Victoria. 3930, Australia
Tel: +61–3–97871246
e-mail: newfolk@satlink.com.au

Holland
Brain-Train,
Sikkelstraat 28,
4904AB Oosterhout, Netherlands
Tel: +31–162–455882
e-mail: advdlely@westbrabant.net

Ireland
The European Centre for Brain
   Injuries,
18, Old Kilmainham,
Dublin. 8, Ireland
Tel/Fax: +353–1–6602886
e-mail: nodaunts@yahoo.com

Italy
Antonio DiMeglio,
Via C. Angiolieri 26,
Siena. 53–100, Italy
Tel: +39–0577–287956
e-mail:
dimeglio@campo.comune.siena.it

Malta
The Institute for Brain Injured
   Children,
Villa Indiana, Anglu Gatt Street,
Mosta, Malta
Tel: +356–432843, Fax: +356–420382
email: ibic@camline.net.mt

Poland
'Daj Szanse',
ul. Piskorskiej 11,
87–100 Torun, Poland
Tel/Fax: +48–566–482363

United Kingdom
The Brain-Net Family Unit,
The Alison Centre
8, Cypress Drive,
Puriton, Bridgwater,
Somerset, United Kingdom
Tel/Fax: +44–(0)1278–683588
e-mail:
Keith.Pennock@btinternet.com

U.S.A.
Carolyn Ward,
4306, Chas. Jeff. Road, Jeffersonville,
Indiana. IN47130
Tel: 001–812–293–4480
e-mail: ctward@otherwise.com

Copies of this book are also available from:
The Brain-Net Family Unit, 8, Cypress Drive, Puriton, Bridgwater,
Somerset. TA7 8AQ, United Kingdom

BRAIN-NET

THE ALISON CENTRE

For computer and communications buffs, the BRAIN-NET Internet WebSite
can be found on http://www.btinternet.com/~brain.net